Sankofa

Sankofa

*African American Perspectives on Race and Culture
in US Doctoral Education*

Edited by

Pamela Felder Small, Marco J. Barker,
and Marybeth Gasman

SUNY
PRESS

Published by State University of New York Press, Albany

For information, contact State University of New York Press, Albany, NY
www.sunypress.edu

Library of Congress Cataloging-in-Publication Data

Names: Felder Small, Pamela Petrease, editor. | Barker, Marco J., 1978– editor. | Gasman, Marybeth, editor.
Title: Sankofa : African American perspectives on race and culture in US doctoral education / [edited by] Pamela Petrease Felder Small, Marco J. Barker, and Marybeth Gasman.
Description: Albany : State University of New York Press, [2020] | Includes bibliographical references and index.
Identifiers: LCCN 2019036173 | ISBN 9781438477992 (hardcover : alk. paper) | ISBN 9781438478005 (pbk. : alk. paper) | ISBN 9781438478012 (ebook)
Subjects: LCSH: African American doctoral students—Social conditions. | African American doctoral students—Attitudes. | African Americans—Education (Graduate) | Universities and colleges—United States—Graduate work. | African American universities and colleges. | African Americans—Race identity. | United States—Race relations.
Classification: LCC LC2781 .S26 2020 | DDC 378.1/982996073—dc23
LC record available at https://lccn.loc.gov/2019036173

10 9 8 7 6 5 4 3 2 1

Contents

Tables

Acknowledgments

We would like to thank the African American and Black doctoral students and completers who participated in the research presented in this volume. Their stories have provided research communities and institutions with greater awareness of how race and culture shapes the doctoral experience.

Editors' Introduction

PAMELA FELDER SMALL, MARCO J. BARKER,
AND MARYBETH GASMAN

Sankofa, *Se wo were fi na wosankofa a yenkyi*, is an Akan philosophical tradition of the Adinkra cultural heritage system, and a way of knowing for the communities of Ghana and throughout the Diaspora (Temple, 2010). It translates into "it is not wrong to go back for that which you have forgotten" and "offers a solution to reconstituting a fragmented cultural past" (p. 128). In this volume, Sankofa is the process of expanding ways of understanding and critiquing the doctoral education experience through a racial and cultural lens, contributing the Black/African American perspective to doctoral education scholarship, and honoring pathways and lived experiences of Black/African American[1] doctoral students. To achieve this, Sankofa acknowledges educational history where Black/African American doctoral students have been forgotten, ignored, or minoritized; presents research on the value and impact of race and culture in the doctoral process; and centers the experiences of historically marginalized students and their journey toward the PhD and beyond with consideration of existing research on doctoral education.

Previous research on doctoral education and the impact of culture often focused on departmental and disciplinary norms, program milestones, doctoral activities, and academic engagement (Gardner, 2008; Gardner & Barnes, 2007; Girves & Wemmerus, 1988; Golde, 2005; Lovitts, 2001, 2007; Tinto, 1993; Weidman & Stein, 2003; Weidman, Twale, & Stein, 2001). Early scholarship on doctoral socialization provided frameworks for how

1

individuals developed a "congruence and assimilation orientation" toward understanding and adopting the norms and values of the profession or field and identifying a career choice without attention being given to academic individuality of the doctoral student (Antony, 2002). Meanwhile, early research on Black/African American doctoral students was limited to statistical portraits of degree attainment and persistence (Willie, Grady, & Hope, 1991; Tinto, 1993). However, in the last 10 to 15 years, greater attention has been given to the racial and cultural dynamics of doctoral education (Antony, 2005; Cleveland, 2004; Davidson & Foster-Johnson, 2001; Ellis, 2001; Felder & Barker, 2013; Gardner & Barker, 2015; Griffin, Muñiz, & Espinosa, 2012; Gildersleeve, Croom & Vasquez, 2011). Scholars have focused more intensively on the Black/African American doctoral experience (Bertrand Jones, Osborne-Lampkin, Patterson, & Davis, 2015; Bertrand Jones, Wilder, & Osborne-Lampkin, 2013; Cleveland, 2004; Davidson & Jones, 2000; Mabokela & Green, 2000) and personal stories of navigating the doctoral process (e.g., Brothers of the Academy and Sisters of the Academy). There also has been a significant increase in studies that challenge traditional notions of socialization and the doctorate (Gardner, 2008; Weidman & Twale, 2001; Weidman, Twale, & Bethea, 2016), examine the role of race in the doctoral process (Gildersleeve, Croom, & Vasquez, 2011; Taylor & Antony, 2000; Twale, Weidman, & Bethea, 2016), and identify the complexities of identity development in socialization (Gardner & Barnes, 2007; Sweitzer, 2009). Overall, though, the volume of research on Black/African American doctoral students does not compare with the growing research on the Black/African American undergraduate experience or on doctoral education or doctoral socialization in general.

This anthology builds on this scholarship by introducing the intersecting identities of doctoral students (e.g., race and gender or race and professional identity) and the racial and gender dynamics of the doctoral experience. Further, it presents a collective voice of empirical research on Black/African American doctoral student experiences; observations of efforts that build diversity among doctoral programs; and implications for policy, practice, and research. This volume also raises awareness about the barriers to student success and degree completion, especially in "chilly" academic environments, where students may not feel a sense of belonging or support. Through the Sankofa lens, we bring to light those issues (e.g., challenges with academic identities, environments, and relationships) that have historically excluded Black/African American doctoral students from fully participating in their doctoral programs and that demonstrate how institutional racism makes navigating doctoral programs difficult and challenging for Black/African American doctoral students. We use the research findings and assessments in this volume to further inform policy and practice and to cultivate new conceptual and structural approaches that support individuals with historically marginalized experiences. We advocate for strategies that consider the ways in which race and its intersections with gender, discipline, and institutional context influence and shape doctoral education, career development, socialization, and student support. While the Sankofa tradition encourages us to look back at the past to understand the Black/African American presence in doctoral education, the growing research on race and culture is forging new methods for conceptualizing what success, degree completion, and transition into the academy means and looks like.

Trends in Black/African American Doctoral Degree Completion

Statistical trends have been helpful in guiding an understanding of Black/African American doctoral degree completion, but less informative about specific issues concerning student experience. For instance, in *Three Magic Letters: Getting to the Ph.D.*, Michael Nettles and Catherine Millett present data on the status of the PhD over a nearly 25-year period. Between 1977 and 2000, there was a 70.8% increase in Blacks/African Americans earning doctoral degrees albeit a 34.8% increase in the total number of doctoral degrees awarded. According to Nettles and Millett, this increase reflected a focus on reducing the disparity between the representation of Blacks and Latina/os[2] in the U.S. population and their underrepresentation among doctorates. Subsequently, the Survey of Earned Doctorates reported an increase in doctoral degrees awarded to underrepresented students between 1957 and 2016 (National Science Foundation, 2017). In particular, doctorates earned by Blacks and/or African Americans increased by 70% between 1994 and 2014, which certainly contributed to the overall substantial growth in doctoral degree completion. While these data point to a period of growth, less is known about how institutions and doctoral programs have prepared for or responded to this greater diversity and how the student experience would be different for doctoral students of color. Additionally, how might doctoral student engagement need to shift or to be more culturally specific for Black/African American students?

The Sankofa tradition facilitates renewed purpose and understanding of statistical trends regarding Blacks/African Americans in doctoral education by connecting findings across this volume to an Afrocentric conceptual framework and providing a qualitative, sociological, and phenomenological analysis of Black doctoral education.

In examining disciplinary nuances, we find that Blacks/African Americans are unevenly represented in different fields. Blacks/African Americans represent the largest ethnic minority among education and non-science/engineering programs (National Center for Science and Engineering Statistics, 2015). However, there is significant underrepresentation in science, engineering, technology, and mathematics (STEM) fields. According to 2016 IPEDS (2017), Blacks earned 8.6% of doctoral STEM degrees awarded, compared with 63.6% of White doctoral STEM degree recipients, 12.1% of Hispanic or Latinx recipients, and 11.6% of Asian recipients. Despite the lack of representation of African Americans among STEM doctoral completers, there is promise, given the contributions of historically Black colleges and universities (HBCUs).

HBCUs contribute to the increased enrollment and success of Black/African American doctoral students in three major ways. First, HBCUs award a significant number of doctoral degrees to Blacks/African Americans. *The Journal of Blacks in Higher Education* (2016) released an article noting the increase of doctoral degree recipients produced by HBCUs. While these degrees may not be exclusively awarded to Black/African American students, these institutions still reach a high number of Blacks/African Americans. According to the Survey of Earned Doctorates (NCSES, 2015), from 2010 to 2014, two of the top five producers of Black/African American doctoral degree recipients included HBCUs—Howard University and Jackson State University—with Howard producing the highest number of recipients for not-for-profit institutions.

Furthermore, there has been a history of HBCUs graduating a significant number of Black/African American degree holders, building the availability of graduate school applicants. In the NCES report "Historically Black Colleges and Universities 1976 to 2001," Provasnik and Shafer (2004) found that HBCUs accounted for 12.9% of Black enrollment in postsecondary education while making up only 1.8% of total enrollment. HBCUs have been proven pathways for building the pipeline for Blacks/African Americans in STEM (Borum, Hilton, & Walker, 2016; Gasman & Nguyen, 2016). The American Institute on Research reported that approximately one-third of Blacks/African Americans in STEM doctoral programs attended HBCUs as undergraduates (Upton & Tanenbaum, 2014).

HBCUs have a long-standing tradition of engaging practical strategies designed and tailored to foster academic success and degree completion for historically marginalized students (Allen, Epps, & Haniff, 1991). When many historically White institutions have ignored the academic contributions by students of color, HBCUs are credited for supporting the academic excellence and success of this student population. They have played a significant role in doctoral degree completion, serving as institutions for baccalaureate origin as well as for the conferral of doctoral degrees (Fry Brown, Flowers, Hilton, & Dejohnette, 2018; Joseph, 2013; Ross-Sheriff, Edwards, & Orme, 2017). The rate of Blacks/African Americans participating in doctoral education indicates growth and promise, but these data must be juxtaposed with the lived experiences and retention of Blacks/African Americans. We argue that analyzing the success of the diversification of the doctorate must be done through a critical, racial lens to develop and shape the doctoral experience into an inclusive and culturally responsive environment.

Sankofa and the Black/African American Doctoral Experience: Situating the Research

Given the strong emphasis on seminal statistical portraits illustrating doctoral degree attainment for Blacks/African Americans, situating racially and culturally focused research in the field of doctoral education involves three important factors. First, in keeping with the research developments about race and culture in higher education, it is imperative to *interrogate* the meaning of policies and practices and their impact on the experiences of historically marginalized groups (Bonilla-Silva, 2013; Hurtado, Milem, Clayton-Pedersen, & Anderson 1999; Harper, 2012). In higher education research, this interrogation is based on the use of critical frameworks that raise questions about the impact of academic environments on the experiences of historically marginalized groups. Thus, the cultural practice of Sankofa centralizes race and culture as an act of resistance to the misrepresentation of the Black/African American doctoral experience within the history of doctoral education research. Further, it calls for a reconsideration of how socialization occurs in the doctoral process; how the traditional practices of mentoring may privilege White doctoral students and exclude Black/African American doctoral students; and how disaggregation of data and more detailed analyses of admission, progression, retention, and time-to-completion rates may all indicate the existence of racial bias.

Second, the practice of Sankofa *reveals* the importance of culturally relevant practice in doctoral education and its applicability to the larger body of research on the student experience in doctoral education. Sankofa permits critical discussion of racial and cultural experiences that are often unheard in mainstream doctoral education literature. For instance, seminal research on student experiences within doctoral study has typically addressed the nature of academic culture to mean the role and function of departments and disciplines (Golde, 2005) without emphasis on the role of students' racial or cultural experiences. This volume offers studies and a review where race and culture serve as points of analysis—either solely or in connection with other theoretical frameworks.

Third, there have been calls for a "renewed national effort" to support and prepare African American students for doctoral degree completion and career/professional success (Council of Graduate Schools & Educational Testing Service, 2010). Scholarly recommendations insist on identifying vulnerabilities that hinder our national capacity for innovation. Improving completion rates, preparing future faculty, and broadening participation have been identified as key recommendations for universities, employers, and policy makers to consider for doctoral programs. However, not considering how students of varying races experience their academic environments is a disservice, and it jeopardizes our nation's ability to produce the brightest and most innovative thinkers—fostering economic and intellectual vulnerability and consequently affecting the ability of the United States to compete globally. As the nation becomes increasingly racially and ethnically diverse, understanding diverse experiences becomes essential to the current and future development of higher education (Smith, 2016). The practice of Sankofa promotes the value of race and culture as meaningful in the process of producing Black/African American doctoral degree completers. This means analyzing and further evaluating aspects of graduate education: the role of faculty in supporting and facilitating degree completion, doctoral socialization into the discipline and within the department and institution, and learning and living environments. A Sankofan approach recognizes cultural ways of knowing and doing, and it respects the history, traditions, and values of individuals of the African Diaspora.

Critical Focus Areas Regarding the
Doctoral Student Experience

As represented in this volume, there are multiple aspects of the doctoral experience: identity, socialization, organizational context, and interactions with faculty. The Sankofa tradition may be applied to each of these areas by challenging traditional notions or literature and using theories, concepts, and frameworks that incorporate a racial analysis and provide discussion and a synthesis that centers on the African Diaspora or, in the case of this volume, the African American experience.

Doctoral student socialization research has focused on the following areas: student response to institutional cultural dynamics, levels of student involvement, preparation for the profession, student adjustment and assimilation, the faculty perspective, and the part-time experience (Antony, 2002; Austin, 2002; Gardner, 2008, 2010; Gardner & Barnes, 2007; Taylor & Antony, 2000). Scholarship focused on the organizational perspective of the doctoral experience tends to contextualize socialization to highlight the role of academic environments (i.e., departments) as an important way to make distinctions among the ways in which students are socialized in a variety of contexts (Weidman, 2006; Weidman & Stein, 2003; Weidman et al., 2001). While this work emphasizes the value of organizations, it aptly considers that socialization processes are complex and that they vary according to individual characteristics. In this volume, authors demonstrate how race becomes a factor in socialization and career development within doctoral programs and how students experience their socialization as non-affirming. Through Sankofa, there becomes a greater appreciation for the needs and interests of Black/African American doctoral students and how preparing students for future careers might reflect more of a blending of students' academic and cultural identities.

Identity in the context of doctoral education is dynamic and complex when one considers the doctoral programs' goal of socializing and preparing students for contributing to the profession. Doctoral or graduate identity development is considered to occur as students complete their doctoral milestones and activities, which means a student's personal identity development becomes only a byproduct of navigating these doctoral requirements (Gardner & Barker, 2015). This approach does not make personal identity development a priority. However, it is during socialization that students begin to connect their social, professional, and academic identities or see these identities in conflict with their area of research or the core principles of the profession or discipline. More specifically, doctoral students of color face the challenge of negotiating the paradigms of their academic disciplines or exclusion of their programs and institutions (i.e., doctoral student identity) with their cultural identities, citing how graduate or doctoral programs tend to be Eurocentric and patriarchal (Christman, Pepion, Bowman, & Dixon, 2015; González, 2006, 2009; Sulé, 2009). Black doctoral students—especially those in predominantly white institutions (PWIs)—report these same challenges. Students share how their race, and in some cases their gender, plays a role in how they choose advisors, what research they pursue, if and when they address discrimination or bias, how they are supported or leveraged in their doctoral programs, and what career fields are presented as options (Barker, 2014; Felder & Barker, 2013). The works in this volume recognize and speak to the ways that doctoral student identity for Black/African American students is complex and how race intersects with cultural and professional identities.

Across this volume, there are references made to the varying institutional, disciplinary, and geographical contexts in which students are matriculating. This focus on context acknowledges that where Black/African American doctoral students study and live is as important as what they study is to their long-term success. It reminds us that the type of institution, the history of an organization or environment, and student lived experiences can influence matriculation and career trajectory. Earlier in this introduction, we highlighted the role of HBCUs in the preparation of successful Black/African American doctoral students. The HBCU context fosters the conditions where students, undergraduate and graduate alike, thrive. Additionally, they provide students with the affirmation and self-efficacy in their identity to go on to doctoral programs at PWIs. Conversely, PWIs may create conditions where Black/African American students do not feel supported or their ideas and scholarly interest are not valued. These concerns are further amplified depending on where the institution is located. Barker (2014) found that Black/African American doctoral students in the American South reported that part of overcoming challenges as a Black/African American doctoral student meant overcoming racialized experiences in the city and institution.

Because context can shape a student's experience, the role of faculty members and advisors in negating these harmful environmental and contextual factors heightens. Faculty impact the doctoral socialization process, and they are central to doctoral education (Lovitts, 2001). Black/African

American doctoral student success and degree attainment is largely the result of faculty members who work diligently to support the academic process (Graham, 2013). This involves recruitment and transition into doctoral programs, supervising the doctoral experience (and retention efforts), and preparation for career opportunities beyond degree completion. The role of race in the doctoral advising relationship influences how students navigate their programs, develop their professional identity, and manage their own social identity (Barker, 2012).

The African practice of Sankofa in this work is influenced by orientation toward cultural consciousness, and it facilitates resistance by interrogating systems of oppression and misrepresentation and by insisting on the relevance of culture to defining and characterizing contemporary circumstances and experiences for historically marginalized doctoral students (Temple, 2010). Critically examining literature related to these issues is essential to addressing systemic barriers of injustice and inequity that impede degree completion. These barriers serve to hinder doctoral socialization of historically marginalized doctoral students, thus creating and sustaining vulnerabilities in our national system of graduate education. Furthermore, this volume presents racial implications for doctoral student socialization that may serve to more effectively and successfully support Black/African American doctoral students' engagement, development, and completion.

Overview of Chapters

This volume emphasizes Sankofa as a viable tool for engaging a culturally relevant examination of the doctoral experience. Chapters focus on multiple themes, including the role of context in the Black or African American doctoral experience, disciplinary experiences, and the role and impact of faculty–student engagement. The Sankofa practice of "going back" involves the acknowledgement of a key historical trend at the beginning of each chapter that is related to the chapter's topic and current relevance to student experience. Historical trends are drawn from *U.S. Doctorates in the 20th Century* (National Science Foundation, 2006).

To set the context for the volume, Felder Small provides an overview on the status of Black/African American doctoral students. Her chapter, "Understanding Race, Culture and the Doctorate," draws on several important statistical portraits of doctoral degree completion to present a broad-based discussion of how race and culture are represented (or not represented) in the presentation of data and student experience. The Sankofa perspective speaks to "going back" to fully understand the contributions of African Americans and the implications for higher education in previous representations of data. Specifically, Felder Small offers several recommendations for strategies for building institutional capacity to support the development of racial and cultural understanding.

In chapter 2, "Programmatic Efforts Supporting Doctoral Student Socialization in Education: A Literature Review," Felder Small, Liggans, Chirombo, and Freeman shed light on how programmatic efforts impact doctoral student socialization. Drawing on the field of education and concepts of socialization and student success, they examine African American doctoral student socialization within specially designed programs that primarily address marginalization due to historic legacies of exclusion. In this work, Sankofa represents a focus on the programmatic efforts to develop practices that center race and culture. Understanding the role of these efforts is critical to addressing the ways African Americans are marginalized during the doctoral process and their transitions into the academy as faculty.

In chapter 3, Yi and Ramos explore how African American women have placed their race and gender at the center of their education. Their work enacts Sankofa by speaking to the experiences women of color face when their identities are excluded and/or challenged by academic norms, resulting in women of color being isolated, their research not embraced, and their experiencing racial and gender bias. Through the powerful counter-stories in "Resistance Narratives: Counter-stories of Black Female Doctoral Students," the authors highlight how these women have navigated the doctorate and their previous education through the lenses of race and gender. These perspectives allowed them to increase their awareness of structural inequities and to better navigate racist and sexist spaces.

A growing body of literature examines the experiences of doctoral students who are pursuing doctoral degrees in STEM and how they come to navigate their academic identity as scientists along with their racial, gender, and other identities. Two chapters in this work contribute to this scholarship by focusing on the disciplinary areas where Blacks/African Americans have been represented by low participation and degree completion rates. Burt's research, presented in chapter 4, "Demystifying the Monolithic Black Male Mystique," builds on theoretical frameworks and research through his own empirical study. Burt emphasizes that existing research tends to characterize Black males as being monolithic and to suggest "one-size-fits-all" policies and practices. In his chapter, he explores the within-group differences of 11 Black male doctoral students in engineering. The findings from this chapter provide implications for taking more nuanced approaches to aiding in the educational experiences of Black males that may apply to researchers, practitioners, and policy makers. Recent trends suggest that while there has been some progress made toward increasing the representation of Black students in science graduate education, they are less likely to transition into academic or research positions at the end of their training.

In Chapter 5, "Being One of Few: Examining Black Biomedical PhDs' Training Experiences and Career Development through a Campus Racial Climate Lens," Griffin, Gibbs, and English interviewed 21 Black doctoral degree recipients in the biomedical sciences to better learn what messages trainees received about what it means to be a scientist and to work in academia throughout their training. The authors' study examines how these messages are sent and received by the doctoral recipients, as well as the recipients' processes of determining whether the values of science aligned with their own values.

Additionally, chapters in this volume focus on the impact of institutional mission and the engagement of faculty on the student experience beginning at the start of the PhD path and across the institutional contexts of HBCUs and PWIs. In chapter 6, Felder Small and McCallum represent Sankofa by challenging traditional mentoring models and examining the power of the HBCU institutional mission on the student commitment to pursue the PhD and examining how HBCUs guide African American students into the academy. In their chapter, "From Firm Foundations to Where? Understanding the Role of HBCUs in Black/African American PhD Student Commitment," the authors highlight undergraduate socialization experiences, with a particular focus on (1) the relationship between institutional mission and student experience, and (2) the ways such relationships inspire students to pursue graduate education and the professoriate. Suggestions from this chapter reveal opportunities for building the doctoral pipeline.

In chapter 7, "Rethinking Engagement: Examining the Role of Faculty–Student Interactions and Black Doctoral Student Success at HBCUs," Boykin facilitates Sankofa through her discussion of the variance within and the impact of faculty–student interaction on doctoral students' positive academic experiences and perceived persistence. Specifically, external engagement—social components for student success external to a student's academic program and research practices—has been found to be a critical component for and best predictor of optimal experiences and increased belief in self in regard to program completion. Boykin provides recommendations for dissertation supervisors, faculty, and administrators.

Examining the outcomes of the cross-race faculty and doctoral student relationships, Barker and Washington examine how Black doctoral students negotiate and manage their identities when working with White advisors and within predominantly White institutions or spaces. In chapter 8, "Double Consciousness: Exploring Black and Doctoral Student Identity within Cross-Race Advising Relationships," they use Du Bois's concept of double consciousness to better explain the experiences where Black doctoral students encounter situations to reflect on their identities. In this chapter, Barker and Washington provide recommendations for research and practice where programs and institutions may create spaces for students to be supported both academically and culturally. Sankofa emerges through an interrogation of student–faculty relationships within challenging academic situations and marginalizing academic functions.

In the concluding chapter, Felder Small and Barker summarize findings presented across the volume and put forth recommendations for policy, practice, and research. Sankofa is further addressed to draw conclusions about its applicability within the volume as well as within the larger body of academic research on doctoral education.

Conclusion

There is a growing percentage of Black/African American students enrolling in doctoral programs. While this growth indicates success, it is important to remember that Black/African American students still experience racism and discrimination and differential treatment in advising, mentoring, and career development. Additionally, many Black/African American doctoral students continue to struggle with their racial and doctoral identities in ways that are not understood by program administrators or faculty. In many instances, PWIs broadly and doctoral programs specifically have failed in designing experiences and developing culturally responsive socialization approaches that recognize and reflect a student's personal and cultural interests. Sankofa presents a more Afrocentric and culturally inclusive perspective for better understanding the experiences of Black/African American doctoral students. The volume contributors demonstrate the varying ways that race matters in developing support mechanisms, advising doctoral students, building doctoral pipelines, developing doctoral processes, and cultivating faculty–student engagement. The goal of this volume is to bring greater attention to why Black doctorates matter and how ethnic principles like Sankofa can inform practices and policies that support not only Black doctoral students but other students of color as well. Further, we hope the work presented in this volume contributes to the research in this field by providing new ways of framing and critiquing doctoral education and offering new considerations for programmatic design and policy.

Notes

1. In this manuscript, *African American* and *Black* may be used interchangeably, as determined by the authors.
2. Millett and Nettles used the U.S. Census term *Hispanic*. The authors have opted to use *Latina/o* instead.

Works Cited

Allen, W. R., Epps, E., & Haniff, N. Z. (Eds.). (1991). *College in Black and White: African American students in predominantly White and in historically Black public universities*. Albany, NY: State University of New York Press.

Antony J. S. (2002). Reexamining doctoral student socialization and professional development: Moving beyond the congruence and assimilation orientation. In J. C. Smart & W. G. Tierney (Eds.), *Higher education: handbook of theory and research* (pp. 349–380). New York, NY: Springer, Dordrecht.

Barker, M. J. (2012). An exploration of racial identity among Black doctoral students involved in cross-race advising relationships. In J. Sullivan & A. Esmail (Eds.), *African American identity: Racial and cultural dimensions of the Black experience* (pp. 384–414). Lanham, MD: Lexington Books.

Barker, M. J. (2014). Critiquing doctoral education: Moving toward a cross-race doctoral advising model. In P. P. Felder & E. P. St. John (Eds.), *Supporting graduate students in the 21st century: Implications for policy and practice* (Vol. 27, pp. 109–134). New York, NY: AMS Press.

Bertrand Jones, T., Osborne-Lampkin, L., Patterson, S. M., & Davis, D. J. (2015). Creating a "safe and supportive environment": Mentoring and professional development for recent Black women doctoral graduates. *International Journal of Doctoral Studies, 10*, 483–499.

Bertrand Jones, T., Wilder, J. A., & Osborne-Lampkin, L. (2013). Employing a Black feminist approach to doctoral advising: Preparing Black women for the professoriate. *Journal of Negro Education, 82(3)*, 326–338. doi:10.7709/ jnegroeducation.82.3.0326

Borum, V., Hilton, A., and Walker, E. (2016). The role of Black colleges in the development of mathematicians. *Journal of Research Initiatives, 2*(1), 1–15.

Cleveland, D. (Ed.) (2004). *A long way to go: Conversations about race by African American faculty and graduate students.* New York, NY: Peter Lang.

Council of Graduate Schools and Educational Testing Service. (2010). *The path forward: The future of graduate education in the United States. Report from the Commission on the Future of Graduate Education in the United States.* Princeton, NJ: Educational Testing Service.

Davidson, M. N., & Foster-Johnson, L. (2001). Mentoring in the preparation of graduate researchers of color. *Review of Educational Research, 71*(4), 549–574.

Ellis, E. M. (2001). The impact of race and gender on graduate school socialization, satisfaction with doctoral study, and commitment to degree completion. *The Western Journal of Black Studies, 25*, 30–45.

Felder, P. P., & Barker, M. J. (2013). Extending Bell's concept of interest convergence: A framework for understanding the African American doctoral experience. *International Journal of Doctoral Studies, 8*, 1–20.

Felder, P. P., Stevenson, H. C., & Gasman, M. (2014). Understanding race in doctoral student socialization. *International Journal of Doctoral Studies, 9*, 21–42.

Fry Brown, R. L., Flowers, A. M., Hilton, A. A., & Dejohnette, M. (2018). Beyond respectable: Why earn an advanced degree from an historically Black college and university. In T. F. Boykin, A. A. Hilton, & R. T. Palmer (Eds.), *Professional education at historically Black colleges and universities* (pp. 123–140). New York, NY: Routledge Publishing.

Gardner, S. K. (2008). Fitting the mold of graduate school: A qualitative study of socialization in doctoral education. *Innovative Higher Education, 7*, 1–21.

Gardner, S. K. (2009). Conceptualizing success in doctoral education: Perspectives of faculty in seven disciplines. *The Review of Higher Education, 32*(3), 383–406.

Gardner, S. K. (2010). Keeping up with the Joneses: Socialization and culture in doctoral education at one striving institution. *The Journal of Higher Education, 81*(6), 728–749.

Gardner, S. K., & Barker, M. J. (2014). Engaging graduate and professional students. In S. R. Harper & S. J. Quaye (Eds.), *Student engagement in higher education: theoretical perspectives and practical approaches for diverse populations* (2nd ed., pp. 339–350). New York, NY: Taylor & Francis.

Gardner, S. K., & Barnes, B. J. (2007). Graduate student involvement: Socialization and the professional role. *Journal of College Student Development, 48*, 269–387.

Gardner, S. K., & Mendoza, P. (Eds.). (2010). *On becoming a scholar: Socialization and development in doctoral education.* Sterling, VA: Stylus Publishing.

Gasman, M., & Nguyen, T.-H. (2016). *Historically Black colleges and universities as leaders in STEM*. Retrieved from http://www2.gse.upenn.edu/cmsi/sites/gse.upenn.edu.cmsi/files/MSI_HemsleyReport_final_0.pdf

Girves, J. E., & Wemmerus, V. (1988). Developing models of graduate student degree progress. *Journal of Higher Education, 59*(2), 163–189.

Graham, E. (2013). The experiences of minority doctoral students at elite research institutions. In K. A. Holley & J. Joseph (Eds.), *Increasing diversity in doctoral education: Implications for theory and practice* (No. 163, pp. 77–87). New Directions for Higher Education. San Francisco, CA: Jossey-Bass.

Green, A. L., & Scott, L. V. (2003). *Journey to the Ph.D.: How to navigate the process as African Americans*. Sterling, VA: Stylus.

Griffin, K. A., Muñiz, M. M., & Espinosa, L. (2012). The influence of campus racial climate on diversity in graduate education. *The Review of Higher Education 35*(4), 535–566.

Golde, C. M. (2005). The role of department and discipline in doctoral student attrition: Lessons from four departments. *The Journal of Higher Education, 76*(6), 669–700.

González, J. C. (2009). Latinas in doctoral and professional programs: Similarities and differences in support systems and challenges. In M. F. Howard-Hamilton, C. L. Morelon-Quainoo, S. D. Johnson, R. Winkle-Wagner, & L. Santiague (Eds.), *Standing on the outside looking in* (pp. 103–123). Sterling, VA: Stylus.

Hurtado, S., Milem, J., Clayton-Pederson, A., & Allen, W. (1999). Enacting diverse learning environments: Improving the climate for racial/ethnic diversity in higher education. *ASHE-ERIC Higher Education Report, 26*(8). Washington, DC: The George Washington University, Graduate School of Education and Human Development.

Jones, L. (2000). *Brothers of the academy: Up and coming Black scholars earning our way in higher education*. Sterling, VA: Stylus Publishing.

Joseph, J. (2013). The impact of historically Black colleges and universities on doctoral students. In K. A. Holley & J. Joseph (Eds.), *New directions for higher education: Increasing diversity in doctoral education: implications for theory and practice* (pp. 67–76). San Francisco, CA: Jossey-Bass.

Journal of Blacks in Higher Education. (2016). HBCUs awarded 448 doctorates in 2014, an all-time high. Retrieved from https://www.jbhe.com/2016/01/hbcus-awarded-435-doctorates-in-2014-an-all-time-high/

Lovitts, B. E. (2001). *Leaving the ivory tower: The causes and consequences of departure from doctoral study*. Lanham, MD: Rowman & Littlefield Publishers.

Lovitts, B. E. (2007). *Making the implicit explicit: Creating performance expectations for the dissertation*. Sterling, VA: Stylus Publishing.

Mabokela, R. O., & Green, A. L. (2000). *Sisters of the academy: Emerging Black women scholars in higher education*. Sterling, VA: Stylus Publishing.

National Science Foundation, National Center for Science and Engineering Statistics. (2017). *Doctorate recipients from U.S. universities: 2016*. Special Report NSF 18-304. Alexandria, VA.

National Science Foundation, National Center for Science and Engineering Statistics. (2015). *Doctorate recipients from U.S. universities: 2014*. Special Report NSF 16-300. Arlington, VA.

Nettles, M. T., & Millett, C. M. (2006). *Three magic letters: Getting to Ph.D.* Baltimore, MD: Johns Hopkins University Press.

Okahana, H., Allum, J., Felder, P. P., & Tull, R. G. (2016). *Implications for practice and research from Doctoral Initiative on Minority Attrition and Completion* (CGS Data Sources PLUS #16-01). Washington, DC: Council of Graduate Schools.

Provasnik, S., & Shafer, L. L. (2004). *Historically Black colleges and universities, 1976 to 2001, NCES 2004–062*. Retrieved from http://nces.ed.gov/pubs2004/2004062.pdf

Ross-Sheriff, F., Edwards, J. B., & Orme, J. (2017). Relational mentoring of doctoral social work students at historically Black colleges and universities. *Journal of Teaching in Social Work, 37*(1), 55–70.

Smith, D. (2016). The diversity imperative: Moving to the next generation. In M. N. Bastedo, P. G. Altbach, & P. J. Gumport (Eds.). *American higher education in the twenty-first century: Social, political, and economic challenges.* Baltimore, MD: John Hopkins University Press.

Smith, W. A., Altbach, P. G., & Lomotey, K. (2002). *The racial crisis in American higher education: Continuing challenges for the twenty-first century.* Albany, NY: State University of New York Press.

Sulé, V. T. (2009). Oppositional stances of Black female graduate students. In M. F. Howard-Hamilton, C. L. Morelon-Quainoo, S. D. Johnson, R. Winkle-Wagner, & L. Santiague (Eds.), *Standing on the outside looking in* (pp. 147–168). Sterling, VA: Stylus.

Taylor, E., & Antony, J. S. (2000). Stereotype threat reduction and wise schooling: Towards the successful socialization of African American doctoral students in education. *The Journal of Negro Education, 69*(3), 184–198.

Temple, C. (2010). The emergence of Sankofa practice in the United States. *Journal of African American Studies, 41*(1), 127–150.

Thurgood, Lori, Golladay, Mary J., & Hill, Susan T. (2006). *U.S. doctorates in the 20th century* (NSF Publication No. 06-319). Alexandria, VA: National Science Foundation, Division of Science Resources Statistics.

Tierney, W. G. (1997). Organizational socialization in higher education. *The Journal of Higher Education, 68*, 1–16.

Tinto, V. (1993). *Leaving college: Rethinking the causes and cures of student attrition* (2nd ed.). Chicago, IL: University of Chicago Press.

Twale, D., Weidman, J., & Bethea, K. (2016). Conceptualizing the socialization of graduate students of color: Revisiting the Weidman, Twale, & Stein Framework. *The Western Journal of Black Studies, 40*(2), 80–94.

Upton, R., & Tanenbaum, C. (2014). The role of historically Black colleges and universities as pathway providers: Institutional pathways to the STEM PhD among Black students. *American Institutes for Research Broadening Participation in STEM Graduate Education Issue Brief.* Retrieved from http://www.air.org/sites/default/files/downloads/report/Role%20of%20HBCUs%20in%20STEM%20PhDs%20for%20Black%20Students.pdf

U.S. Department of Education, National Center for Education Statistics, Integrated Postsecondary Education Data System. (2017). *Digest of Education Statistics.* Retrieved from https://nces.ed.gov/programs/digest/d17/tables/dt17_318.45.asp

Weidman, J. C., & Stein, E. L. (2003). Socialization of graduate students to academic norms. *Research in Higher Education, 44,* 641–656.

Weidman, J. C., Twale, D. J., & Stein, E. L. (2001). *Socialization of graduate and professional students in higher education: A perilous passage?* San Francisco, CA: Jossey-Bass.

Willie, C. V., Grady, M. K., & Hope, R. O. (1991). *African Americans and the doctoral experience: Implications for policy.* New York, NY: Teachers College Press.

Yosso, T. J. (2005). Whose culture has capital? A critical race theory discussion of community cultural wealth. *Race Ethnicity and Education, 8*(1), 69–91.

Chapter 1

Understanding Race, Culture, and the Doctorate

PAMELA FELDER SMALL

The purpose of this chapter is to present an examination of racial and cultural issues influencing Black/African Americans and their experience pursuing the doctoral degree. Higher education research on diversity, race, and culture has evolved considerably over the past thirty years to influence the development of policy, institutional contexts, institutional leadership, and our understanding of student experiences (Smith, 2016; Smith, Altbach, & Lomotey, 2002). The process of going back to learn about the past so that we may move forward is a core principle of the Sankofa tradition, and it emphasizes the value of what can be learned from previous scholarship on doctoral education from a Black/African American perspective. This prospective doctoral process must involve careful consideration of research focused on race and culture that brings to bear critical and important insights missing from scholarship where mainstream perspectives are emphasized. More specifically, practical strategies addressing barriers to academic and degree completion for historically marginalized populations must explicitly embrace notions of race and culture. Such work must be interrogated for its meaningfulness regarding intention, applicability, and effectiveness.

In addition to this chapter identifying several areas of racial and cultural research commonly known in education, a collective presentation underscores their valuable role in shaping practices that strengthen social and academic success for Blacks/African American doctoral students specifically. Discussing how these concepts align with useful practical strategies serves to facilitate a broader dialogue about the important contributions of these Black/African American doctoral degree recipients to the future of higher education and society.

The terms *African American* and *Black* are used interchangeably to discuss statistical information and/or experiences consistent with the way cited sources have identified racial and cultural groups in the literature. These identities are aligned with the following 2010 United States Census Brief racial definition: "Black or African American" refers to "a person having origins in any of the Black racial groups of Africa" (OMB, 2011). As such, in this work there is primary focus on degree attainment by exploring the experiences of African American doctoral degree recipients and their representation within the system of higher education. The primary audience includes individuals and organizations interested in learning more about the impact of the African American doctoral experience on higher education. Analyses of trends from the late 20th century to the present are particularly informative and useful for faculty administrators and students who have an interest in doctoral study and the future of graduate education.

Foreground of Important Statistics

This section foregrounds significant data trends from the Survey of Earned Doctorates and emphasizes key issues relevant to Black/African American participation in doctoral study. Racial and cultural nuances reveal critical aspects of academic preparation, recruitment and retention, research and practical interests, and transitions beyond degree completion into career pathways. Trends focused on baccalaureate origins, top-producing institutions, representation in broad fields of study, and notable achievements highlight the impact and valuable contributions of Blacks/African Americans to graduate education, specific disciplinary and industry areas, and society. Pathways toward Black/African American doctoral degree attainment were ways made out of 'no way.' Sankofa tradition allows for acknowledgement of a fragmented past (Temple, 2010) of academic exclusion from academic opportunities of all levels of higher education.

The practice of Sankofa reveals the importance of acknowledging the exclusion of Blacks/African Americans amid efforts to cultivate renewed cultural perspectives of doctoral education. For example, this work acknowledges disparities between the representation of African American doctoral degree holders and the African American population as an effect of systemic inequities deeply rooted in the racial segregation (Allen & Jewell, 1995; Anderson, 2002; Thomas, 1981; Tillman, 2009). When comparing the representation of earned African American doctorates with the general African American population, similar imbalances exist (Nettles & Millett, 2006). In 2000, African Americans accounted for 12.9% of the population (approximately 34 million of 281 million) yet represented approximately 4% of those who held doctoral degrees (U.S. Census Bureau, 2000; Hoffer et al., 2001).

James Anderson (2002) describes racial conditions of the Black/African American doctoral experience in the following way: "The origins and development of American higher education paralleled the evolution of a national system of racially qualified slavery and its attendant ideologies of racism and class subordination" (p. 3). Unfortunately, this suggests the existence and/or potential of these ideologies to influence our academic systems and their constituents. This consequence illustrates the uniqueness of the African American doctoral experience and its inextricable connection with the tenets of slavery. Origins of doctoral degree attainment for the masses of Blacks/African Americans emerged from racial segregation and the development of historically Black colleges and universities (HBCUs).

Statistics on Black/African American participation in the twentieth century largely represents this growth (National Science Foundation, 2006). Between 1975 and 1999, approximately 26,000 doctorates were conferred upon Blacks/African Americans. The top five baccalaureate institutions for these degree completers were HBCUs, representing approximately 9% of all baccalaureate institutions for Blacks/African Americans. Between 1995 and 1999, approximately 6,600 degrees were conferred upon Black/African Americans. The top six institutions were HBCUs, representing approximately 9%. Though HBCUs are often recognized as institutional origins for the top producers of Black/African American doctoral degree recipients during the twentieth century, only two doctoral degree–granting HBCUs existed by 1975: Howard University and Clark Atlanta University (National Science Foundation, 2006). By the end of the century, fifteen HBCUs existed (see Tables 1.1 and 1.2 on the next page).

Table 1.1. Top 5 and Top 6 Baccalaureate Institutions of Black
U.S.–Citizen PhDs: 1975–1999 and 1995–1999

1975–1999		1995–1999	
Baccalaureate institution	*PhDs*	*Baccalaureate institution*	*PhDs*
All U.S. institutions	25,872	All U.S. institutions	6,631
Howard U. * †	752	Howard U. * †	174
Southern U. †	419	Spelman College * †	100
Hampton U. * †	386	Hampton U. * †	82
Florida A&M U. †	382	Florida A&M U. †	78
Tuskegee U. * †	361	Jackson State U. †	71
		Southern U. †	71
Top 5 as percentage of total	8.9	Top 6 as percentage of total	8.7

Note: Institutions that were tied are listed alphabetically.
*Privately controlled.
†Historically Black college or university.

Table 1.2. Doctorates Awarded to Black U.S. Citizens by HBCUs:
1975–1999

Institution	Doctorates
All HBCUs	1,804
Howard U.	716
Clark Atlanta U.	508
Texas Southern U.	187
South Carolina State U.	76
Meharry Medical College	74
Jackson State U.	56
Morgan State U.	48
Tennessee State U.	45
Grambling State U.	43
Florida A&M U.	23
Alabama A&M U.	18
North Carolina A&T State U.	5
Southern U. A&M College–Baton Rouge	2
U. Maryland–Eastern Shore	2
Hampton U.	1

Note: HBCU = historically Black college or university.

While the number of degrees achieved has increased over generations, the representation of Black/African American doctoral degree recipients remains a cause for concern. For example, in 1977, African Americans earned approximately 4% of all doctoral degrees, and by 2005 that increased to 5.8% (DOE, 2006). This has contributed to the paucity of Blacks with doctoral degrees and the lack of representation of Black faculty at American colleges and universities. In 2003, Blacks comprised 6% of all full-time faculties, with 5% as full professors, 6% as assistant professors, 7% as instructors, and 5% as lecturers (DOE, 2006; DOE, 2005). These data remained the same more than a decade later, with 6% of full-time faculty represented as Black/African American (U.S. Department of Education, 2017).

Data reveal insights relevant to the transitions toward career pathways for Black/African American doctoral students. The Survey of Earned Doctorates (2017) reports that 5,234 doctoral degrees were conferred upon Blacks/African Americans among 54,094 total doctoral degree recipients for all groups, slightly less than 10% total representation. Blacks/African Americans are likely to attain doctorates later in their lives compared to other racial/ethnic groups. For instance, the median age for Black/African doctoral recipients is 35.9 years, the second-highest age reported among historically marginalized groups: American Indian or Alaska Native, 39.2; White, 31.8; Asian, 31.4; more than one race, 31.2; and other race or race not reported, 33.1. Blacks/African Americans are likely to pursue their degrees for a longer period of time compared to other racial/ethnic groups. Blacks/African Americans have the second-highest time-to-degree completion rate, 12.0 years, compared to other groups: American Indian or Alaska Native, 13.4; Asian, 8.8; more than one race, 8.6; other race or race not reported, 10.3; and ethnicity not reported, 9.0. Blacks/African Americans are more likely to have a master's degree related to their doctoral degree, with 83.3 doctoral recipients with master's degrees reported for all fields. Furthermore, of all doctoral degree recipients reporting attainment of a community college degree, 19.5% of them were Black/African American.

Black/African American doctoral degree attainment and representation in the field of education during the 20th century is significant for several important reasons. There were more doctoral degrees conferred in education between 1962 and 1999 compared to any other field of study during the same time period (National Science Foundation, 2006). Appendix 1 represents education as a major field of study by race and ethnicity for 2016 (National Science Foundation, 2016). Education continues to be a vehicle to improve public and societal conditions and to transform socioeconomic situations for people from all backgrounds. For the Black/African American experience specifically, education remains vital to our survival and success in transcending oppressive spaces of exclusion.

The doctorate represents this vitality at some of the highest levels of our society. In the field of education, this vitality is demonstrated in seminal transformative research on race and culture, including a focus on critical race theory and interest convergence (Felder and Barker, 2013; Gildersleeve, Croom, & Vasquez, 2011; Ladson-Billings, 1995; Milner, 2007; Harper, Patton, & Wooden, 2009). An underlying goal of this seminal research is to present pedagogical strategies to improve educational opportunities for historically marginalized populations. This is an approach in alignment with the Sankofa tradition to address a fragmented cultural past. The chapter by Felder, Liggans, Chirombo, and Freeman examines literature focused on research and practical interests in the field of education in greater detail.

Continued study of race, culture, and the doctorate will further illuminate our impact and contribution to education, society, and the world. A notable model of a Black/African American doctoral degree recipient who both illustrates the value of the U.S. doctoral education system and addresses our nation's fragmented cultural past is Nobel Peace Prize Laureate Dr. Martin Luther King Jr., who led the most significant civil rights movement in the United States. Numerically, King is represented both as doctoral degree completer and Nobel Laureate in 20th century statistical reporting on the doctorate (National Science Foundation, 2006).

Racial and Cultural Concepts Supporting Marginalized Doctoral Students

At the center of many institutional diversity efforts is the goal of transforming academic environments away from systemic exclusion toward environments that are more inclusive. For instance, consideration of systemic exclusion in the seminal work of Hurtado, Milem, Clayton-Pedersen, and Allen (1999) includes the purpose of enhancing our understanding of racial/ethnic experiences to strengthen institutional contexts and improve academic success and degree completion rates for students who experience systemic exclusion from college and university environments. This research has largely addressed the racial experiences of undergraduate students with less attention to their application within the context of doctoral education.

Research in this area must increase to address wider practical implications related to the academic pipeline and transitions toward the professoriate, where there is continuing underrepresentation of historically marginalized populations. Hence, the need to engage research that promotes practical strategies facilitating academic support and doctoral degree attainment is critical to any objectives to diversify doctoral education and the professoriate. In this section, two essential racial and cultural concepts in education are discussed to emphasize their importance in reshaping our understanding of the doctoral process: critical race theory (CRT) and cultural wealth.

Critical Race Theory and Interest Convergence

CRT is a conceptual framework that evolved out of critical legal scholarship based on a collective frustration about the slow progression of racial reform in the United States (Ladson-Billings, 1995, 1999; Delgado, 2002). The components of this framework address historic and contemporary issues of African American educational achievement in the United States and provide a structure for qualitative analysis of student experience (Allen, 1992; Anderson & Hrabowski, 1977; Brazziel, 1983; Brazziel & Brazziel, 1987) and is well aligned with Sankofa principles by addressing issues resulting from a fragmented cultural past. CRT lends itself to interpreting marginalized student experiences of African Americans who pursue the doctoral degree by allowing the process of developing counternarratives to address barriers to academic success. Yet this framework is generous in facilitating an understanding about how students balance their experiences of persistence with stories of resilience and success.

CRT offers a lens to explore a shared history of achievement based on experiential knowledge about overcoming barriers to degree completion. Considering race as a key element of persistence toward doctoral degree completion should be an integral aspect of analyzing the marginalized student experience. Progression toward the doctorate evolves out of a system of racial and culturally based challenges that are considered "normal" and "enmeshed in the fabric of our social order" (Ladson-Billings, 1999, p. 12). Some key factors affecting African American belief systems and behaviors associated with the doctoral process include prior socialization, advising, development of disciplinary identity, commitment to the goal of getting the degree, and post-degree completion career objectives.

CRT evolved out of Derrick Bell's (1980) early scholarship on interest convergence, which explains that racial relations in the context of social justice for people of color occurs when the interests, ideas, and realities of both people of color and Whites converge. Interest convergence is at the nexus of interaction and exchange within the doctoral process. For doctoral students, faculty, and administrators, much of what drives an emerging scholar during the doctoral process is understanding how to manage interests and their contribution to the institution and larger disciplinary community. The relational aspects of interest convergence and the racial and power dynamics involved in this negotiation are essential toward the building of racial equality awareness.

Previous scholarship has engaged the use of CRT regarding the educational experiences of Blacks/African Americans to examine the analytic tools in teacher education policies and practices (Milner, 2007) and the enrollment and degree attainment rates across the life span of higher education (Harper, Patton, & Wooden, 2009). In doctoral education, the role of interest convergence for the Black/African American experience has been discussed within the context of doctoral student advising (Felder & Barker, 2013). In describing Bell's own educational experience with his professor, the process of intellectual interests converging to facilitate the process of intellectual creativity serves to broaden Bell's perspective in his disciplinary area of interest—racial inequality. CRT is a critical component and tool for advising Black/African American doctoral students.

As Harper, Patton, and Wooden (2009) assert, CRT as an analytical framework can be used to interrogate systems of oppression, exclusion, racism, and inequity that are prevalent in the educational histories of Blacks/African Americans. As such, CRT tenets adapted from previous research are applicable to the Black/African American doctoral student advisement experiences in the following ways: seeing racism as a normal part of the experiences of Black/African American doctoral students, rejecting notions that all doctoral student experiences are the same regardless of race, valuing the lived experiences of Black/African American doctoral students as being central to their experiences as emergent scholars, identifying any tolerance that encourages racial advances to promote whiteness in an effort to strengthen the academic and social mobility of

Black/African American students, identifying systemic and institutionalized legacies of oppression that serve to marginalize the existence of Black/ African American doctoral students, and ongoing interrogation of systems of exclusion influencing the academic and social mobility of historically marginalized doctoral students.

Cultural Wealth

The concept of cultural wealth provides specific guidance for embracing the lived experiences of communities of color, this involves consideration of race when it impacts responses to structures, practices, and discourses (Yosso, 2005). In particular, five areas regarding these responses are considered: the intercentricity of race and racism, the challenge to dominant ideology, the commitment to racial and social justice, the centrality of experiential knowledge of people of color, and the use of interdisciplinary approaches. Yosso's work is particularly useful in its practicality for implementation of strategies that combat practices that don't promote doctoral student success and are not attuned to the ways the racial experience shapes individual and institutional culture.

The cultural wealth model centralized the lived experiences that nurture communities of color in the six forms of capital. Aspirational capital refers to the ability to maintain hopes and dreams for the future, even in the face of real and perceived barriers. It is important to consider the ways race influences aspiration to pursue the doctorate and, once enrolled, degree completion. Linguistic capital includes the intellectual and social skills attained through communication experiences in more than one language and/or style.

Historically marginalized students have struggled in environments that have not been receptive to cultural difference and language expression. Familial capital refers to cultural knowledge nurtured among familial (kin) that carry a sense of community history, memory, and cultural intuition. Social capital can be understood as networks of people and community resources. Over the last decade, social media has become an increasingly valuable platform to build community, networks, and sources of support for students who do not benefit from cultural wealth in their home academic environments (Felder, Parrish, Collier, & Blockett, 2016). Navigational capital refers to skills of maneuvering through social institutions. Successful doctoral students attain both theoretical and heuristic knowledge to gain access with gatekeepers. Finally, resistant capital refers to knowledge oppositional behavior that challenges inequality.

Race, Culture, and Doctoral Student Socialization

Doctoral student socialization continues to be a seminal concept for examining the process for doctoral degree attainment and provides a key framework for understanding the impact of racial and cultural issues. As research on race and culture evolves, understanding this work within the context of doctoral education will be important to institutional diversification efforts that serve to transform academic environments toward inclusivity. Research on the student aspects of socialization (Gardner, 2008, 2010; Gardner and Barnes, 2007) and the organizational elements of socialization has been cited widely (Tierney, 1997; Weidman, 2006; Weidman, Twale, & Stein, 2003; Weidman and Stein, 2001), but more research on the racial and cultural aspects of the doctoral is needed to provide guidance on creating strategies to increase participation and degree completion from underrepresented groups (Ellis, 2001; Felder, Stevenson, & Gasman, 2014; Twale, Weidman, & Bethea, 2016). While scholars have considered the ways the racial experience complicates the doctoral process when students must address discrimination and racism, including academic preparation, parental educational background, interactions with faculty, and advisement (Antony & Taylor, 2004; Barker, 2011; Cleveland, 2004; Ellis, 2001; Gay, 2004; Green & Scott, 2003; Willie, Grady, & Hope, 1991), additional empirical study is needed to understand why there has been little increase in doctoral degree completion and transition into the professoriate among Black/African Americans and other underrepresented groups.

While there are many critical issues to consider when examining the racial experience, practical strategies presented in this chapter attempt to prioritize supporting the psychosocial aspects of the racial experience and how student perception is a guiding feature in multiple processes associated with doctoral student socialization. In examining the differences in doctoral student success among Black, Hispanic, and White students, Nettles (1990) discusses the severe (and systemic) underrepresentation of Black doctoral students and asserts that Black and Hispanic students perceive more feelings of racial discrimination and receive less research and teaching assistantships than their White counterparts. He notes that of the three groups, Black doctoral students require the most intervention for support because of challenges with undergraduate preparation, availability of research opportunities, and reliance on personal resources to finance doctoral study. Nettles's quantitative study does not identify specific psychosocial issues regarding the racial discrimination experienced by Black students. However, his work underscores that perception of experience is essential to understanding the role race plays in the doctoral process.

Morehouse and Dawkins (2006) also discuss the severe underrepresentation of Black doctoral degree recipients as a long-standing pattern and suggest that more research must be developed to understand how students could be supported once they are enrolled in doctoral programs. Their work with the McKnight Doctoral Fellowship program demonstrates the importance of seamlessness as an effective approach to supporting African American degree completion and success beyond the doctorate. They assert that opportunities should facilitate a connection between research activities and student interests and suggest that these research interests may be related to the African American experience. A seamless approach also considers the environmental constraints associated with the African American student experience in predominantly White spaces where accounts of indirect discrimination and racism may occur about their participation as students as well as the ways in which their research interests are supported. Consideration of these experiences can inform program organizers of practices that typically have served to complicate intellectual development that emerges from student research interests.

A seamless approach involves a series of activities that serves to counteract racist norms through supportive activities designed to embrace students' research interests and empower their intellectual development. In addition to these important motivational elements, Morehouse and Dawkins also discuss program essentials such as providing funding for doctoral study and mentors who are willing to provide guidance on research activities. Taylor and Antony (2000) find that motivation about research was directly linked to the racial experience of doctoral students. They assert that African American doctoral students feel pressure to respond to stereotype threats of not being able to meet standards of academic achievement and feel the need to prove themselves. Furthermore, the need to prove themselves often puts them at risk of responding to false standards that do not encourage their intellectual development. Taylor and Antony note that African American students carry the weight of wanting to improve education for their communities, and this obligation is deeply intertwined with their research agendas. Moreover, African American doctoral students' obligation to social justice is often correlated with an objective to strengthen historically underserved, marginalized communities (Gasman et al., 2008; Hopp et al., 2003).

In fact, for some doctoral students, their racial experience may extend beyond the goal of degree completion toward a commitment to a broad agenda of social justice where racial politics are central to a lifelong obligation of service, research, and teaching—serving to uplift the very communities they represent. To understand doctoral student socialization holistically, we argue that race must be considered to be an aspect of students' research orientation in an effort to facilitate meaning-making of the learning experience, strides toward greater intellectual development, degree completion, and success. Furthermore, considering the racial experience will serve to inform faculty and administrators who are interested in strengthening their capacity to support marginalized doctoral students. As scholars supportive of students of color, we assert that an impetus of this work is to share strategies to improve educational environments where members have been marginalized, thus enacting our commitment to uplifting our community.

Because this work examines race from a psychosocial perspective, it is important to acknowledge scholarship on racial identity/ideology and its significant contribution to the discussion on the psychosocial experiences of Blacks/African Americans, including Cross's (1991) *Shades of Black: Diversity in African American Identity* and Helms's (1990) perspectives on racial identity theory in her work *Black and White Racial Identity: Theory, Research, and Practice.* Cross and Helms present measurement scales and interventions regarding the ways African Americans perceive their identities in relation to their personality development, interpersonal interactions, and environment.

Within the context of doctoral student socialization, Cross's and Helms's perspectives on personality development may be aligned with scholarly intellectual development (scholarly personality or scholarly voice); interpersonal interactions may be aligned with the student–faculty relations (or relationships with other academic community members); and doctoral students' academic setting might be considered for environment. The relevance of Cross's (1991) and Helms's (1990) work brings to bear the psychology of the racial experience as being a critical and significant aspect of socialization for Black/African American doctoral students. Perspectives on the role of racial identity within the doctoral experience is addressed in the examination of doctoral students' interactions with faculty mentors and curriculum design (Felder, 2010; Hall & Burns, 2009). Furthermore, the concept of racial identity is relevant to Black doctoral students' perceptions of their struggle to persist toward degree completion (Gildersleeve, Croom, & Vasquez, 2011) and in understanding their experiences in cross-race advising relationships (Barker, 2012).

Strategies to Support Black/African American Doctoral Students

The doctoral experience is multifaceted and complex, with numerous issues to consider for understanding how to develop holistic support efforts/strategies for historically marginalized doctoral students. There are three areas of socialization that are critical to the ongoing support Black/African American doctoral student success and degree completion: *prior socialization,* or how race and culture can inform the process of preparing students for doctoral study; augmented *advisement* strategies that create support for developing new relational opportunities for building cultural wealth; and understanding the ways *disciplinary interests* are expanding and transforming in response to shifting societal needs. This section recommends several practical strategies based on policy and research focused on doctoral education (Council of Graduate Schools and Educational Testing Service, 2010). Strategies in this section might be considered for all doctoral students, especially those representing historically marginalized communities.

Prior Socialization

The concept of prior socialization addresses a wide range of issues influencing academic preparation for pursuit and completion of the doctoral degree for Black/African American students (Felder, Stevenson, & Gasman, 2014; Twale, Weidman, & Bethea, 2016; Weidman & Twale, 2001). For instance, scholarship has addressed the development of cognitive mapping as an essential aspect of preparation (Lovitts, 2001). That is to say, some students grow up around family members with doctorates who translate experiences of doctoral student success that become ingrained. Prior socialization has also addressed the role of institutions in building support capacity to facilitate transition into graduate education for historically marginalized students (Tierney, 1997). This work has included the impact of programmatic efforts designed to increase recruitment, retention, and degree completion.

For most of the 20th century, HBCU institutions were the primary providers of opportunities for graduate education for Blacks/African Americans (and continue to make substantive contributions). Research on HBCUs as baccalaureate origins, as well as producers of doctoral degree completers for Black/African American doctoral degree recipients, provides foundational background information for understanding the institutional cultural traditions fundamental to academic success at the doctoral level.

Policy research suggests our graduate education system is vulnerable regarding the recruitment and retention of students from historically marginalized backgrounds (Council of Graduate Schools and Educational Testing Service, 2010). HBCUs facilitate opportunities for graduate schools to identify and attract talented students. Furthermore, these institutions specialize in creating interventions that increase degree completion for Blacks/African Americans. In this way, these institutions are key national assets in facilitating institutional diversity and building capacity to support historically marginalized doctoral students by minimizing vulnerability in the graduate education system. Much of this work has developed out of programmatic efforts facilitated by HBCUs (Conrad and Gasman, 2015).

ADVISEMENT

When considering policy research suggestions focused on the academic advisement of Black/African American doctoral students, two important issues should be considered: how to advise students regarding nonacademic career pathways and preparation for future faculty roles. In terms of advising Black/African doctoral students about nonacademic career pathways, strategies must be multifaceted to advise students about opportunities (Barker, 2007, 2011, 2012; Felder & Barker, 2013). In addition to traditional gatekeeping systems, supportive and holistic advisement must involve reviewing prospective networking and professional development opportunities within one's institution in addition to students' relevant disciplinary and industrial communities. Students must be aware of the ways their knowledge and skills can be honed to contribute in alignment with how they make meaning of their academic experiences, disciplines, and practices.

For many Black/African American students, this may involve acknowledging and understanding the ways their racial and cultural perspectives inform their research and practice agendas and incorporating this into advisement strategies (Ellis, 2001). Realities about the availability of faculty opportunities must be considered to address the racial and cultural interests of students. These realities may include advising students about faculty opportunities related to a student's research interests, the ways faculty may or may not be supportive of these interests, and identifying other opportunities where a student may be able to thrive both professionally and personally. For instance, if a Black/African American student's research agenda prioritizes race and culture, an adviser should consider how this agenda will be supported in post-degree completion within a faculty role. Furthermore, professional development at the doctoral level must address students' ability to hone transferable skills and how these skills might address their interest in racial and cultural issues.

Disciplinary Interests

Disciplinary areas focused on education, social sciences, and humanities have been identified to represent the largest concentration of Black/African American doctoral degree completers (Survey of Earned Doctorates, 2006, 2016). Therefore, understanding trends about career opportunities related to these areas is essential to supporting academic success, degree attainment, and transition beyond degree completion. Also, an understanding of these trends must involve consideration of the racial and cultural aspects of the doctoral student experience. To maximize interest in disciplines of students from underrepresented backgrounds, grant programs that leverage the interests represented by the academy and industries should consider the ways racial and cultural issues inform research and practice. In doing this, they will be better positioned to understand and support contributions from doctoral students from historically marginalized communities.

Furthermore, strategies that increase awareness and understanding of these issues can serve to strengthen institutional and organizational diversity initiatives. How and why these students persist through to completion can be integral for learning more about their persistence in other disciplines. Given the significant representation of Blacks/African Americans in these areas, examining their scholarly impact will lend insight to understanding academic achievement at all levels of education. This also includes discussion about the fields of science, technology, engineering, agriculture, and mathematics (STEAM) and the growing emphasis on recruitment and retention strategies for doctoral students of color in these disciplinary areas (Allum, Okahana, Felder, & Tull, 2015).

Discussion

There are several benefits to studying the racial and cultural aspects of the doctoral experience as they relate to understanding Black/African American doctoral students. First, issues contributing to racial and cultural inequities in doctoral education that relate to a student's prior socialization, advisement needs, and institutional commitment to supporting students' interests inform our understanding of how to support academic success, degree completion, and transitional experiences beyond the doctoral process. Second, looming sociohistorical factors and the existence of racism and exclusionary policies in higher education have contributed to systemic educational marginalization.

CRT and interest convergence provide important foundational philosophical frameworks for building practical strategies that align with the historical and intellectual needs of Black/African American doctoral students related to historic legacies of exclusion. Third, the study of racial and cultural experiences at the doctoral level contributes to the existing body of knowledge about the ways Black/African American students experience the doctoral process by examining issues that have contributed to the underrepresentation of Blacks/African Americans.

Research on the racial and cultural aspects of the doctoral experience must expand to support the value of storytelling and narratives about student experience. Finally, research-based recommendations are practitioner focused; specifically, they are focused on programmatic and policy interventions for graduate school programs. These efforts emphasize the racial and cultural experiences associated with socialization for historically marginalized students.

Conclusion

Future research must consider the value of the racial and cultural aspects of the doctoral students for any meaningful strategies designed to support Black/African American doctoral students (and students from historically marginalized backgrounds). Practical strategies might address how faculty members who support students in doctoral programs could modify their advising so that it encompasses more mentoring and cross-cultural competence. Mentoring relationships between faculty and students of color, particularly at the doctoral level, are critical to doctoral degree completion for African Americans and other students of color (Davidson & Foster-Johnson, 2001; Taylor & Antony, 2000).

To better understand successful models for student persistence at the doctoral level, future research should consider the institutional impact on the experiences of students of color, particularly those at predominantly White institutions, HBCUs, and Hispanic-serving institutions. Chapters in this volume address research focusing on how these students' racial and cultural perspectives may influence their disciplinary experiences.

Furthermore, understanding the impact of HBCUs is of particular importance, as many of these institutions serve to facilitate African American doctoral degree attainment. Cultural frameworks like Sankofa, as well as CRT, can be used to develop these recommendations and to explore implications for the development of institutional and student policy. Also, research must continue to provide research on doctoral degree attainment to include personal narratives of Black/African American doctoral students.

Works Cited

Anthony, J. S., & Taylor, E. (2004). Theories and strategies of academic career socialization: Improving paths to the professoriate for Black graduate students. In D. H. Wulff, A. E. Austin, & Associates, *Paths to the professoriate: Strategies for enriching the preparation of future faculty* (pp. 92–114). San Francisco, CA: Jossey-Bass.

Antony, J. S. (2002). Reexamining doctoral student socialization and professional development: Moving beyond the congruence and assimilation orientation. In: J. C. Smart & W. G. Tierney, (Eds.), *Higher education: handbook of theory and research* (Vol. XVII, 349–380). New York, NY: Agathon Press.

Austin, A. E. (2002). Preparing the next generation of faculty: Graduate school as socialization to the academic career. *The Journal of Higher Education*, 73, 94–121.

Austin, A. E., & McDaniels, M. (2006). Preparing the professoriate of the future: Graduate student socialization for faculty roles. In: John C. Smart (Ed.), *Higher education: Handbook of theory and research* (Vol. XXI, 397–456). New York, NY: Agathon Press.

Barker, M. J. (2007). Cross-cultural mentoring across institutional contexts. *Negro Educational Review, 58*(1/2), 85–103.

Barker, M. J. (2012). An exploration of racial identity among Black doctoral students involved in cross-race advising relationships. In J. Sullivan & A. Esmail (Eds.), *African American identity: Racial and cultural dimensions of the Black experience*. Lanham, MD: Lexington Books.

Barker, M. J. (2011). Racial context, currency, and connection. Black doctoral student and white faculty advisor perspectives on cross-race advising. *Innovative Education & Teaching International, 48*(4), 387–400.

Cleveland, D. (Ed.). (2004). *A long way to go: Conversations about race by African American faculty and graduate students*. New York, NY: Peter Lang.

Cross, W. E., Jr. (1991). *Shades of Black: Diversity in African-American identity*. Philadelphia, PA: Temple University Press.

Davidson, M. N., & Foster-Johnson, L. (2001). Mentoring in the preparation of graduate researchers of color. *Review of Educational Research, 71*(4), 549–574.

Ellis, E. M. (2001). The impact of race and gender on graduate school socialization, satisfaction with doctoral study, and commitment to degree completion. *The Western Journal of Black Studies, 25,* 30–45.

Felder, P. (2010). On doctoral student development: Exploring faculty mentoring in the shaping of African American doctoral student success. *The Qualitative Report, 15*(3), 455–474.

Felder, P. P., & Barker, M. J. (2013). Extending Bell's concept of interest convergence: A framework for understanding the African American doctoral experience. *International Journal of Doctoral Studies, 8,* 1–20.

Felder, P. P., Parrish, W. P., Collier, J., & Blockett, R. (2016). Understanding programmatic support of doctoral student socialization via social media. *Teachers College Record*. Retrieved from http://www.tcrecord.org, ID Number: 19451

Gardner, S. K. (2008). Fitting the mold of graduate school: A qualitative study of socialization in doctoral education. *Innovative Higher Education, 7,* 1–21.

Gardner, S. K. (2010). Keeping up with the Joneses: Socialization and culture in doctoral education at one striving institution. *The Journal of Higher Education, 81*(6), 728–749.

Gardner, S. K., & Barnes, B. J. (2007). Graduate student involvement: Socialization and the professional role. *Journal of College Student Development, 48,* 269–387.

Gasman, M., Gerstl-Pepin, C., Aderson-Thompkins, S., Rasheed, L., & Hathaway, K. (2004). Developing trust, negotiating power: Transgressing race and status in the academy. *Teachers College Record, 106*(4), 689–715.

Gasman, M., Hirschfield, A., & Vultaggio, J. (2008). "Difficult yet rewarding": The experiences of African American graduate students. *Journal of Diversity in Higher Education, 1*(2), 126–138.

Gay, G. (2004). Navigating marginality en route to the professoriate: Graduate students of color learning and living in academia. *International Journal of Qualitative Studies in Education, 17*(2), 265–288.

Green, A. L., & Scott, L. V. (2003). *Journey to the Ph.D.: How to navigate the process as African Americans.* Sterling, VA: Stylus.

Gildersleeve, R., Croom, N., & Vasquez, P.L. (2011). Am I going crazy?: Critical race analysis in doctoral education. *Equity & Excellence in Education, 44*(1), 93–114.

Harper, S. R., Patton, L. D., & Wooden, O. S. (2009). Access and equity for African American students in higher education: A critical race historical analysis of policy efforts. *Journal of Higher Education, 80*, 389–414.

Harper, S. R., & Hurtado, S. (2007). Nine themes in campus racial climates and implications for institutional transformation. In S. R. Harper & L. D. Patton (Eds.), *Responding to the realities of race on campus* (pp. 7–24). *New Directions for Student Services, 120.* San Francisco, CA: Jossey-Bass.

Helms, J. E. (1990). *Black and White racial identity: Theory, research, and practice.* Westport, CT: Praeger.

Hopp, C., Mumford, V., & Williams, F. (2003). The role of mentoring for future academicians. In A. L. Green & L. V. Scott (Eds.), *Journey to the Ph.D.: How to navigate the process as African Americans* (pp. 255–269). Sterling, VA: Stylus.

Hughes, D., Rodriguez, J., Smith, E. P., Johnson, D. J., Stevenson, H. C., & Spicer, P. (2006). Parents' racial/ethnic socialization practices: A review of research and agenda for future study. *Developmental Psychology, 42*(5), 747–770.

Hurtado, S., Milem, J., Clayton-Pederson, A., & Allen, W. (1999). Enacting diverse learning environments: Improving the climate for racial/ethnic diversity in higher education. *ASHE-ERIC Higher Education Report, 26*(8). Washington, DC: The George Washington University, Graduate School of Education and Human Development.

Ladson-Billings, G. (1995). Toward a theory of culturally relevant pedagogy, *American Educational Research Journal, 32*(3), 465–491.

Lovitts, B. E. (2001) *Leaving the ivory tower: The causes and consequences of departure from doctoral study.* Lanham, MD: Rowman & Littlefield.

Milner, H. R. (2007). Race, culture, and researcher positionality: Working through dangers, seen, unseen, and unforeseen. *Educational Researcher, 36*(7), 388–400.

Morehouse, L., & Dawkins, M. P. (2006). The McKnight Doctoral Fellowship Program: Toward a seamless approach to the production of African American doctorates. *Journal of Negro Education, 75*, 563–571.

National Science Foundation, National Center for Science and Engineering Statistics (NCSES). (2012). *Doctorate recipients from U.S. universities: 2011.* Special Report NSF 13-301. Arlington, VA. Available from http://www.nsf.gov/statistics/doctorates

Nettles, M. T. (1990). Success in doctoral programs: Experiences of minority and White students. *American Journal of Education, 98*(4), 494–522.

Nettles, M. T., & Milliett, C. M. (2006). *Three magic letters: Getting to Ph.D.* Baltimore, MD: Johns Hopkins University Press.

Okahana, H., Allum, J., Felder, P. P., & Tull, R. G. (2016). *Implications for practice and research from Doctoral Initiative on Minority Attrition and Completion* (CGS Data Sources PLUS #16-01). Washington, DC: Council of Graduate Schools.

Rentz, T. (2003). The role of mentorship in developing African American students and professionals within the academy. In A. L. Green & L. V. Scott (Eds.), *Journey to the Ph.D.: How to navigate the process as African Americans* (pp. 255–269). Sterling, VA: Stylus.

Smith, D. (2016). The diversity imperative: Moving to the next generation. In M. Bastedo, P. G. Altbach, and P. J. Gumport (Eds.), *American higher education in the twenty-first century: Social, political, and economic challenges* (pp. 375–400). Baltimore, MD: Johns Hopkins University Press.

Smith, W., Altbach, P., & Lomotey, K. (2002). *The racial crisis in American higher education: Continuing challenges in the twenty-first century.* Albany, NY: State University of New York Press.

Steele, C. M., & Aronson, J. (1995). Stereotype threat and the intellectual test performance of African Americans. *Journal of Personality and Social Psychology, 69*, 797–811.

Stevenson, H. C. (2014). *Promoting racial literacy in schools: Differences that make a difference.* New York, NY: Teachers College Press.

Stevenson, H. C., & Arrington, E. G. (2009). Racial/ethnic socialization mediates perceived racisms and the racial identity of African American adolescents. In D. Slaughter-Defoe, H. C. Stevenson, E. G. Arrington, & D. Johnson (Eds.), *Black educational choice: Assessing the private and public alternatives to tradition K–12 public schools.* Santa Barbara, CA: Praeger.

Taylor, E., & Antony, J. S. (2000). Stereotype threat reduction and wise schooling: Towards the successful socialization of African American doctoral students in education. *The Journal of Negro Education, 69*(3), 184–198.

Thurgood, Lori, Golladay, Mary J., & Hill, Susan T. (2006). *U.S. doctorates in the 20th century* (NSF Publication No. 06-319). Alexandria, VA: National Science Foundation, Division of Science Resources Statistics.

Tierney, W. G. (1997). Organizational socialization in higher education. *Journal of Higher Education, 68*(1), 1–16.

Twale, D., Weidman, J., & Bethea, K. (2016). Conceptualizing socialization of graduate students of color: Revisiting the Weidman-Twale-Stein framework. *The Western Journal of Black Studies, 4*(2), 80–94.

U.S. Department of Education, National Center for Education Statistics. (2017). *The Condition of Education 2017* (NCES 2017-144), Characteristics of Postsecondary Faculty.

Walker, G. E., Golde, C. M., Jones, L., Bueschel, A. C., & Hutchings, P. (2008). *The formation of scholars: Rethinking doctoral education for the twenty-first century*. San Francisco, CA: The Carnegie Foundation for the Advancement of Teaching, Jossey-Bass.

Weidman, J. C. (2006). Socialization of students in higher education: Organizational perspectives. In C. Conrad & R. C. Serlin (Eds.), *The SAGE handbook for research in education: Engaging ideas and enriching inquiry* (pp. 253–262). Thousand Oaks, CA: Sage.

Weidman J. C., & Stein E. L. (2003). Socialization of doctoral students to academic norms. *Research in Higher Education 44*(6), 641–656.

Weidman, J. C, Twale, D. J., & Stein, E. L. (2001). Socialization of graduate and professional students in higher education: A perilous passage? *ASHE-ERIC Higher Education Report*. Washington, DC: The George Washington University, School of Education and Human Development.

Willie, C. V., Grady, M. K., & Hope, R. O. (1991) *African Americans and the doctoral experience: Implications for policy*. New York, NY: Teachers College Press.

Chapter 2

Programmatic Efforts and the Black Doctoral Experience in Education

A Literature Review

Pamela Felder Small, Girvin Liggans,
Fanuel Chirombo, and Sydney Freeman Jr.

There have been numerous efforts to support the experiences of students moving toward doctoral degree completion. A chief concern of these efforts is the level of effectiveness at student, program, and institutional levels. Sankofa provides guidance when exploring a fragmented cultural past and identifying how this may minimize the value of students' racial and cultural values (Temple, 2010). Institutional selectivity and prestige are consistent with legacies of exclusion that have historically excluded and marginalized Black/African American students in higher education (Allen, 1985, 1992). Predominantly White institutions (PWIs) have a long history of facilitating highly selective doctoral programs. Many of these programs are housed within the most competitive national and internationally renowned universities (Hernández, 2010).

Emergent scholarship examines Black/African American students pursuing doctoral study within these environments and their doctoral student socialization in an effort to strengthen support of their academic success, doctoral degree completion, and positionality of their cultural focus (Bertrand Jones, Osborne-Lampkin, Patterson, & Davis, 2015; Blockett, Felder, Parrish, & Collier, 2016; Felder & Barker, 2013; Gildersleeve, Croom, & Vazquez, 2011; Rowley, 2014; Taylor & Antony, 2000; Weidman, Twale, & Bethea, 2016).

Themes regarding the significance of mentoring and advising, peer support, academic isolation, financial stress, and spirituality serve to emphasize the value of racial and ethnic student perspectives. However, continued research is needed to better understand programmatic efforts that support doctoral socialization, facilitate academic success and degree completion, and stem attrition. The role of attrition is characterized in our national system of graduate education as a critical area of sustained vulnerability in need of further development (Council of Graduate Education & Educational Testing Service, 2010, 2012).

The attrition rate of doctoral students in the United States has consistently been estimated to be around 40% to 50% (Wendler et al., 2010). The attrition rate of doctoral students is traditionally calculated as the percentage of fully admitted students who do not complete the degree (Pauley, Cunningham, & Toth, 1999). Several factors are linked to this attrition. For example, Jairam and Kahl investigated the role of social support in the successful completion of a doctoral degree. They found that stress and the possibility that students who leave programs might not have received adequate social support from academic friends, family, and faculty to be major factors contributing to doctoral student attrition (Jairam & Kahl, 2012). Thus, understanding how to facilitate greater levels of support for doctoral students may strengthen approaches to achieving academic success.

Many researchers studying doctoral attrition (particularly for students of color) have looked to models of attrition applied at the undergraduate level to see how those concepts could apply at the doctoral level (Girves & Wemmerus, 1988; Boyd 1977; Lovitts, 2001; Mallinckrodt & Sedlacek, 1987). A theoretical base has been generated, and several models of attrition have been developed and tested empirically (Girves & Wemmerus, 1988). However, models have not been prevalent in guiding the study of doctoral attrition for specific racial and ethnic groups.

African American doctoral student retention as a research area is fairly undeveloped. In fact, many researchers have suggested that more studies should examine this topic (Brown et al., 1994; Clewell, 1987). For example, the Minority Graduate Education Project of the Educational Testing Service released an update of its research agenda and urges further research on the factors shaping minority graduate students' persistence, attrition, and degree completion rates (Brown et al., 1994). Clewell (1987) asserts that the "identification of the most significant factors affecting success or failure of minority graduate students is an important step in understanding the problem of low persistence rates among minority graduate students" (p. 19).

This growing body of work contributes new insight into the complexities of the doctoral process and moves the discussion toward understanding student experience beyond statistical portraits of degree completion. Research that expands the discussion of the racial and cultural significance of this experience is essential to this dialogue and serves to strengthen the foundation of this scholarship.

The purpose of this chapter is to provide a discussion of literature focused on doctoral student socialization specific to the education field, issues related to marginalization, and doctoral student success for the Black/ African American experience. We discuss why these areas of literature are important for a better understanding of programs designed to support historically marginalized students, and we review several programs that have been successful in strengthening Black/African American doctoral student success and degree completion. We discuss nuances of programmatic models and explain their strengths and capacity to support students within a variety of institutional contexts.

Socialization is viewed as a process of becoming part of an organization through learning the culture, values, attitudes, and expectations of that organization (Austin, 2002). Sankofa emphasizes the role and value of race and culture as being central to this process. We seek to understand the programmatic functions facilitating socialization by exploring the following questions in this chapter: What programmatic efforts are in place to support socialization of Black/African American doctoral students in the field of education, specifically teacher education, STEM education, and higher education? In what ways do these programmatic efforts support and/or hinder the socialization of doctoral students? In what ways do these programmatic efforts support and/or hinder transition into the professoriate?

Understanding the Relationship between Socialization, Marginalization, and African American Doctoral Persistence

Researchers have explored aspects of race and gender as well as student and faculty perspectives as they relate to the doctoral student socialization experience (Gardner, 2010). Graduate students experience socialization to the role of graduate student and academic life, to the profession, and to a specific discipline simultaneously (Austin 2002). According to Gardner (2010) and Felder (2010), faculty members play a central role in the student socialization process. Gardner (2010) points to Bragg's (1976) statement that program structures, goals, and values may be clearly expressed in a program catalog, but it is the faculty members who serve as the primary means for student socialization. Doctoral programs differ by institution, and no two students will experience the socialization process the exact same way (Weidman, Twale, & Stein, 2001). Faculty transmit culture, values, attitudes, and expectations of their programs through their formal and informal functions and interactions as instructors, advisors, supervisors, and academic professionals (Gardner, 2010). Differences in doctoral programs are seen across academic disciplines at different institutions (Weidman, Twale, & Stein, 2001).

SOCIALIZATION

Socialization is the process by which people learn the characteristics of their group, and these include the knowledge, skills, attitudes, values, norms, and actions thought appropriate for them (Henslin, 2014). According to Merton (1957) in Gopaul (2011), socialization is the process through which a person develops a sense of self through values, attitudes, knowledge, and skills that govern behavior in a wide variety of situations. Gopaul (2011) identified the four stages of socialization as anticipatory, formal, informal, and personal.

The anticipatory stage involves developing an awareness of the characteristics of the desired group. Gopaul pointed out that this stage involves observations and interactions with peers and faculty members that a new doctoral student undertakes when he or she enters the doctoral program. The formal stage of socialization is concerned with learning the expectations, standards, and rewards of the organization. The informal stage is about individuals learning informal expectations and degrees of flexibility associated with the roles they play. At the personal stage, individuals internalize the parameters and dimensions of particular roles and begin to integrate a new identity with the existing self-image.

Gopaul (2011) extends the four stages of socialization to identifying knowledge acquisition, investment, and involvement as the three core elements of socialization. Knowledge acquisition involves learning the language, history, problems, and ideology of the profession. This involves the integration of self-image and professional image as group members mirror and model the behaviors of established members. Investment is concerned with channeling time, energy, and self-esteem into the group and thereby giving up or foregoing other options. Involvement is about role identification and commitment where individuals participate in various professional activities and internalize their identification with the commitment to the professional role. Critical to this involvement is the way culture shapes an understanding of the socialization experience.

Marginalization

The concept of marginalization was discussed in depth by Duchscher and Cowin (2004). Historically, it referred to status-based social attributes afforded to the elite relative to that afforded the impoverished. However, this has since changed, as it now refers to the process through which people are pushed to the periphery on the basis of their identities, associations, experiences, and environments (Hall & Meleis, 1994, in Duchscher & Cowin, 2004). Doctoral students come to the learning environment with different identities, associations, experiences, and from different environments, which can lead to their marginalization.

According to Duchscher and Cowin (2004), the marginalizing situation is the purposeful, time-limited process of passing from the center of one cultural group to the center of another cultural group, while the marginalized personality results from the long-standing misappropriation of individuals into a binding subordinate social or economic stratum within which the realization of their full sense of self is prohibited, and from which they are unable to ascend. In the case of marginalized doctoral students, ineffective or unattended programmatic efforts designed to facilitate socialization may create a marginalizing situation that can lead to permanent marginalization of some of them through attrition.

Where Programmatic Efforts Make a Difference

When considering differences in degree completion regarding the Black/African American doctoral experience, statistical evidence suggests degree attainment is highly likely to occur within the field of education compared to other fields of study represented by other racial and ethnic groups (Survey of Earned Doctorates, 2014, 2016). Thus, in addition to examining attrition, recruitment, and retention efforts to increase enrollment and degree completion, understanding belief systems about commitment to specific disciplines and areas of interest are critical to understanding Black/African American participation at the doctoral level. For example, Gasman, Hirschfield, and Vultaggio (2008) explored African American doctoral student socialization in the field of education and sought to understand the nature of the graduate school experience, the types of support available for success, and the process for doctoral student socialization for future faculty and professional roles in these environments. Findings of this work support Rowley's (2014) perspectives on the importance of centering students' racial identity, their understanding of disciplinary knowledge, and their historical background into the development of institutional systems of support.

In reporting U.S. citizen and permanent resident doctoral recipients by major field of study, ethnicity, and race for 2015, the Survey of Earned Doctorates (2016) determined that 4,029 doctorates in education were conferred out of the 35,117 doctorates represented by all fields. The field of education is represented by five major subfields, with Blacks/African Americans receiving the most degrees, by percentage, beyond every other racial and ethnic group: education administration (24.8), education research (13.5), teaching education (15. 2), teaching fields (9.3), and other (16.4). To strengthen Black/African American doctoral student socialization, consideration of student experience within this field of study represents significant potential for building programmatic support. Specifically, we review three areas of this field: (1) teacher education; (2) science, technology, engineering and mathematics (STEM) within teacher education; and (3) higher education. We review effective strategies for programmatic support in these areas, and models where there is significant potential to build capacity for these efforts. Teacher education (with an emphasis on urban education), STEM, and higher education have received noteworthy attention in the literature (McLachlan, 2006; Wolf-Wendel, Baker, Twombly, Tollefson, & Mahlios, 2006).

TEACHER EDUCATION

In the United States, schools of education are facing the dilemma of finding qualified applicants who are interested in filling faculty positions in teacher education programs (Wolf-Wendel et al., 2006). Wolf-Wendel et al. see this dilemma affecting two major features of the educational system: the development of new knowledge and the creation of new leaders within the academy. While these issues appear to be daunting aspects of education in general, their impact on the racial and cultural aspects of teacher education appear to be more complex regarding career preparation (Ladson-Billings, 1999).

In their analysis of data from the National Survey of Postsecondary Faculty and the Survey of Earned doctorates, Wolf-Wendel et al. (2006) found that minorities pursued academic careers at lower rates than non-minorities. This information is not surprising given the general rates of doctoral degree completion in general. However, their findings on the likelihood of individuals pursuing faculty careers addresses the larger issue of the lack of racial and cultural representation in the academy and along the educational spectrum. For instance, their work indicates that only 7% of public schoolteachers nationwide attended highly selective colleges and that attendance at the "top 50 graduate schools of education" increased the likelihood of a doctoral student entering a faculty career in teacher education (Wolf-Wendel, et al., 2006).

This raises concerns about African American doctoral degree completion in the field of teacher education and their participation as leaders in the nation's public school system. According to Cooper and Jordan (2009), an achievement gap continues to exist as African American students continue to lag behind their White and Asian student counterparts. Cooper and Jordan assert that most of the emerging school leadership tends to be out of touch with the racial, cultural, and socioeconomic backgrounds of the students and communities they teach. Given these realities, an important question to consider is: What are the belief systems of doctoral students in the field of teacher education regarding these realities? Furthermore, in what ways are African American doctoral students committed to addressing the achievement gap and lack of leadership?

STEM EDUCATION

Perhaps no other area within the discipline of education highlights disparities among African American doctoral degree completers more than STEM. Previous research on underrepresented minorities (URM) in this area suggests that racial and cultural differences are significant factors in shaping relationships that impact degree completion (MacLachlan, 2006). While in the past low doctoral degree completion rates for URM was a cause for concern, researchers suggest this issue is now a matter of national importance and is viewed as a vulnerability, as this affects the nation's global educational position for the future (Wendler et al., 2010).

As previously stated, achievement gaps at every other level preceding the doctorate have shaped African American doctoral degree completion in particular. MacLachlan (2006) suggests that recruitment strategies are helpful in getting African Americans to matriculate into doctoral study. However, MacLachlan implies that greater support strategies may be needed to support students through periods of adjustment, especially for those students who make a transition into doctoral programs with institutional structures that are very different from the undergraduate or master's degree programs.

Higher Education

The field of higher education is significant in understanding the African American doctoral degree experience mainly because more research regarding this population is needed in general. This includes more research concerning the factors outlined in chapter 3. But beyond this, the study of higher education explores the "knowledge business" as it relates to access, creation, dissemination, and certification of knowledge relative to African American participation. Two important features of higher education should be considered when evaluating the impact of this field on African American doctoral degree attainment. They include the study of the African American doctoral degree experience within elite institutional environments and historically Black colleges and universities (HBCUs).

According to a report of the *Data-Based Assessment of Research-Doctorate Programs in the United States* (National Research Council, 2010), doctoral education is dominated by public universities, which housed 72% of the doctoral programs ranked in the study. Of the 37 universities that produced the most PhDs from 2002 to 2006, only 12 were private universities. Furthermore, the report indicated that the faculty is not diverse with respect to underrepresented minorities, who make up 5% or less of faculty in all broad fields except the social sciences (7%) and the humanities (11%). One conclusion drawn from these statistics is that research efforts should be focused on doctoral degree completion within the public university system. However, challenges regarding matriculation and degree completion tend to be emphasized within institutions where the historic legacy of exclusion tend to be the greatest: within the private elite institutions.

African American participation within PWI environments will continue to be a challenge given its history. As the Local Model of Doctoral Student Success suggests, more information about student commitment toward degree completion will contribute to an understanding of promoting the faculty–student relationships that are vital to developing ongoing faculty and administrative leadership within higher education. This model draws on research on student integration, student involvement, and student attrition (Astin, 1984, 1985; Bean, 1980, 1982, 1983; Padilla, 1991; Tinto, 1987, 1993).

WHY PROGRAMMATIC EFFORTS ARE IMPORTANT

As the culture, beliefs, and norms of the institution are not innately understood by students entering a degree program, it has primarily fallen to the student's educational institution to establish strategies and actions that promote socialization and academic success of doctoral students. Programmatic efforts emphasizing factors of success, such as those outlined in the Local Model of Doctoral Student Success in Table 2.1, are essential to

Table 2.1. Model of Doctoral Student Success

Components of Socialization	Factors of Success
Pre-matriculation characteristics of commitment to degree completion	Academic: undergraduate grade point average, graduate school entrance exams; and personal: socioeconomic status and family educational level
Belief systems about academic socialization include degree completer perceptions of the following:	Faculty and staff interactions; academic adjustment; and student involvement
Belief systems about environment include degree completer perceptions of the following:	Racial climate; alienation; and prejudice, racism, and discrimination
Belief systems about support include degree completer perceptions of the following:	Financial support; family; and organizational support
Commitment to the institution (while enrolled and post-degree completion)	While enrolled: participation in events; relationships with faculty, administrators, and current students; and post-degree completion: engagement with institution and relationship to faculty, administrators, current students and alumni

socialization in general, and specifically to the socialization of historically marginalized doctoral students. These efforts include financial support, professional development, faculty interactions, and networking opportunities. Often, programs are designed to convey and establish these factors of success; however, when factors of success are not aligned with student belief systems and fail to consider the impact of racial, cultural, institutional, and regional nuances, processes of socialization may be complicated for students who may experience a lack of support. As described earlier, the process of socialization is largely characterized as a relationship between the educational institution and the student. However, independent from the student's home institution, various programs seek to provide support for the academic success of historically underrepresented students enrolled in doctoral programs. Such student support may be offered indirectly through institutional and academic program support or directly to doctoral students themselves. While variation exists, the consistent components central across these programs include financial support, professional development, evidence-based strategies, and networking opportunities.

For educational institutions interested in implementing strategies that support historically marginalized students, the following recommended programs may be helpful in developing strategies of support within specific contexts. These recommendations consider the disciplinary areas discussed in this chapter along with research-based factors of success represented in (but not limited to) state-wide, institutional, and regional examples (see Table 2.2). Programs such as these imbed a consideration of cultural nuance in the role traditionally played by the faculty and staff of the home institution and combat marginalization through activities that normalize and strengthen identities, associations, experiences, and environments of historically marginalized students.

The Alliance for Graduate Education and the Professoriate Program (AGEP) provides a good example of a national program offering student support indirectly through institutional and academic program and faculty support. These institutions and academic programs receiving support then provide support directly to doctoral students themselves. AGEP has set forth a national goal of increasing the number of underrepresented minorities in STEM and faculty positions that are achieved through regional and state-level partnerships. Financial and organizational support is provided directly to institutions for projects focused on strategic alliances and empirical research designed to study and implement evidence-based strategies, models, and practices.

Table 2.2. Examples of Programmatic Efforts Supporting Doctoral
Student Socialization

National Example	Alliance for Graduate Education and the Professoriate Program (AGEP); The National Science Foundation funds the Alliances for Graduate Education and the Professoriate (AGEP) program. The primary goals of AGEP are to (a) significantly increase the number of underrepresented minorities (i.e., African Americans, Hispanics, American Indians, Alaska Natives, and Native Hawaiians or other Pacific Islanders) obtaining graduate degrees in science, technology, engineering and mathematics (STEM); and b) to enhance the preparation of underrepresented minorities for faculty positions in academia. http://www.nsfagep.org/
Regional Example	Southern Regional Education Board Doctoral Scholars Program; The Doctoral Scholars Program provides multiple layers of support—not only financial assistance and research funding, but also career counseling, job postings, and a scholar directory for networking and recruiting. Mentoring and advocacy for scholars is crucial, and support continues into early careers as graduates become faculty members. Also, each fall, 1,000 scholars and young faculty members convene to learn and support one another at the Institute on Teaching and Mentoring. http://www.sreb.org/doctoral-scholars-program)
Institutional Example	Chancellor's Doctoral Incentive Program Scholars; The California State University (CSU) Chancellor's Doctoral Incentive Program (CDIP) aims to increase the number of promising doctoral students applying for future CSU instructional faculty positions by offering financial assistance in the form of a loan and mentorship by CSU faculty.
	Established in 1987, the CSU CDIP is the largest program of its kind in the United States. As of June 2016, the program had loaned $49 million to 2,081 doctoral students enrolled in universities throughout the nation. A total of 1,275 participants have successfully earned doctoral degrees, and more than half (735 participants) have subsequently obtained employment in CSU instructional faculty positions. http://www.calstate.edu/hr/cdip/

The Southern Regional Education Board (SREB) Doctoral Scholars Program and the PROMISE: Maryland's Alliance for Graduate Education and the Professoriate, respectively, stand as current regional and state-level examples that take work in collaboration and with support from AGEP to provide support directly to the doctoral student. SREB shares the same goal as AGEP and works directly with its 16 member universities via the Doctoral Scholars Program (DSP) to provide financial assistance, research funding, career counseling, job postings, and mentoring to doctoral students from underrepresented groups. DSP participants and young faculty also meet annually in a networking and support event. PROMISE is Maryland's AGEP and consists of an alliance of the 14 colleges, universities, and regional education centers in the University System of Maryland. PROMISE provides underrepresented minority doctoral students with seminars on professional development, dissertation writing, a Summer Success Institute (SSI), and a Professors-in-Training program.

The Chancellor's Doctoral Incentive (CDIP) program is an institutional example within the California higher education system. CDIP provides multiple levels of support to include loans up to $10,000 per year over five years, with a maximum amount of $30,000. The loans are repayable over a 15-year period commencing one year after completion of, or withdrawal from, full-time doctoral study. A key support strategy is loan forgiveness, with a forgivable rate of 20% for each year of full-time postdoctoral teaching employment in the CSU or 10% for each year of part-time postdoctoral teaching employment in the CSU. A mentorship component ensures the success of the doctoral students by combining the loan program with faculty support through collaborative teaching research and/or service activities. Faculty mentors support the CDIP Scholars' successful completion of their doctoral studies. They also work to enhance the CDIP Scholars' potential for employment in an instructional faculty position at CSU.

The national, regional, and institutional examples are considered models based on the breadth and depth of capacity regarding impact of their programmatic components reaching multiple constituents: students, faculty, and policy makers. They also represent the development of critical mass for the areas they represent. For instance, a primary outcome of all AGEP projects is significant capacity building with respect to administrative infrastructure. More specifically, the successful and effective implementation of strategies to coordinate innovative graduate education activities across multiple departments at participating institutions and across multiple partnering institutions requires the establishment of new administrative infrastructure (i.e., policies, practices, offices, and staffing). These newly established administrative infrastructures involve a variety of resources, including (but not limited to) space, equipment, and staff. This administrative infrastructure will exist after the term of the NSF-supported activity. Additionally, practices by the SREB specifically focus on facilitating successful transition into faculty pathways. CDIP also encourages postdoctoral degree completion success by supporting participants through the attainment of full-time faculty positions with the California State University system.

There are many programmatic efforts supporting historically marginalized students in a variety of ways. They are too numerous to include in this chapter. The goal of this chapter is not to focus on every program available supporting doctoral degree completion, but rather to focus on how critical nuances of programmatic efforts could serve as guidance for existing programs and the development of new ones. For instance, there are gender-based efforts such as Sisters of the Academy (SOTA), with a focus on providing undergraduate and graduate women of color with the skills and motivation necessary to complete post-baccalaureate degrees. SOTA offers programs focused on professional development, the development of relationships, and collaborative scholarship. SOTA participants receive opportunities to identify their strengths and passions and mentoring by scholars in residence. A unique feature of SOTA's efforts emphasizes the value of sisterhood and networking among its participants.

WHEN MARGINALIZATION COMPLICATES SOCIALIZATION: IMPLICATIONS FOR FUTURE RESEARCH AND PRACTICE

In the context of this work, we see marginalization as a potential complication of socialization, serving as a hindrance to the facilitation of a thriving sense of academic success, movement toward degree completion, and transition into the professoriate. Drawing on concepts of socialization, we seek to explore this complication of underrepresented students as a contradiction between the historically oppressive spaces and structures associated with PWIs and their race, culture, and values. Students bring belief systems with them to doctoral programs. However, often these belief systems become marginalized during the socialization process.

Students must learn how to become agents of transformation of their marginalized realities in order to combat oppressive racial and cultural exclusion. When there is a lack of programmatic support or it doesn't exist, students are at risk of leaving their doctoral program, and this leads to attrition. This is why the existence of programmatic efforts supporting academic success and degree completion for historically marginalized students is critically important.

However, more information is needed to understand facets of the African American experience not captured in this literature. The legacy of exclusion associated with the doctoral experience and the potential of its impact on developing future leadership are reasons to expand the scope of exploration beyond the doctoral program itself. That is, substantive growth of African American doctoral student participation and degree completion must involve a concerted effort to understand achievement both before and after the doctoral process. This must also include an examination of causes of student attrition.

Learning about the African American doctoral experience from students engaged in study, causes of African American doctoral student attrition can be gleaned from experiences prior to doctoral program matriculation. Also, African American doctoral degree completers can offer insight about the process that served to promote their persistence while engaged in doctoral study (Felder, 2005). This is consistent with Tinto's notion of attrition and graduate student persistence. Tinto (1991) modified his undergraduate student integration model to examine persistence at the doctoral level. He posits that graduate school attrition is more strongly related to departmental characteristics and specific relationships within the department. "Unlike undergraduate persistence, the process of graduate persistence cannot be easily described by any one simple model" (Tinto, 1991, p. 81). Furthermore, given the disproportionate representation of African American doctoral degree holders, study of this experience should include extensive knowledge about undergraduate student persistence and its impact on student success.

Discussion

Statistics demonstrate that the fields of education, social sciences, and the humanities continue to be productive for Black/African American doctoral students (National Science Foundation, 2016). However, the nature of reality regarding this student experience continues to be misunderstood and undervalued, leading to differences in expectations for academic success.

Institutional definitions and intended programmatic outcomes are often different from what students need to transition beyond their doctoral programs into careers where they can draw on what they have learned and extended networks of support. Students may come to their programs with important stores of cultural wealth, but if institutions are not in a position to support them, students struggle with success, and institutions are at risk for minimizing valuable racial and cultural investments in their students and the potential for enriching the academic environments.

Understanding the contributions of doctoral students must involve fully describing the socialization process to be inclusive of racial and cultural elements, including the ways students may experience marginalization coupled with the role of multiple stakeholders supporting their experience. Embracing Sankofa as a framework for examining the role of cultural influence within the socialization experience is important. Support of socialization for Black/African American (and other underrepresented) students should consider transformative practices that are creative, yet critically address processes that maximize their interests, social and academic abilities, and contributions to their programs and communities. Leveraging what is known about the contributions of students in fields where there is a larger concentration of participation for Blacks/African Americans lends insight about this student experience in other disciplines where there are higher levels of underrepresentation.

Conclusion

Future research must delve more deeply into the development, implementation, and intended outcomes of programmatic efforts that consider the value and contributions of historically marginalized student populations. This chapter has examined racially and culturally relevant aspects of doctoral student socialization, ways that marginalization complicates the doctoral process for Black/African American students, academic areas where students are more likely to be successful in managing the socialization process, and examples of programmatic efforts supporting academic success and doctoral degree completion (particularly in PWI environments).

The programs presented consider components of the doctoral process and factors of success, but more research is needed to understand how these issues inform support for Blacks/African Americans in other disciplines. What is unknown about this support may facilitate hindrances to academic and degree completion and hinder transition into the professoriate. Additional research in other disciplinary areas might examine disciplinary differences in expectations and values within the socialization process through cultural frameworks like Sankofa. Furthermore, shifting dialogue about socialization toward Blacks/African Americans thriving within academic cultures and disciplines will be important in facilitating sustained paradigms of success that embrace the importance of race and culture as lifelong institutional legacies.

Works Cited

Allen, W. R. (1985). Black student, white campus: Structural, interpersonal, and psychological correlates of success. *Journal of Negro Education, 54,* 134–150.

Allen, W. R. (1992). The color of success: African-American college student outcomes at predominantly White and historically Black public colleges and universities. *Harvard Educational Review, 62*(1), 26–42.

American Council on Education. (2000). *Status report on minorities in higher education.* Washington, DC: Author.

Anderson, E. F., & Hrabowski, F. A. (1977). Graduate school success of Black students from White colleges and Black colleges. *The Journal of Higher Education, 48*(3), 294–303.

Astin, A. W. (1975). *Preventing students from dropping out.* San Francisco, CA: Jossey-Bass.

Astin, A. W. (1977). *Four critical years.* San Francisco, CA: Jossey-Bass.

Astin, A. W. (1982). *Minorities in American higher education.* San Francisco, CA: Jossey-Bass.

Astin, A. W., Astin, H. S., Green, K. C., Kent, L., McNamara, P., & William, M. R. (1982). Two theories of college persistence. *Journal of Higher Education, 63,* 143–164.

Attiyeh, Gregory M. (1999). *Determinants of persistence of graduate students in Ph.D. programs* (RR-99-04, GREB-95-18R). Princeton, NJ: Educational Testing Service.

Baird, L. (1990). Disciplines and doctorates: The relationships between program characteristics and the duration of doctoral study. *Research in Higher Education, 31*(4), 369–385.

Bean, J. P. (1980). Dropouts and turnover: The synthesis and test of a causal model of student attrition. *Research in Higher Education, 12*(2), 155–187.

Bean, J. P. (1982). Student attrition, intention, and confidence: Interaction effects in a path model. *Research in Higher Education, 17*(4), 291–320.

Bean, J. P. (1983). The application of a model of turnover in work organizations to the student attrition process. *Review of Higher Education, 6*(1), 129–148.

Bean J. P. (1985). Interactional effects based on class level in an explanatory model of college student dropout syndrome. *American Educational Research Journal, 22*(1), 35–64.

Bean, J. P. (1990). Why students leave: Insights from research. In D. Hossler, J. P. Bean, et al. (Eds.), *The strategic management of college enrollments* (pp. 147–169). San Francisco, CA: Jossey-Bass.

Bean, J. P., & Metzner, B. S. (1985). A conceptual model of nontraditional and undergraduate student attrition. *Review of Educational Research, 55*(4), 485–540.

Bennett, C., & Bean, J. C. (1984). A conceptual model of black student attrition at a predominantly white university. *Journal of Equity & Leadership, 4,* 173–188.

Bertrand Jones, T., Osborne-Lampkin, L., Patterson, S., & Davis, D. J. (2015). Creating a "safe and supportive environment": Mentoring and professional development for recent black women doctoral graduates. *International Journal of Doctoral Studies, 10,* 483–499. Retrieved from http://ijds.org/Volume10/IJDSv10p483-499Jones1748.pdf

Boyd, W. M. (1977). Black undergraduates succeed in white colleges. *Educational Record, 58*(3), 309–315.

Brazziel, M. E., & Brazziel, W. F. (1987). Impact of support for graduate study on program completion of Black doctorate recipients. *The Journal of Negro Education, 56*(2), 145–151.

Brazziel, W. F. (1983). Baccalaureate college origins of Black doctorate recipients. *The Journal of Negro Education, 52*(2), 102–109.

Brown, S. V., Clewell, B. C., Ekstrom, R. B., Goertz, M. E., & Powers, D. E. (1994). *Research agenda for the Graduate Record Examinations Board Minority Graduate Education Project: An update* (MGE-94-01). Princeton, NJ: Educational Testing Service.

Clewell, B. C. (1987). *Retention of Black and Hispanic doctoral students.* Princeton, NJ: Educational Testing Service.

Cole, D., & Griffin, K. A. (2013). Advancing the study of student–faculty interaction: A focus on diverse students and faculty. In M. B. Paulsen (Ed.), *Higher education: Handbook of theory and research* (Vol. 28, pp. 561–611). Dordrecht, Netherlands: Springer.

Council of Graduate Schools and Educational Testing Service. (2010). *The path forward: The future of graduate education in the United States.* Report from the Commission on the Future of Graduate Education in the United States. Princeton, NJ: Educational Testing Service.

Council of Graduate Schools and Educational Testing Service. (2012). *Pathways through graduate school and into careers.* Report from the Commission on Pathways Through Graduate School and Into Careers. Princeton, NJ: Educational Testing Service.

Davidson, M. N., & Foster-Johnson, L. (2001). Mentoring in the preparation of graduate researchers of color. *Review of Educational Research, 41*(4), 549–574.

Duchscher, J. E. B., & Cowin, L. S. (2004). The experience of marginalization in new nursing graduates. *Nursing Outlook, 52*(6), 289–296.

Felder, P. (2010). On doctoral student development: Exploring faculty mentoring in the shaping of African American doctoral student success. *The Qualitative Report, 15*(2), 455–474.

Gardner, S. K., & Mendoza, P. (2010). On becoming a scholar: Socialization and development in doctoral education (1st ed.). Sterling, VA: Stylus.

Gary, S. (2008). Bennett and Spelman colleges: Creating Black female Ph.D.s in the sciences. In M. Gasman & C. Tudico (Eds.), *Historically Black colleges and universities: Triumphs, troubles, and taboos* (pp. 41–52). New York, NY: Palgrave MacMillan.

Gasman, M., Hirschfield, A., & Vultaggio, J. (2008). "Difficult yet rewarding": The experiences of African American graduate students. *Journal of Diversity in Higher Education, 1*(2), 126–138.

Golde, Chris (1998, Spring). Beginning graduate school: Explaining first-year doctoral attrition. *New Directions for Higher Education, 101*, 55–64.

Golde, C. M., & Dore, T. M. (2001). *At cross purposes: What the experiences of doctoral students reveal about doctoral education.* Philadelphia, PA: Pew Charitable Trusts. Retrieved from www.phd-survey.org

Golde, C. M., & Walker, G. E. (Eds.) (2006). *Envisioning the future of doctoral education: Preparing stewards of the discipline—Carnegie essays on the doctorate.* San Francisco, CA: Jossey-Bass.

Graham, L. (1999). *Our kind of people: Inside America's Black upper class* (1st ed.). New York, NY: HarperCollins.

Guarino, C. M., Santibanez, L., & Daley, G. A. (2006). Teacher recruitment and retention: A review of recent empirical literature. *Review of Educational Research, 76*(2), 173–208.

Hoffer, T. B., Selfa, L., Welch, V., Jr., Williams, K., Hess, M., Friedman, J., . . . Guzaman-Barron, I. (2004). *Doctorate recipients from United States universities: Summary report 2003.* Chicago, IL: National Opinion Research Center.

Hoffer, T., Dugoni, B., Sanderson, A., Sederstrom, S., Ghadialy, R., & Rocque, P. (2001). *Doctorate recipients from United States universities: Summary report 2000.* Chicago, IL: National Opinion Research Center.

Hood, S., & Freeman, D. (1995). Where do students of color earn doctorates in education? The top 25 colleges and schools in education. *The Journal of Negro Education, 64*(4), 423–436.

Jairam, D., & Kahl, D. H., Jr. (2012). Navigating the doctoral experience: The role of social support in successful degree completion. *International Journal of Doctoral Studies, 7*, 311–329.

King, J. E. (Ed.). (2005). *Black education: A transformative research and action agenda for the new century.* Mahwah, NJ: Lawrence Erlbaum Associates.

Ladson-Billings, G. (1999). Just what is critical race theory, and what's it doing in a nice field like education? In L. Parker, D. Deyhle, & S. Villenas (Eds.), *Race is . . . race isn't: Critical race theory and qualitative studies in education* (pp. 7–30). Boulder, CO: Westview Press.

Lovitts, B. E. (2001). *Leaving the ivory tower: The causes and consequences of departure from doctoral study.* Lanham, MD: Rowman & Littlefield.

Lovitts, B. E., & Wert, E. L. (2009). *Developing quality dissertations in the humanities: A graduate student's guide to achieving excellence.* Sterling, VA: Stylus.

MacLachlan, A. J. (2006). *Developing graduate students of color for the professoriate in science, technology, engineering, and mathematics (STEM)* (Research & Occasional Paper Series: CSHE.6.06). University of California, Berkeley, Center for Studies in Higher Education.

Mallinckrodt, B., & Sedlacek, W. (1987). Student retention, social support, and dropout intention: Comparison of black and white students. *Journal of College Student Development, 29,* 60–64.

Mommsen, K. G. (1974). Black doctorates in American higher education: A cohort analysis. *Journal of Social and Behavioral Sciences, 21,* 101–117.

Moses, Y. T. (1994, Spring). Quality, excellence and diversity. *New Directions for Institutional Research, 81,* 9–20.

National Center for Education Statistics. (1993). Student financing of graduate and first professional education (NCES 93-076). Washington, DC: U.S. Department of Education, Office of Educational Research and Improvement.

National Research Council. (1989). *Summary report 1988: Doctorate recipients from United States universities.* Washington, DC: National Academy Press.

National Research Council. (1995). *Summary report 1995: Doctorate recipients from United States universities.* Washington, DC: National Academy Press.

National Research Council. (2010). *A revised guide to the methodology of the data-based assessment of research-doctorate programs in the United States.* Washington, DC: The National Academies Press.

National Science Foundation, National Center for Science and Engineering Statistics. 2017. *Doctorate Recipients from U.S. Universities: 2015.* Special Report NSF 17-306. Arlington, VA. Retrieved from https://www.nsf.gov/statistics/sed/2017/nsf17306/

Nettles, M. T. (1990). Success in doctoral programs: Experiences of minority and White students. *American Journal of Education, 98*(4), 494–522.

Nettles, M. T., & Millett, C. M. (2006). *Three magic letters: Getting to Ph.D.* Baltimore, MD: Johns Hopkins University Press.

Padilla, R. V., Trevino, J., Trevino, J., & Gonzalez, K. (1997). Developing local models of minority student success in college. *Journal of College Student Development, 38*(2), 125–135.

Pascarella, E. T., & Terenzini, P. T. (1991). *How college affects students*. San Francisco, CA: Jossey-Bass.

Pauley, R., Cunningham, M., & Toth, P. (1999). Doctoral student attrition and retention: A study of a non-traditional Ed.D. program. *Journal of College Student Retention*, 1(3), 225–238.

Rowley, L. (2014). The socialization of African American PhD students: Race, sociology of knowledge, and historical concepts for contemporary contexts. In P. P. Felder and E. P. St. John (Eds.), *Supporting graduate students in the 21st century: Implications for policy and practice*. New York, NY: AMS Press.

Snyder, T. D., Tan, A. G., & Hoffman, C. M. (2006). Digest of Education Statistics 2005 (NCES 2006-030). Washington, DC: U.S. Government Printing Office.

St. John, E. P., Hu, S., & Fisher, A. (2011). *Breaking through the access barrier: How academic capital formation can improve policy in higher education*. New York, NY: Routledge.

Taylor, E., & Antony, J. S. (2000). Stereotype threat reduction and wise schooling: Toward the successful socialization of African American doctoral students in education. *Journal of Negro Education*, 69(3), 184–198.

Temple, C. (2010). The emergence of Sankofa practice in the United States. *Journal of African American Studies*, 41(1), 127–150.

Thurgood, L., Golladay, M. J., & Hill, S. T. (2006). *U.S. doctorates in the 20th century* (NSF 06-319). Arlington, VA: National Science Foundation, Division of Science Resources Statistics.

Tinto, V. (1993). *Leaving college: Rethinking the causes and cures of student attrition* (2nd ed.). Chicago, IL: University of Chicago Press.

Turner, C. S. V., & Thompson, J. R. (1993.) Socializing women doctoral students: Minority and majority experiences. *The Review of Higher Education*, 16(3), 355–370.

U.S. Department of Education (DOE), National Center for Education Statistics (NCES). (2005). 2003 *Integrated Postsecondary Education Data System* (IPEDS), Winter 2003–04. Washington, DC.

Walker, G. E., Golde, C. M., Jones, L., Bueschel, A. C., & Hutchings, P. (2008). *The formation of scholars: Rethinking doctoral education for the twenty-first century*. San Francisco, CA: Jossey-Bass.

Wendler, C., Bridgeman, B., Cline, F., Millett, C., Rock, J., Bell, N., & McAllister, P. (2010). *The path forward: The future of graduate education in the United States*. Princeton, NJ: Educational Testing Service.

Willie, C. V., Grady, M. K., & Hope, R. O. (1991). *African-Americans and the doctoral experience*. New York, NY: Teachers College Press.

Wolf-Wendel, L., Baker, B. D., Twombly, S., Tollefson, M., & Mahlios, M. (2006). Who's teaching the teachers? Evidence from the national survey of postsecondary faculty and the survey of earned doctorates, *American Journal of Education*, 112(2), 273–300.

Chapter 3

Resistance Narratives

Counterstories of Two Black Women Doctoral Students

DELMA RAMOS AND VARAXY YI

Over the years, Black women have slowly but steadily achieved great success in academia despite many barriers (e.g., negative stereotypes, racial and gender oppression, and caring for family members) (Baumgartner & Johnson-Bailey, 2010; Bertrand Jones, Osborne-Lampkin, Patterson, & Davis, 2015; Dortch, 2016; Ong, Wright, Espinosa, & Orfield, 2011; Patterson-Stephens, Lane, & Vital, 2017; Robinson, 2013). According to the National Center for Education Statistics (2012), of the degrees awarded to all Black students in 2009–2010, Black women earned 68% of associate's degrees, 66% of bachelor's degrees, 71% of master's degrees, and 65% of doctoral degrees. Black women are attaining degrees at the highest levels compared to women from other racial/ethnic groups (National Center for Education Statistics, 2012). Overall, the degrees awarded in master's and doctoral programs increased from 1999–2000 to 2009–2010 for women in all racial/ethnic groups. The trend indicates that women, specifically Black women, are pursuing their graduate degrees at increasing rates.

As more and more Black women enter doctoral programs across the country, it is imperative that educators across the nation strive to understand their experiences and build support structures that account for the uniqueness and assets of Black women. The Sankofa tradition lends itself to better understanding and critiquing doctoral programs through racial, gender, and intersectional lenses. Furthermore, it allows for examining the constructs of identity, context, and socialization from the African American perspective. Temple (2010) noted that modern practice or use of Sankofa may be witnessed through "resistance with respect to rejecting Eurocentric language and world views and insisting on the relevance of using African conceptual possibilities to define and characterize African life in the contemporary era" (p. 128). In this chapter, we provide a critical analysis of the doctoral experience by offering African American narratives. Overall, there is a need to better understand the experiences of Black women, especially as they relate to issues of race and gender, as disparities continue to exist for this population relative to other groups.

Despite the increasing numbers of Black women doctoral students in the United States, it is important to note that they are still relatively underrepresented when compared to their White male counterparts in terms of degree attainment and faculty positions (National Center for Education Statistics, 2012, 2015). While not all Black women doctorates aspire to positions in academia, the data indicate that the underrepresentation of Black women doctorates, in general, is still an issue worthy of concern. Furthermore, it is important to recognize that Black women are not immune to the effects of inequity and marginalization that have impacted the overall representation of populations of color in academia (e.g., Alexander & Hermann, 2016; Baumgartner & Johnson-Bailey, 2010; Boulding, 1983; Dortch, 2016; Gay, 2007; Martin, 2015; Nettles, 1990; Ong, Wright, Espinosa, & Orfield, 2011). There is still a need to further explore the doctoral experiences of Black women. While the scholarship has shifted in recent years toward a more assets-, strengths-, and knowledge-based perspective of racially minoritized populations (e.g., Carson, 2009; Kiyama, 2011; Montiel, 2016; Rios-Aguilar, Kiyama, Gravitt, & Moll 2011; Yosso, 2005), many scholars have called for more empirical understandings of the impacts of race and gender and their impacts on the success of students of color (e.g., Agosto, Karanxha, & Bellara, 2015; Jones, Wilder, & Osborne-Lampkin, 2013; Ong et al., 2011; Patterson-Stephens, Lane, & Vital, 2017; Solórzano & Yosso, 2001). Indeed, for Black women, it is necessary and relevant to consider the ways race and gender impact their experiences while also foregrounding an assets-based perspective of the ways they inherently resist and are resilient in their quests for their doctoral degrees.

In the spirit of Sankofa, this chapter seeks to explore the lived experiences of two Black women doctoral students as they exist, persist, and resist within a system of oppression. The concept of looking in and looking back to move forward closely mirrors the intent of critical race theory (CRT), which seeks to uncover and make visible the system of racism in the pursuit of liberatory justice for oppressed communities. In exploring the doctoral experiences of two Black women, we seek to uncover and learn from the depths of their experiences to envision new ways of doing better as educators.

In this chapter, we use a CRT perspective that accounts for the centralization of race and racism as well as the intersectionality (Delgado & Stefancic, 2001) of race and gender as conditions that impact the doctoral experiences of Black women. We rely on critical race methodology (CRM) to examine how Black women navigate experiences with racism and sexism and what women tell about their own experiences as narratives that reflect the inherent resilience and acts of resistance that motivate them to persist. We seek to explore the counterstories of Black women doctoral students in the ways they disrupt and challenge dominant narratives of the doctoral student experience and, specifically, the ways Black women are viewed in academia. This is important, as it informs and further advances perspectives of persistence and resistance while highlighting the ways that Black women subvert and resist oppressive spaces in order to succeed. The research questions guiding this study are (1) What stories do Black women doctoral students tell about their experiences with racism and sexism?; and (2) How do Black women doctoral students resist deficit ideologies, racism, and sexism in their doctoral journeys?

Challenges for Black Women Students

Black women face a myriad of challenges, especially as they pertain to issues and instances of racism and sexism, and these experiences are intensified within academic programs of study (Patterson-Stephens, Lane, & Vital, 2017; Simmons, 2016). Scholars have noted that academic environments are characterized by isolation and exclusion for Black students (Johnson-Bailey, Valentine, Cervero, & Bowles, 2008). Also, Black women are faced with assumptions that they were admitted because of affirmative action (Margolis & Romero, 1998; Patterson-Stephens, Lane, & Vital, 2017). Overall, Black women students must contend with tokenism (Robinson, 2013), hostility (Johnson-Bailey & Cervero, 2008), isolation (Ellis, 2001; Jones et al., 2013), deficit assumptions about their intelligence and ability (Carter-Black, 2008; Margolis & Romero, 1998), negative and stereotypical imagery (Patterson-Stephens, Lane, & Vital, 2017; Margolis & Romero, 1998), lack of or poor mentoring and advising opportunities (Bertrand Jones, Osborne-Lampkin, Patterson, & Davis, 2015; Felder, 2010), and in general lack of support for their research interests (Woods, 2001).

Such barriers have potentially detrimental impacts on their persistence in doctoral programs, as they create unsupportive and hostile environments that students must navigate in complex ways. Students may experience elements such as "blaming the victim" and "cooling out," in which they are led to believe they are the problem and their issues are individual instantiations rather than structural patterns; consequently, students may begin to lower their expectations about their education (Margolis & Romero, 1998, p. 13). These experiences produce major psychological consequences such as depression, low self-esteem, and self-hatred (King, 2005). Attention is effectively diverted away from the systemic issues that make it difficult for marginalized students to access the same support as their White counterparts, while the same marginalized students must deal with the psychological distress on their own.

Despite these hostile environments, and as evidenced by the preceding data on doctoral attainment rates, Black women continue to persist in their degrees. As such, more attention has been given toward exploring the ways that they persist (Fries-Britt & Turner Kelly, 2005; Johnson-Bailey, 2004; Shavers & Moore III, 2014; Winkle-Wagner, 2009). For example, Shavers and Moore III (2014) determined that Black women shift between academic masks and their private selves in an attempt to conduct themselves in a professional manner while hiding their true selves in a protective fashion. Such actions can produce psychological impacts, as they can foster a denial of self. However, Black women have also turned to informal networks and sister circles to create a space for authentic connections, to share in vulnerability and trust, and to mentor each other through doctoral programs (Fries-Britt & Turner Kelly, 2005; Ross, 2003). Many scholars have explored the importance of mentoring relationships and their impact on the persistence and success of Black women (Grant & Simmons, 2008; Grant & Gee, 2015). For example, Grant and Simmons (2008) recommended formal mentoring programs for Black women at a predominantly White institution (PWI). More recently, given the limited number of Black women in the professoriate overall to formally mentor incoming Black women doctoral students, nontraditional and informal mentoring have come under focus as important sources of support and as beneficial for the success of Black women in doctoral programs (Grant & Gee, 2015).

Black women have persisted and continue to persist through developing inclusive communities and networks that counter their own isolation, effectively retaining each other (Fries-Britt & Turner Kelly, 2005). This is a necessity given that many doctoral programs are still (re)producing inequitable climates and environments for Black women doctoral students. Even as Black women are successfully navigating their academic environments, there are important costs and consequences that Black women continue to pay, and much more still needs to be explored in relation to their doctoral experiences, especially their experiences with oppression.

Foundations and Framework of Critical Race Methodology

CRT asserts that racism is endemic in our society; as such, placing race at the center of analysis is important (Parker, 1998). Since its inception, CRT has facilitated a deeper understanding of the impacts of race, and other forms of oppression, on the lives of people of color specifically. As researchers of color, we hold the same perspectives regarding the centrality of race in society. Furthermore, as women, we also recognize that sexism, another form of oppression, continually impacts the lives of women in nefarious ways. With these understandings, CRT offers a useful lens for exploring how these two forms of oppression individually and mutually impact the lives of Black women as they pursue their doctorates.

Informed by CRT, critical race methodology (CRM) was developed as an approach that seeks to "foreground race and racism in all aspects of the research process" (Solórzano & Yosso, 2002). In education research, five major tenets of CRT and CRM intersect:

1. Intercentricity of race and racism with other forms of subordination: Given the nature of racism as endemic and permanent in society, the centrality of race deeply impacts individual lives; however, CRM also acknowledges the intersections of different layers of oppression and marginalization according to, but not limited to, class, gender, immigration status, and sexuality;

2. Challenge to dominant ideology: CRT problematizes traditional narratives of objectivity, meritocracy, colorblindness, and race neutrality, which serve to protect the interests of those groups in power. CRM exposes deficit-oriented narratives about oppressed groups;

3. Commitment to social justice: CRT is committed to a transformative, liberatory process that counters racism and other other systems of oppression. CRM acknowledges multiple layers of oppression;

4. Centrality of experiential knowledge: The experiences of people of color are prioritized as legitimate, powerful sources of knowledge for understanding racial and other forms of subordination. CRM challenges traditional forms of knowledge, text, and theories. It uncovers deficit-oriented approaches that seek to distort the experiences of people of color;

5. Transdisciplinary perspective: Historical and contemporary contexts of racism are underscored in order to challenge ahistorical or unidisciplinary understandings of race. Relying on a variety of disciplines in women's studies, ethnic studies, sociology, history, and law, CRM uses transdisciplinary knowledge to better understand the effects of racism, sexism, and classism. (Solórzano & Yosso, 2002).

CRM centers the experiential knowledge of marginalized and oppressed groups and challenges dominant or majoritarian narratives about success and opportunity in U.S. society. Counterstories are one critical strategy that centers race and highlights the importance of voice and of "naming one's own reality" as a mode and method of countering the stock explanations or false narratives about equity in education (Ladson-Billings & Tate, 1995, p. 56). Stock explanations are stories that justify the power of dominant groups as they are constructed in ways that maintain dominant group privilege (Delgado, 1989; Ladson-Billings & Tate, 1995). These are also known as "master narratives," which act as scripts that specify and control how social processes occur (Stanley, 2007, p. 14). These scripts often overshadow the realities experienced by oppressed groups and are frequently used to justify their oppression.

However, the stories of marginalized groups seek to subvert, counter, and challenge reality—they also have the power to undermine complacency and challenge the status quo (Delgado, 1989). Delgado (1989) argued that counterstories can open new windows into reality in ways that present new possibilities regarding how we can see life beyond the stock ways that we have been led to believe. As such, the authentic voices and stories of marginalized groups are critical for understanding equity in education (Ladson-Billings & Tate, 1995). Counterstories in and of themselves are acts of resistance from marginalized populations (Muñoz & Maldonado, 2012). Solórzano and Yosso (2002) also assert that counterstories can build community among those within the margins, challenge perceived notions through transforming established belief systems, open new windows for marginalized persons to see new possibilities and connections to other marginalized groups, and teach others through the construction of a world beyond both the story and the reality. Consequently, we rely on CRT as a theoretical foundation for how we view the world and CRM as a framework for how we understand and present the stories of participants within this chapter as forms of resistance enacted by Black women.

Method

Qualitative research methods allow us to explore the life stories and narratives of participants (Denzin & Lincoln, 1994). Qualitative methods empower researchers to develop a deep understanding of how participants perceive and understand their social realities and attempt to identify connections between participants' perceptions, and experiences (and their context) (Denzin & Lincoln, 1994). To these ends, we relied on semistructured interviews (Yin, 2013) to engage in an in-depth understanding of doctoral women of color, including Black/African American women's life stories and experiences with racism and sexism in the academy. Qualitative research methods coupled with the theoretical influence of CRM served as tools to engage in research that exposes and expands our understanding of the experiences of marginalized communities, with an explicit focus on race as it intersects with other forms of oppression.

Sultana (2007) highlights the importance of positionality when engaging in research inquiry to engage in the process ethically. As researchers of color, we are committed to the belief that our lenses shape how we view this work. Consequently, it is important that we share our identities and consider how they shape our analyses of the experiences of the study's participants. One of us identifies as an immigrant, first-generation, Latina doctoral student. The second identifies as a Khmer American woman, a child of refugees, and a doctoral student. We are deeply passionate in the pursuit of equity. These interests influence our desire to contribute in ways that seek to challenge the status quo and redefine long-standing deficit perspectives of students of color in college. As women of color, we stand in unity with all oppressed individuals while also acknowledging that our lenses and our experiences are shaped by systems of oppression in different ways than our participants. In highlighting the experiences of two Black women doctoral students, our goal is always the pursuit of liberatory justice and equity for all.

Two Women, Multiple Identities

We highlight the narratives of two participants whom we selected from a larger sample within a broader study on the experiences of doctoral women of color and their experiences with racism and sexism. We used purposeful sampling to achieve intensity and variation, to include information-rich cases, and to achieve diversity within the sample (Patton, 2002). Recruitment was limited to the Mountain region of the United States, where three sites were selected—two public research universities and one private research university. Each of these institutions was a PWI. We sent recruitment emails to contacts in graduate programs at each institution. Of the total participants in the larger study, two identified as Black/African American women, with one also identifying as multiracial. For the purposes of this chapter, we focus specifically on their narratives as they provide rich insights regarding their experiences as Black women and doctoral students having navigated and continuing to navigate racist and sexist environments. Their narratives counter the master narratives that dominate conversations about the doctoral student experience and erase their struggles in the academy.

Gina is a first-year doctoral student in education at a PWI in the Rocky Mountain area. She identifies as Black/African American and multiracial. She is a first-generation college student. Gina's mother, initially a stay-at-home mother who transitioned successfully into the workplace as a teacher, played a pivotal role in shaping her motivation to pursue her education. Growing up, Gina has been saliently aware that she has had access to fewer opportunities and resources than her peers at college. Gina's experiences with racism tell a story of struggles where she has had to prove herself and demonstrate that she is capable of fulfilling the tasks at hand. She has navigated racist contexts and seeks to identify safe spaces where she can talk openly about her experiences.

Andrea identifies as a Black woman and second-year doctoral student in leadership at a PWI. Her experience in executive leadership led her to pursue a doctoral degree that would support her continued success in this field. Gender was an important component of her life growing up, as she was encouraged to become a teacher or nurse. As a mother, she describes how she had to advocate exhaustively for her daughters to have access to certain sports; advanced math courses; and classes in science, technology, engineering, and mathematics (STEM). Likewise, racism has always been present in her life, with the most recent incident involving facing hostility as the only Black person at a funeral. Despite many experiences with racism, her family instilled a sense of resolve in Andrea to not allow people to treat her unfairly.

We do not attempt to make generalizations about Gina and Andrea's experiences to the larger group of Black women in academia; however, the narratives expressed by these two women offer important and relevant insights about their individual experiences and suggest some implications for better understanding the nuances, both explicit and subtle, of the racist and sexist incidents that shape their doctoral experiences. These are important, as they offer perspectives and experiences rarely considered in academia.

DATA COLLECTION

We collected interview data in fall 2014 through in-person, semistructured interviews (Yin, 2013). Each interview lasted approximately 60 to 90 minutes. In alignment with CRM, which acknowledges the intersectionality of different forms of oppression, the interview protocol for the study solicited information on the ways intersecting identities of participants played out within multiple systems of oppression. Additional questions encouraged participants to narrate specific experiences related to race and gender; the questions solicited data that enabled us to identify strategies participants employed to negotiate their doctoral journeys.

Data Analysis

Our framework, CRM, guided our analysis for this chapter. First, we transcribed all interviews, conducted multiple reads of each of the interview transcripts, and identified emerging themes that expanded our understanding of participants' experiences with racism and sexism. We uploaded the transcripts into NVivo and individually coded the data to develop emergent themes. This process allowed for intercoder agreement and consistency in preliminary findings (Creswell, 2007). Once this step was completed, we expanded data analysis in NVivo, reread all interview transcripts, and created additional nodes as necessary. Throughout this process, we met four times (every other week) to discuss the coding scheme and emerging findings. This approach further strengthened reliability and consistency within the coding process.

Codes related to racist and sexist incidents served as the cornerstone of the analysis for this chapter and are an example of how CRM informed data analysis. These codes included sexist and racist experiences, responses to incidents, and reflections on ways in which participants responded to and described their experiences with racism and sexism. The codes in our analysis referred to oppressive structures that expanded our understanding of how these structures shaped participants' narratives and how their stories disrupted dominant narratives of Black women in doctoral programs. Our findings then led us to conceptualize participants' narratives as counterstories that challenge stock stories of Black doctoral women in academia. Specifically, their counterstories serve as powerful sources of knowledge that open new windows to understanding experiences of Black doctoral women through resistance, resilience, and persistence.

Limitations

Findings from this study are not to be generalized to all Black women doctoral students because of the various limitations of this inquiry. First, insights presented in this chapter only reflect experiences of two Black women doctoral students who faced racism and sexism in their doctoral programs. Additionally, their narratives were excavated from a larger study exploring doctoral women of color experiences. Given that eligibility to participate in the study called for participants who wanted to share their experiences with racism and sexism, their experience is reflective of those who tackle similar struggles but not all Black women enrolled in doctoral programs. Second, another limitation of this study is that both participants were enrolled at the same institution, which would not allow readers to establish comparisons with the experiences of other Black women doctoral students enrolled at different institutions. Third, while we identify as women of color, we are not Black women. As such, while our positionality influenced study design (i.e., focus, methods, protocols) and elevated some important characteristics and dimensions of the experiences of Black women participants in this study, we acknowledge that it also masks other aspects that require further exploration. Nevertheless, we contend that participants' experiences, as reflected through our positionality as women of color, offer important considerations for the advancement of knowledge on Black women doctoral student experiences. We seek not to represent these narratives as generalizable to all Black women doctoral experiences; however, in the vein of CRM and CRT, we seek to illuminate their experiential knowledge so that we can begin to better understand.

Findings

The findings in this study highlight the ways Gina and Andrea define themselves as women of color, the manners in which they navigate oppressive societal contexts, and the approaches they take to resist Western and Eurocentric forms of education. Their understandings of their identities as Black women were informed by their lifelong journeys from childhood to the present. From growing up to attending graduate school, they reframed and challenged stereotypical and deficit-based perspectives about themselves and members of their communities. The counterstories they tell speak of important factors that shaped their experiences, including familial networks, their experiences within the U.S. education system, and the critical positions that both race and gender occupy within their lives. Specifically, we highlight six modes of resistance related to the participants' counterstories of race and of gender. With relation to race, Gina and Andrea underscore the central position that race comprises in their lives and leverage strategies to resist and challenge negative messages, which include seeking out inclusive spaces; reframing negative messaging; and relying on their knowledge to challenge ahistoric, incomplete, and incorrect assumptions about their communities. Regarding gender, Gina and Andrea reinforce the importance of strong familial ties and networks as sources of strength, highlight the critical role other women played in their lives, and assert their value and self-worth.

It is important to note that while we distinguish the themes into distinct sections related to race or gender, we recognize that participants' experiences with racism and sexism are often, if not always, intertwined and difficult to separate. As such, we do not imply that the resistance strategies used by participants are solely attributed to individual experiences with either racism or sexism. Rather, such strategies will always be informed by the multiple layers and intersections of Black women identities and the societal systems within which they exist.

Counterstories of Race

Both Gina and Andrea conveyed personal understandings of their racialized experiences, which shaped their trajectories in life and in education. Both recognize the importance of reframing their experiences with racism as a means to reshape the deficit stories told about them and to empower others around them. Andrea also points out the frequency with which race impacts her everyday life and the magnitude of race in her lived experience, primarily with regard to her expectations regarding encounters with racism:

> But it doesn't matter, it's happened in my career, it's happened with my kids. I have three grown children. It's happened with my just everyday experiences with people. This is what their expectations—Lack of positive expectations [about Blacks], and like I said, it's a fascinating thing, but you just roll with the punches and do what you need to do, and a lot of it. You were asking about feelings, you get frustrated and you get shocked, but it's so much a part of your life that you just keep keeping on.

Andrea recounts a sense of resolution and expectation that racism has happened and will continue to happen. The matter-of-fact way that she refers to the existence and impact of racism in her life mirrors her own response to such experiences—that is, such incidents happen, and they happen often, yet it is critical to keep moving forward. In this example, Andrea acknowledges the important position that race plays in her life and also details it as a source of motivation to continue to persist. In her narrative, Andrea uses her experiences with racism to build resistance. Consequently, this resolute awareness, not acceptance, of racism forms a foundation for the ways Gina and Andrea seek to challenge their oppression. The ways they accomplish this are to seek out inclusive spaces and people who share their identities, reframe negative messaging as motivation to persist, and use knowledge and education to challenge ahistoric, incomplete, or incorrect assumptions.

Seek out inclusive spaces. Gina and Andrea conveyed the importance of race as an influential external and internal system that helps shape who they are and the spaces where they exist. Specifically, Gina shares the way she seeks out inclusive spaces:

> I'd say some ways also, as a person of color in predominantly white institutions, it's been really easy to define myself based on this small community that I belong to. And that we are there—separated from the White populus, from the majority on campus. And so, it's always been important to me to find spaces of color, to connect with people of color and to build those relationships has always been really important. And so, I'd say that's a really big part of my identity to foster that and seek that out. But yeah, I struggle with, I'd say I primarily see myself as a person of color, then a woman.

Gina's understanding of the lack of diversity in predominantly white college campuses and how it pushes race to the center of her identity demonstrates her awareness of inequitable educational spaces that push communities of color into isolation (Allen, 1992; Ellis, 2001; Greer & Chwalisz, 2007; Johnson-Bailey et al., 2008). She relies on a strategy that students of color at PWIs often resort to in their quest to find support on chilly campus environments, which is to identify spaces where they can coexist with and seek support from others like them (Bentley, Edwards, & Chapman Hillard, 2015). The way she responds to college environments that are not inclusive challenges traditional notions about students of color, who are framed as lacking understanding of the college context and as not being in possession of knowledge and strategies to overcome barriers in those spaces. In actuality, Gina's knowledge that these spaces were not built for her that led her to use strategies to seek out spaces where she can feel supported.

Reframe negative messaging. In alignment with the centrality of race to their identities as women of color, Gina and Andrea identify ways of resistance. Although these strategies take place in a different fashion for each of our participants, they are both actively invested in resisting and challenging systems of oppression. Gina's awareness of how society views members of her community propels her desire to challenge stereotypes. She shares:

> To some extent, it's been kind of contrarian of me. Oh, that's what you think? You think I'm a dangerous minority? You think I'm this? I'm going to show you. I am going to outperform you and outsmart you, and out-whatever I feel like I can do to thump my chest to prove, to validate, both my own experiences and to uplift within my community that we can do this. And we are important. So to some extent, yeah, flipping the middle finger off at these people who, you may be pumping my gas some day and I'm going to have a PhD. So, there's that.

Gina desires to actualize success not only for herself but for her entire community. Instead of fulfilling low standards placed on people of color, she decides to break out of the box in which society has put her in (Carter-Black, 2008; Margolis & Romero, 1998) and demonstrate that she is a successful woman of color and that she and members of her community can and will succeed despite the oppression and oppressive systems she constantly navigates. Such narratives are not unique, as many individuals of color often find solace and power in developing high-achieving goals in education.

Challenge ahistoric, incomplete, and incorrect assumptions. The counterstories told by Andrea and Gina reveal that both of them rely on (formal and informal) knowledge and education and in different ways, to shape how they challenge oppression. Andrea shares her early experiences in school as pivotal in shaping her attitude toward racism:

> I'm really proud of my accomplishments, of my people's accomplishments. I fortunately went to a middle school in Maryland where they taught Black history all through middle school. Even though I had it in my family anyway, that very much solidified what my contributions were internationally and nationally. And so I thought when people say crazy things to me, I'm like, 'they don't know their own history.' So I'm just like, 'I know mine and I know yours.'

Andrea recounts the importance of learning and knowing the accomplishments and contributions of her community. Long term, this knowledge became an essential part of her ability to contest racist incidents. Not only does this knowledge give power to these participants, but it also inherently shapes the values and sense of self-worth that enable Gina and Andrea to resist oppression.

Andrea also shares a similar narrative of using this knowledge of history as a powerful tool for countering ahistoric or incorrect assertions about her community:

> . . . Since I've been in this doctoral program, probably the most offensive comment was made by a professor who's talking about slavery . . . I'd done a lot of my genealogy research, so I descended from both freed blacks who were landowners since the 1700s . . . So they had to carry their free papers at the beginning of the 1800s to prove that they were born of a couple that was biracial, in a sense, White father and a Black mother. And I remember him saying something to the effect of, "Oh yeah . . . all these Black slave women and their White slave masters, the reason why there's all these mixed-race Black people." And I said, "that's not the only reason that there's mixed-race," and I'm mixed and I have both, but it's mostly from free Blacks, so I said, "No, that's not true . . ." I had sent him some documents that I had from my family just so he could understand. But this man had gone to Harvard, was clueless about U.S. history, was clueless about my history, or any Black history . . . And yet I thought, gosh, you're teaching doctoral level folks in Education, and you don't know a thing.

Andrea's account of doing her own research and her own knowledge of her family's history became the means through which she built understanding, a knowledge base, and the confidence to openly disrupt the (re)production of false dominant narratives. The saliency of race and making sense of contemporary racism through the reference to history is another use of Sankofa—"looking to the past to prepare for the future" (Jones & Leitner, 2015, p. 201). Jones and Leitner posit that "drawing on lessons of the past" is a careful process of collecting past thoughts, memories, and stories (p. 202) in the way exhibited by Andrea and Gina. Andrea's counterstory is one that challenges ideologies about the low-educational capital of underrepresented communities (Carter-Black, 2008; Cokley & Chapman, 2008; Margolis & Romero, 1998) and influences her ability to challenge racist ideals in the classroom. Furthermore, Andrea's comment highlights the pervasiveness of miseducation about Black history and underrepresented communities in our education systems, such that even highly educated scholars can spread misinformation, which incidentally serves to bolster negative messages about Black communities. However, both Gina and Andrea continually challenge these ahistoric, incomplete, and incorrect assumptions in powerful and public ways.

COUNTERSTORIES OF GENDER

While race occupied a central role in Gina and Andrea's lives, gender also played an important, if, by their admission, a less visible or overt role. While both participants readily identified specific instances of racism in their lives, when it came to identifying experiences of sexism, both indicated that they had not given it too much prior thought. Gina shared:

> I have never really thought about it in those terms. . . . Wow, I'd say to some extent, I always put the person of color ahead of the woman part. And part of that maybe—so I consider myself a feminist or a womanist and that is very much integrated into the way I see myself as a person of color . . . So that's more primary in my thought, where I feel like a lot more is happening based on race than for me personally based on gender. So yeah, I usually—I'd say I have forefronted race in the way I identify myself and the way I approach that.

Gina's point also supports the central role that race plays in her life; however, gender also impacts her life significantly in difficult ways. Both Gina and Andrea shared experiences ranging from dealing with sexist comments from their peers and educators to sexual harassment. Throughout these experiences, both participants shared a sense of resolve in persisting despite these experiences. Their resistance strategies included relying on familial networks that support strong narratives of Black women, identifying women of color role models, and making use of policies and processes that assert their self-worth.

Familial networks support strong Black woman roles. Early literature that explores the role of family and communities of color in shaping academic aspirations and trajectories for underrepresented students has portrayed them negatively. Some scholars posit that families represent a barrier for students to pursue higher education for a variety of reasons, including deficient cultural values and attributes of their communities (Carney-Hall, 2008; LeMoyne & Buchanan, 2011; Lopez Turley, Desmond, & Brunch, 2010; Taub, 2008). It is less frequent that we see families framed as valuable supporters of their children's postsecondary educational attainment (Barnett, 2004; Gloria, Kurpius, Hamilton, & Wilson, 1999; Kiyama et al., 2015; Lamborn & Nguyen, 2004). The same goes for communities of color, which are frequently labeled as deficient and lacking role models who can expand educational possibilities for their members. However, Andrea's counterstory demonstrates the value of family support in shaping not only her educational aspirations and her identity as a strong woman of color. She also points out role models in her community (Brown, 2008; Miller, 1999; Neblett, Philip, Cogburn, & Sellers, 2006; Wilson, 1989). Andrea shared that when she was growing up, Black women were expected to only become nurses or teachers, and she expresses how her family helped her challenge these ideas:

> Well, it's an interesting thing. I fortunately grew up in a family where there's the diversity, just like any family, socio-economically, and as far as academic achievement, but I was given the insight that I could do anything that I wanted. And I always had family members and community leaders nationally that my family members would cling to as examples of what was possible. So, I actually wouldn't change being black any more than I would change being a woman, or when I was born, or anything about my life.

The significant role of family and community is consistent with Sankofa education tradition. Tedla (1995) stated that in Amara traditional thought, the individual does not exist without the community: "For it is impossible to think of an individual as a person unless s/he has become a bonded part of the community who is incorporated into the community and who has incorporated the community into her/himself" (p. 57). Furthermore, when asked about how her experience with sexism and racism impacted her decision to pursue an advanced degree, Andrea responded that her family had a strong impact on her decisions and goals around education, again challenging deficit-based ideologies around families of students of color. Strong familial networks form a foundation for the participants to develop a strong sense of self-concept and value as women.

Women of color role models. Dominant notions in educational research attribute the low educational attainment of communities of color to the lack of role models that can position educational success within reach for members of their communities (Barber, 2014; Barnes & Piland, 2010). Gina and Andrea challenge these ideologies as they share the existence and importance of women role models in their ability to navigate oppressive spaces and advance their education. For Gina, role models were predominantly other women of color:

> And even choosing my advisor. She brings a lot of feminism of color into her writing. Lots of critical race theory. Lots of critical whiteness. And as a woman of color . . . And so, having that connection to it, where to some extent, I feel it more deeply . . . And then just in reading more of her [advisor's] work and getting to know her, I honestly think I wouldn't have applied to this program if she wasn't here. And so, kind of having that understanding of here's a person who—she's a single mother as well. Knowing what she's been through and what she's done. I'm cool with her. She's my people. She is my community. She gets it. She understands. She has that history with racism and sexism. And so yeah, having that instant community, that instant bond.

Gina highlights the importance of finding role models who understand the experience of being a woman of color in the academy, which serves to expand access and support for communities of color to advance their education. It is also a clear example that there are role models in these communities who can and do pave the way for future generations to fulfill academic aspirations. The alarmingly low numbers of faculty of color in academia are yet another reason to concentrate efforts that support faculty diversity. Creating the conditions to foster such impactful connections between Black women and other women of color role models can positively socialize these students into positions in academia.

Assert self-worth and value as women of color. Ultimately, Gina's and Andrea's experiences have highlighted how they have developed a strong sense of self-worth and value because of the foundational influence of familial networks and support, education, and myriad experiences with both racism and sexism. These experiences culminated in a strong sense of determination for both participants. Each developed methods for asserting her position as a strong woman of color and challenging oppression. For example, Andrea asserts:

> I've been sexually harassed, especially when I was younger, so the last time that I was sexually harassed, I actually filed a complaint against a pretty high-powered person. And every time that person sees me to this day, I think he was shocked, because he's never really had anyone stand up to him. I said, "I'd rather be homeless or dead before I let you talk to me like this." And it was a combination, it was the sexism and then he added the racism on top of it . . . I felt when you have that foundation, you just can't let people treat you any kind of way, so I was raised that . . . if you don't see my value that's your issue, it's not mine. But I put the boundaries on how you treat me.

Clearly, Andrea is assured in her identity as a Black woman with inherent value and worth. Furthermore, Andrea successfully uses institutional policies to assert this value and to send a message about what types of treatment are unacceptable. It is important to note that this experience also highlights the accumulation of knowledge, power, and other forms of capital that culminated in a significant show of strength to challenge both racism and sexism. For both participants, while they acknowledge the constancy of oppression, many of their stories showcase how they can harness experience, knowledge, support, and understandings of the system to more directly challenge their oppressors.

Discussion

Counterstories offered by Gina and Andrea disrupt long-held ideologies about communities of color in various ways. Both leverage the centrality that race has in their lives and use it to shape their awareness of structural inequities and strategies to navigate racist and sexist spaces. They rely on knowledge and education to strengthen their confidence and ability to address sexist and racist incidents and share with us the importance of family, community, and academic role models in supporting their persistence in exclusionary educational spaces. Although their counterstories share broad commonalities, they are also different. Both Gina and Andrea use their experiences to build an internal resistance to racism and sexism, which fuels their ability to address racism and sexism in their current experiences as doctoral students and professionals. A closer look at their narratives uncovers the pivotal role that familial networks played in the early development of Andrea's counterstory. She often referenced family and familial educational aspirations as a main source of support in disrupting oppression. On the other hand, Gina presents a fluid perspective on family, which includes her doctoral advisor, and expresses the importance of having familial bonds in graduate school. Such familial networks and bonds serve to bolster their thinking with regard to what is possible and attainable for them as Black women. Familial networks and community within their doctoral journeys enable them to persist.

The role that education played in informing their counterstories also varied for both participants. On the one hand, Andrea received formal education that framed her community as valuable and important to society; this knowledge was critical for her to conceptualize her own identity and that of her racial and ethnic group positively and to be confident in challenging dominant deficit thinking. By contrast, Gina went through the education system learning much less positive perspectives on her community. It is important to note that, despite the positively or negatively charged knowledge about their communities that Gina and Andrea acquired in their educational journeys, they both leveraged it to contest assumptions and expectations about their capabilities as Black women.

The intersectionality of race and gender in their counterstories is evident, as they continuously shared experiences that embodied both identities. While they similarly expressed that their race played a more salient role in their lives, their experiences also reveal how gender and race mutually impact their experiences. This demonstrates that race and gender are not mutually exclusive and that, combined, they offer us a greater and more accurate understanding of the experiences of Black women. As Gina shared, "Where I think of myself as a scholar, I think of myself as a teacher and an advisor. And a person of color. And being a woman of color impacts that. And it's not like I can check it at the door." For Gina, race and gender function simultaneously; these are not elements of her identity that she can separate. In turn, the intersectionality of race and gender also points to the combination of systems of oppression our participants encounter and ultimately shapes opportunity in their daily lives.

Implications

The current study underscores the importance of uncovering narratives of marginalization and oppression within the academy, which offers opportunities for addressing inequity. Specifically, the counternarratives of two Black women doctoral students have several implications for how we can better change traditionally inequitable environments to account for their racialized and gendered experiences in the academy. These implications include continuing to bolster inclusivity in faculty training and development, incorporating more culturally relevant doctoral student programming, integration of familial support and community systems, and leveraging networks to create both formal and informal mentoring opportunities for Black women.

First, specific to bolstering inclusivity and the concept of intersectionality in faculty development, educators can better incorporate inclusivity in the classroom through the choices they make in whose scholarship is considered valuable. This is an important factor to consider because classrooms can be settings where the experiences of marginalized communities are rarely reflected in curriculum development and implementation (Gay, 2010). Curricular decisions that showcase diverse examples and theories that reflect experiential knowledge of marginalized communities can cultivate and encourage students to pursue research interests related to issues of equity and can help minimize the stigmatization that Black women may experience (Margolis & Romero, 1998). Additionally, we recommend targeted faculty training in the areas of diversity and inclusion to better incorporate a meaningful engagement with the systemic and structural policies and practices that negatively impact students' experiences. Centering this knowledge positions all faculty as responsible for understanding and responding accordingly to the experiences of Black women. Relying solely on women and faculty of color to support Black women creates an imbalance among faculty workload (Jean-Marie & Brooks, 2011). Future efforts must be made to ensure that all faculty can provide culturally relevant and responsive support that attends to the racialized and gendered experiences of Black women doctoral students.

Second, culturally relevant programming that highlights inclusive spaces can help Black doctoral students to develop strong networks and support systems with people who look like them or understand their experiences. Examples include supporting affinity groups and spaces that offer students from historically marginalized communities the opportunity to share and reflect on their experiences in academia. Institutionalized writing support groups can also create a sense of community for students and offer targeted support for students to strengthen their doctoral writing practice. Studies have signified the importance of sister circles as a space of connection and bonding for African American women (Fries-Britt & Turner Kelly, 2005; Ross, 2003). To honor, support, and help facilitate such spaces can indicate a commitment to the success of Black women in the academy. Further, it is important to offer students guided opportunities to deconstruct their racialized and gendered experiences in ways that support their development as future scholars and professionals. The doctoral experience is often characterized as isolating and alienating as is. To minimize the impact on Black women, doctoral programs must offer the tools and resources necessary to support students in building successful relationships that enable them to form resistance strategies.

Third, it is in the best interest of institutions to find ways to integrate familial student support in the academy. There is a need to consider more holistic support that considers students' families and support networks. This can include inviting family members to campus events and functions that engage students or bringing the valuable knowledge among members of these communities to the classroom—for instance, having friends, family, and members of students' community guest speak in class. There are opportunities for students to connect the social implications of their research and professional goals with their own families' experiences. To acknowledge the experiential knowledge of Black women is to also honor their families' roles in shaping who they are as individuals.

Fourth, beyond the critical need to improve the doctoral environment for Black women, there must be intentional efforts to expand their networks and foster mentoring relationships across both formal and informal lines. As noted by our participants, seeing role models from one's community offers inspiration and motivation to persist and graduate. As such, other Black women can offer guidance and advice to current students and support their advancement in academia. This need for mentorship extends into STEM fields, particularly as women of color navigate and develop their science identity (Carlone & Johnson, 2007). MacLachlan (2006) emphasized the role of mentors in shaping and guiding the experiences of women of color in STEM. However, this guidance must be thoughtful and intentional. Additionally, doctoral programs can leverage resources to support the professional development of students through national conference and other institute engagement, as they are prime spaces for students and faculty to connect. For Black women doctoral students, who have limited access to mentors who look like or understand them at their home institutions, supporting them through expanding their networks should be a priority for doctoral programs interested in the souls and spirits of their students and future faculty.

Conclusion

The counterstories presented in this chapter demonstrate the multiplicity of oppressions that two Black women face throughout their lives and in the academy. The oppression they encountered was shaped by structural inequality, where they were caught between racist and sexist systems that worked in tandem to diminish opportunities for them. However, their counterstories bring to light not only the oppressions but also their courage and determination to challenge those systems. In this regard, counterstorytelling served as a comprehensive means through which we learned how they pushed against oppressive structures. Becoming more aware about the ways in which Black women experience doctoral programs and resist oppressive structures provides more insight into how doctoral program faculty and staff can improve persistence, retention, and completion of Black women in general and of doctoral Black women specifically.

In the end, equity-focused strategies can aid faculty and doctoral programs in better addressing the prevailing incidents of racism and sexism that negatively impact the experiences of Black women and enhancing the doctoral student experience in general. Addressing these issues are of the utmost concern as more Black women seek entry into doctoral programs and the academy. Not only is this change inevitable, but it is occurring now. While the counternarratives of two Black women doctoral students highlight a variety of strategies that they use to resist and counter oppressive conditions and experiences, underscoring the inherent resiliency within, it is still the responsibility of institutions, and their various actors, to transform their environments to better serve these students. To chart new pathways ahead within a more equitable system of education, the experiences of two Black women provide new opportunities and understandings for us to do and to be better.

Works Cited

Agosto, V., Karanxha, Z., & Bellara, A. (2015). Battling inertia in educational leadership: CRT praxis for race conscious dialogue. *Race Ethnicity and Education, 18*(6), 785–812.

Alexander, Q. R., & Hermann, M. A. (2016). African-American women's experiences in graduate science, technology, engineering, and mathematics education at a predominantly white university: A qualitative investigation. *Journal of Diversity in Higher Education, 9*(4), 307–322.

Allen, W. (1992). The color of success: African-American college student outcomes at predominantly White and historically Black public colleges and universities. *Harvard Educational Review, 62*(1), 26–45.

Baber, L. D. (2014). When aspiration meets opportunity: Examining transitional experiences of African American males in college readiness programs. *Community College Journal of Research and Practice, 38*(12), 1097–1111.

Bamberg, M., & Andrews, M. (2004). *Considering counter-narratives: Narrating, resisting, making sense.* Amsterdam, Netherlands: John Benjamins Publishing Company.

Barnes, R. A., & Piland, W. E. (2010). Impact of learning communities in developmental English on community college student retention and persistence. *Journal of College Student Retention: Research, Theory & Practice, 12*(1), 7–24.

Barnett, M. (2004). A qualitative analysis of family support and interaction among Black college students at an Ivy League university. *Journal of Negro Education,* 53–68.

Baumgartner, L. M., & Johnson-Bailey, J. (2010). Racism and White privilege in adult education graduate programs: Admissions, retention, and curricula. *New Directions for Adult and Continuing Education, 125*, 27–40.

Bentley-Edwards, K. L., & Chapman-Hilliard, C. (2015). Doing race in different places: Black racial cohesion on Black and White college campuses. *Journal of Diversity in Higher Education, 8*(1), 43.

Bertrand Jones, T., Osborne-Lampkin, L., Patterson, S., & Davis, D. J. (2015). Creating a "safe and supportive environment": Mentoring and professional development for recent black women doctoral graduates. *International Journal of Doctoral Studies, 10*, 483–499.

Boulding, E. (1983). Minorities and women: Even harder times. *Academe, 69*(1), 27–28.

Brown, D. L. (2008). African American resiliency: Examining racial socialization and social support as protective factors. *Journal of Black Psychology, 34*(1), 32–48.

Carlone, H. B., & Johnson, A. (2007). Understanding the science experiences of successful women of color: Science identity as an analytic lens. *Journal of Research in Science Teaching, 44*, 1187–1218.

Carney-Hall, K. C. (Ed.). (2008). Managing parent partnerships: Maximizing influence, minimizing interference, and focusing on student success. *New Directions for Student Services, 122.*

Carson, L. R. (2009). "I am because we are": Collectivism as a foundational characteristic of African American college student identity and academic achievement. *Social Psychology of Education, 12*(3), 327–344.

Carter-Black, J. (2008). A Black woman's journey into a predominately white academic world. *Affilia, 23*(2), 112–122.

Cokley, K. O., & Chapman, C. (2008). The roles of ethnic identity, anti-white attitudes, and academic self-concept in African American student achievement. *Social Psychology of Education, 11*(4), 349–365.

Council of Graduate Schools and Educational Testing Service. (2010). *The path forward: The future of graduate education in the United States.* Report from the Commission on the Future of Graduate Education in the United States. Princeton, NJ: Educational Testing Service.

Council of Graduate Schools and Educational Testing Service. (2012). *Pathways through graduate school and into careers.* Report from the Commission on Pathways Through Graduate School and Into Careers. Princeton, NJ: Educational Testing Service.

Delgado, R. (1989). Storytelling for oppositionists and others: A plea for narrative legal storytelling. *Michigan Law Review, 87,* 2411–2441.

Delgado, R., & Sefancic, J. (2001). Introduction. *Critical race theory: An introduction* (pp. 24–27). New York, NY: New York University Press.

Dortch, D. (2016). The strength from within: A phenomenological study examining the academic self-efficacy of African American women in doctoral studies. *The Journal of Negro Education, 85*(3), 350–364.

Ellis, E. M. (2001). The impact of race and gender on graduate school socialization, satisfaction with doctoral study, and commitment to degree completion. *Western Journal of Black Studies, 25*(1), 30–45.

Felder, P. (2010). On doctoral student development: Exploring faculty mentoring in the shaping of African American doctoral student success. *The Qualitative Report, 15*(2), 455–474.

Fries-Britt, S., & Turner Kelly, B. (2005). Retaining each other: Narratives of two African American women in the academy. *The Urban Review, 37*(3), 221–242.

Gay, G. (2010). *Culturally responsive teaching: Theory, research, and practice.* New York, NY: Teachers College Press.

Gay, G. (2007). Navigating marginality en route to the professoriate: Graduate students of color learning and living in academia. *International Journal of Qualitative Studies in Education, 17,* 265–288.

Gloria, A. M., Kurpius, S. E. R., Hamilton, K. D., & Willson, M. S. (1999). African American students' persistence at a predominantly White university:

Influences of social support, university comfort, and self-beliefs. *Journal of College Student Development, 40*(3), 257.

Grant, C. M., & Ghee, S. (2015). Mentoring 101: Advancing African-American women faculty and doctoral student success in predominantly White institutions. *International Journal of Qualitative Studies in Education, 28*(7), 759–785.

Grant, C. M., & Simmons, J. C. (2008). Narratives on experiences of African-American women in the academy: Conceptualizing effective mentoring relationships of doctoral student and faculty. *International Journal of Qualitative Studies in Education, 21*(5), 501–517.

Greer, T. M., & Chwalisz, K. (2007). Minority-related stressors and coping processes among African American college students. *Journal of College Student Development, 48*(4), 388–404.

Jean-Marie, G., & Brooks, J. S. (2011). Mentoring and supportive networks for women of color in academe. In J.-M. Gaëtane & B. Lloyd-Jones (Eds.), *Women of color in higher education: Changing directions and new perspectives* (pp. 91–108). Bingley, United Kingdom: Emerald Group Publishing Limited.

Johnson-Bailey, J. (2004). Hitting and climbing the proverbial wall: Participation and retention issues for Black graduate women. *Race Ethnicity and Education, 7*(4), 331–349.

Johnson-Bailey, J., & Cervero, R. M. (2008). Different worlds and divergent paths: Academic careers defined by race and gender. *Harvard Educational Review, 78*(2), 311–332.

Johnson-Bailey, J., Valentine, T. S., Cervero, R. M., & Bowles, T. A. (2008). Lean on me: The support experiences of Black graduate students. *The Journal of Negro Education, 77*(4), 365–381.

Jones, J. M., & Leitner, J. B. (2015). The Sankofa effect: Divergent effects of thinking about the past for Blacks and Whites. In M. Stolarski, N. Fieulaine, & W. van Beek (Eds.), *Time perspective theory; review, research, and application: Essays in honor of Philip G. Zimbardo* (pp. 197–211). New York: Springer Publishing.

Jones, T. B., Wilder, J., & Osborne-Lampkin, L. (2013). Employing a Black feminist approach to doctoral advising: Preparing Black women for the professoriate. *The Journal of Negro Education, 82*(3), 326–338.

King, K. R. (2005). Why is discrimination stressful? The mediating role of cognitive appraisal. *Cultural Diversity and Ethnic Minority Psychology, 11*(3), 202–212.

Kiyama, J. M. (2011). Family lessons and funds of knowledge: College-going paths in Mexican American families. *Journal of Latinos and Education, 10*(1), 23–42.

Kiyama, J. M., Harper, C. E., Ramos, D., Aguayo, D., Page, L. A., & Riester, K. A. (2015). Parent and family engagement in higher education. *ASHE Higher Education Report, 41*(6), 1–94.

Ladson-Billings, G., & Tate, W. F. (1995). Toward a critical race theory of education. *Teachers College Record, 97*(1), 47–68.

Lamborn, S. D., & Nguyen, D. G. T. (2004). African American adolescents' perceptions of family interactions: Kinship support, parent–child relationships, and teen adjustment. *Journal of Youth and Adolescence, 33*(6), 547–558.

LeMoyne, T., & Buchanan, T. (2011). Does "hovering" matter? Helicopter parenting and its effect on well-being. *Sociological Spectrum, 31*(4), 399–418.

Lopez Turley, R. N., Desmond, M., & Bruch, S. K. (2010). Unanticipated educational consequences of a positive parent–child relationship. *Journal of Marriage and Family, 72*(5), 1377–1390.

MacLachan, A. J. (2006). The graduate experience of women in STEM and how it could be improved. In J. M. Bystydzienski & S. R. Bird (Eds.), *Removing barriers: Women in academic science, technology, engineering, and mathematics.* Bloomington, IN: Indiana University Press.

Margolis, E., & Romero, M. (1998). "The department is very male, very white, very old, and very conservative": The functioning of the hidden curriculum in graduate sociology departments. *Harvard Educational Review, 68*(1), 1–32.

Martin, J. (2015). *Racial battle fatigue: Insights from the front lines of social justice advocacy.* Santa Barbara, CA: ABC-CLIO, LLC.

Miller, D. B. (1999). Racial socialization and racial identity: Can they promote resiliency for African American Adolescents? *Adolescence, 34,* 493–501.

Montiel, G. I. (2016). Navigating the Ivy League: Funds of knowledge and social capital of undocumented Ivy League students. *Harvard Journal of Hispanic Policy, 28,* 64–79.

Muñoz, S. M., & Maldonado, M. M. (2012). Counterstories of college persistence by undocumented Mexicana students: Navigating race, class, gender, and legal status. *International Journal of Qualitative Studies in Education, 25*(3), 293–315.

National Center for Education Statistics. (2012). Degrees conferred by sex and race. Retrieved August 24, 2016, from https://nces.ed.gov/fastfacts/display. asp?id=72

National Center for Education Statistics. (2015). Race/ethnicity of college faculty. Retrieved July 15, 2016, from https://nces.ed.gov/fastfacts/display.asp?id =61

Neblett, E. W., Jr., Philip, C. L., Cogburn, C. D., & Sellers, R. M. (2006). African American adolescents' discrimination experiences and academic achievement: Racial socialization as a cultural compensatory and protective factor. *Journal of Black Psychology, 32,* 199–218.

Nettles, M. T. (1990). Success in doctoral programs: Experiences of minority and White students. *American Journal of Education, 98*(4), 494–522.

Ong, M., Wright, C., Espinosa, L., & Orfield, G. (2011). Inside the double bind: A synthesis of empirical research on undergraduate and graduate women of color in science, technology, engineering, and mathematics. *Harvard Educational Review, 81,* 172–209.

Parker, L. (1998). "Race is race ain't": An exploration of the utility of critical race theory in qualitative research in education. *International Journal of Qualitative Studies in Education, 11*(1), 43–55.

Patterson-Stephens, S. M., Lane, T. B., & Vital, L. M. (2017). Black doctoral women: Exploring barriers and facilitators of success in graduate education. *Academic Perspectives in Higher Education, 3*(1), 5.

Patton, M. Q. (2002). *Qualitative evaluation and research methods.* Newbury Park, CA: Sage Publications.

QSR International. (n.d.). Cambridge, MA.

Rios-Aguilar, C., Kiyama, J. M., Gravitt, M., & Moll, L. C. (2011). Funds of knowledge for the poor and forms of capital for the rich? A capital approach to examining funds of knowledge. *Theory and Research in Education, 9*(2), 163–184.

Robinson, S. J. (2013). Spoketokenism: Black women talking back about graduate school experiences. *Race Ethnicity and Education, 16*(2), 155–181.

Ross, M. (2003). *Success factors of young African American women at a historically Black college.* Westport, CT: Praeger Publishers.

Shavers, M. C., & Moore, J. L., III. (2014). Black female voices: Self-presentation strategies in doctoral programs at predominately White institutions. *Journal of College Student Development, 55*(4), 391–407.

Simmons, D. (2016). Impostor syndrome, a reparative history. *Engaging Science, Technology, and Society, 2,* 106–127.

Solórzano, D. G. (1998). Critical race theory, race and gender microaggressions, and the experience of Chicana and Chicano scholars. *International Journal of Qualitative Studies in Education, 11*(1), 121–136.

Solórzano, D. G., & Yosso, T. J. (2001). Critical race and LatCrit theory and method: Counter-storytelling. *International Journal of Qualitative Studies in Education, 14*(4), 471–495.

Solórzano, D. G., & Yosso, T. J. (2002). Critical race methodology: Counter-storytelling as an analytical framework for educational research. *Qualitative Inquiry, 8*(1), 23–44.

Stanley, C. A. (2007). When counter narratives meet master narratives in the journal editorial-review process. *Educational Researcher, 36*(1), 14–24.

Sultana, F. (2007). Reflexivity, positionality and participatory ethics: Negotiating fieldwork dilemmas in international research. *ACME: An International E-Journal for Critical Geographers, 6*(3), 374–385.

Taub, D. (2008). Exploring the impact of parental involvement on student development. *New Directions for Student Services, 122,* 15–28.

Tedla, E. (1995). *Sankofa: African thought and education.* New York: Lang Publishing.

Temple, C. N. (2010). The emergence of Sankofa practice in the United States: A modern history. *Journal of Black Studies, 41*(1), 127–150.

Wilson, M. N. (1989). Child development in the context of the Black extended family. *American Psychologist, 44*, 380–385.

Winkle-Wagner, R. (2009). *The unchosen me: Race, gender, and identity among Black women in college.* Baltimore, MD: Johns Hopkins University Press.

Woods, R. L. (2001). Invisible women: The experiences of Black female doctoral students at the University of Michigan. In R. O. Mabokela & A. L. Green (Eds.), *Sisters of the academy: Emergent Black women scholars in higher education* (pp. 94–116). Sterling, VA: Stylus Publishing.

Yin, R. K. (2013). *Case study research: Design and methods.* Thousand Oaks, CA: Sage Publications.

Yosso, T. J. (2005). Whose culture has capital? A critical race theory discussion of community cultural wealth. *Race, Ethnicity and Education, 8*(1), 69–91.

Chapter 4

Demystifying the Monolithic Black Male Mystique

Advancing a Research Agenda on Black Men in Engineering Graduate Programs

BRIAN A. BURT

R edefining and challenging narrow, Western views of the Black male is consistent with the Sankofa theme of this volume (Tedla, 1995). Based on empirical data, this conceptual chapter highlights the intersecting identities and educational experiences of Black males in the context of engineering programs (e.g., professional identity development, persistence, interactions with faculty and peers). Examining one subpopulation of Black male students through an empirical-reflective analysis, in a field in which many colleges and universities currently seek to increase their represen-tation, allows for a deeper examination of their unique experiences and provides greater opportunities for reform. By taking this approach, this chapter also lays out a research agenda for future exploration aimed at better understanding the nuanced experiences of Black men. In the spirit of Sankofa, this chapter looks back at the history of characterization and portrayal of Black men in order to move this work forward.

Background

Black men are plagued with many societal tropes of the monolithic Black male mystique: Black men as lazy, unintelligent, and incapable of learning (Butler, 2013; Jackson & Moore, 2006). On many college campuses, administrators, staff, and faculty aim to improve the plight of their Black male students. However, vestiges of a monolithic Black male identity continue to linger. The assumptions regarding a singular Black male identity manifest both in campus policies and practices and in published scholarly work that assumes that Black men are all the same (Brown, 2011; Dancy, 2014; Dancy & Brown, 2008; Dumas, 2016).

Harper and Nichol's (2008) study of 39 high-achieving Black male collegians poses the rhetorical question, "Are they not the same?" This central question seems absurd, right? Of course, all Black men are not the same. In the article, the authors highlight participants' voices describing not only their own campus identities, but also those of their Black male peers. The authors identified at least six kinds of identities described by student participants: student leaders, members of historically Black fraternity organizations, student athletes, more and less academically engaged men, urban men, and those from suburban and predominantly White environments. Clearly, Black men themselves can recognize the within-group differences among their Black male peers. Why then do assumptions of the monolithic Black male still seem to be present in higher education policies, practices, and research?

Disparaging examples of monolithic stereotypes of Black men are rooted in the historical fabric of the United States (Jackson, 2006; Jackson & Moore, 2008). Symbolic examples can be seen in film (e.g., *Birth of a Nation*, 1915), public and scholarly discourse (e.g., *The Bell Curve*, 1994), and data sources that inform policy (e.g., census surveys that did not/do not disaggregate among Black/African American), to name a few. Where these tropes come from is beyond the scope of this chapter. However, it is important to acknowledge that these stereotypes of Black men have historical significance rooted in racism. What is more important is that higher education scholars, practitioners, and policy makers begin to problematize—and in doing so, demystify and dismantle—these pervasive stereotypes of the monolithic Black male. In assuming that Black men are the same, we consistently overlook their vast within-group differences. And, in overlooking their differences, colleges and universities are not meeting their needs and are possibly creating barriers to their success.

Thus, although Harper and Nichol's (2008) central question might seem pretty simple to some, the practices and policies on most college and university campuses illustrate that the question is anything but easy to answer and that it warrants much discussion. Most germane to this chapter: why is it important to think about Black male college students' differences, and how might researchers, practitioners, and policy makers go about interrogating their differences? This conceptual chapter addresses these enduring questions through a domain-specific focus on Black men in engineering graduate programs.

Study Methods and Context

Black men are vital to addressing persistent calls for broadening participation in engineering (Brazziel & Brazziel, 2001; Chubin et al., 2005; Herzig, 2004; Maton & Hrabowski, 2004; Moore, 2006; National Action Council for Minorities in Engineering [NACME], 2014). In 2015, only 1% (or 1,574 of 156,407) of master's and doctoral students enrolled in engineering graduate programs were Black men (Yoder, 2015), and fewer than 1% (112 of 11,702) of engineering doctoral degrees were awarded to Black men (Yoder, 2015). These data, which do not include Black men with international status, represent a very small pool of potential Black faculty members; education and thought leaders; those likely to give back to their communities; and mentors and role models inspiring and teaching future generations of students in science, technology, engineering, and mathematics (STEM). Expanding the representation of Black men in engineering would increase the talent pool of those contributing to solving the problems of the nation and world.

The data used for this chapter derive from qualitative interviews with 11 Black male doctoral students enrolled in five different engineering specializations at one institution. Table 4.1 on page 94 includes demographic data for study participants.

The methodological choice to focus the sample at one institution allowed for a more nuanced investigation of the men's experiences at Midwestern University (pseudonym). This choice allowed for a deeper understanding of an institution-specific context, which also includes events occurring at the societal and local levels, on students' experiences. For example, at the time at which the data were collected, history was being made with the election of President Barack Obama. Race, gender, and politics permeated the campus climate because they were components of larger social issues at the national and international levels. Simultaneously, attacks on affirmation action at the federal (Supreme Court) and state referendum levels were being felt on the students' campus. Participants noted immediate changes in the College of Engineering's recruitment practices;

Table 4.1. Demographic Data for Study Participants

Pseudonym	Class Level	Engineering Specialization	Citizenship Status	Undergraduate Origin	Postgraduate Career Intention
Alphonso	5th	Electrical	FB	PWI	Industry
Chris	5th	Chemical	NB	PWI	Industry
Jackson	3rd	Mechanical	NB	PWI	Uncertain
Jaden	2nd	Electrical	NB	HBCU	Industry
James	4th	Biomedical	FB	PWI	Faculty
Marcus	3rd	Mechanical	FB	PWI	Uncertain
Paul	4th	Electrical	FB	PWI	Uncertain
Quentin	5th	Electrical	FB	PWI	Uncertain
Terrence	2nd	Material	FB	Intl	Uncertain
Trai	4th	Mechanical	NB	PWI	Industry
Victor	5th	Chemical	NB	PWI	Industry

Note: "Class Level" refers to the number of years a student has been in graduate school; "Citizenship Status" refers to students who are foreign born (FB) or native born (NB); "Undergraduate Origin" refers to the designation of students' undergraduate institution: predominantly White institution (PWI), historically Black college or university (HBCU), or an international institution (Intl).

because of the affirmative action cases being tried and voted on in the state, Midwestern University scaled back its efforts to target and recruit students of color. Thus, how students made sense of themselves in terms of race and gender was influenced—at least in part—by the effects of the political and historical discourses taking place at the time of data collection. (More on how these historical, social, and local *contexts* influence students' identity and development is explained below.)

In addition to the emphasis on one institution, the decision to include a domain-specific design for this study (i.e., focusing on one field of study) instead of studying Black men across the STEM spectrum provided an opportunity to identify and focus on the specific experiences of men in engineering. Although students encountered nuanced engineering experiences based on their varied specializations, this study's focus on students' racialized experiences as being Black and male and being in engineering made it appropriate to include students across engineering specializations. In combination, these intentional methodological choices enabled me to consider issues around cultural contexts (i.e., institutional-, college-, and departmental-level culture) and political contexts (i.e., federal, state, local), in addition to students' individualized experiences.

Because of the dearth of existing scholarship on Black men in engineering graduate programs (Burt et al., 2016; Robinson et al., 2016), broad questions regarding collegiate backgrounds, expectations for graduate school, postgraduate aspirations, and identification with and intentions to remain in engineering were asked during interviews to capture participants' lived and shared experiences in engineering. All interviews were scheduled for one hour, yet many approached two hours. Several participants later acknowledged that the first time someone had asked about their experiences in engineering and graduate school, and for their opinions on how to improve the practices and activities of the college, was during this interview. This observation is similar to what Harper (2014) noted: his participants were rarely asked their opinions, and therefore felt more comfortable sharing. In the present study, many left their interviews feeling affirmed that through their participation they were contributing to an improved experience for future Black men in engineering.

All participants received copies of their interview transcript and were invited to make corrections and clarify—and/or expand upon—their comments. No participants provided changes. Additionally, four of the 11 participants were invited to participate in a follow-up focus group to provide feedback on my preliminary interpretations of the data. During the focus group, participants responded to my few interview prompts by talking to one another, building upon one another's insights, and clarifying where their experiences differed from what they heard from others and from the preliminary research interpretations.

Finally, albeit at different stages on the doctoral continuum, all participants were doctoral students at the time of data collection. Since the conclusion of data collection, all participants have successfully navigated the doctoral program and earned a PhD in engineering.

Future Research Agenda on Black Men in Engineering Graduate Programs

The research agenda advanced in this chapter is not exhaustive of all potential areas that should be explored. I present, however, some of the most salient areas of inquiry that need further attention in efforts to demystify the monolithic Black male mystique: 1) applying different theoretical frameworks; 2) foregrounding demographics and social identities; 3) considering native-born and foreign-born ethnicities; and 4) investigating health and wellness.

APPLYING DIFFERENT THEORETICAL FRAMEWORKS

Applying theoretical frameworks to research provides lenses through which to view previous scholarship, interrogate limitations and assumptions, and guide analyses of new data (Maxwell, 2013). Existing scholarship on graduate education tends to use "socialization" as a theoretical framework to study students' transition to graduate school, advising, mentoring, and preparation for postgraduate careers. This theory is particularly important for its contributions to understanding how graduate students become socialized to the norms, behaviors, and values of their academic community (Austin, 2002; Gardner, 2008; Felder, Stevenson, & Gasman, 2014; Weidman & Stein, 2003). Drawing on alternative theoretical frameworks, however, provides opportunities to ask questions (both new and old) from different perspectives.

Sociocultural Perspectives on Learning. My existing research tends to draw upon sociocultural perspectives on learning, a social constructivist theory that—in its broadest sense—assumes that knowledge is co-constructed through social activities with others (Lave & Wenger, 1991; Wertsch, del Rio, & Alvarez, 1995). This theory is a learning and identity development theory, usually applied to K–12 and undergraduate studies focused on STEM. However, a small yet growing number of STEM scholars are beginning to use sociocultural perspectives on learning when investigating the learning and identity development of graduate students in STEM (Bhattacharyya & Bodner, 2014; Burt et al., 2016; Crede & Borrego, 2013; Vekkaila et al., 2012; Villa et al., 2013). Central to the theory, Burt (2014) outlined three interrelated key concepts that are briefly discussed here: context, mediation, and participation:

1. "Contexts" include historical, political, and economic settings; cultural values and expectations; institutional environments; and disciplines, departments, and research groups.

2. "Mediation" refers to the "interactions" and "tools" that enable individuals to engage with others in specific contexts (e.g., interactions with a faculty advisor, interactions

with peers, learning the necessary language and acronyms within one's field and department, learning how to use the lab equipment).

3. "Participation" refers to individuals' engagement in the community's practices and activities after they have acquired the mediational tools needed to be full members of the community.

Next, I provide an illustration of how sociocultural perspectives on learning can be applied to the study of Black men in engineering graduate programs. I draw on the experiences of one participant in my study's data set.

Alphonso is a Black male engineering doctoral student from a lower-middle-class socioeconomic background who attended a racially diverse K–12 school system [*social identity character-istics*]. He is currently enrolled at a prestigious predominantly White research institution [*context*]. Because he always showed interest in science—and because both of his college-educated parents valued and understood the importance of academic enrichment—they allowed him to watch science shows on the public broadcast station, regularly took him to the local science museum, and bought him chemistry experiment sets [*medi-ation*]. Because of this support from his parents, he was able to overcome barriers such as being called "geeky," "nerd," and "not Black" because of his interest in science. As he continued along the science pathway, he became increasingly aware that he was one of few Blacks in his classrooms. Continuing through college and graduate school, most of his peers and research colleagues were White or non-Black international students, which contributed to his feelings of isolation. He felt as if his peers did not think he was smart enough to be in science (or assumed he was admitted because of affirmative action [*sociohistorical context*]). Thus, his peers were reluctant to study and/or engage in research with him [*context*]. After passing his qualifying exams, he identified a dissertation topic and a new faculty advisor, and began engaging in research (albeit within a research group; he was in a non-experimental group where students work on individualized research projects) [*mediation, participation*]. Now, having a more positive research experience where he had support from a new, nurturing faculty advisor [*mediation*], he had his first paper accepted to a conference, and soon after, a manuscript was accepted for publication [*participation*]. While he did not describe positive experiences with peers, his initial faculty advisor, or the academic department [*context*], once he began having positive experiences with research, he began envisioning himself as capable of being an engineering professor [*identity*]. (Burt, 2010; Burt, 2014, p. 37)

While I name the concepts in parentheses, these are only select examples of the kinds of ideas that are likely to emerge through data collection and analyses related to one of this study's participants. A primary benefit of this theoretical framework is the utility of its three concepts; together they provide a holistic approach to investigating an individual's learning and identity development. Questions that can be asked when using this theoretical framework can include "what" students are learning, "how" they are learning it, "who" interacts with students, and how students' learning influences their emerging identities (both personal and professional).

Critical Race Theory. Understanding the engineering and broader educational contexts is important to understanding how Black men navigate graduate school. Engineering must be situated within a broader science context; this scientific context is steeped in European male traditions of power and privilege. Thus, to better understand how Black men experience their educational spaces (Nasir & Hand, 2006), critical race theory (CRT) is a useful theoretical framework that directly attends to race, racialized systems and structures, and power and privilege in the field of education (Ladson-Billings, 1998; Solorzano, Ceja, & Yosso, 2000; Tate, 1997; Yosso, 2005). Originating from critical legal studies in the mid-1970s, CRT began as a movement among scholars and activists who used a racial lens to interpret legislation (Delgado & Stefancic, 2001, 2005). CRT scholars posit that racism is real but can be difficult to discern when embedded in language, behavior, and governmental interventions rather than explicitly asserted (Bell, 1980; Delgado & Stefancic; Ladson-Billings & Tate, 2016; Tate, 1997). Problematizing power dynamics and structures ingrained in the United States are key goals of CRT. CRT scholars study the ways in which certain policies and practices benefit White Americans and maintain their ideologies (Ladson-Billings, 1998; Tate, 1997).

CRT provides the tools to fully interrogate how race, specifically, informs students' educational experiences (Barker, 2011; Felder & Barker, 2013; McGee & Stovall, 2015). Using CRT as a theoretical framework has prompted three initial questions for the study of Black men in engineering doctoral programs: Whom does Black men's STEM participation help? Why do Black men want to be in STEM? How do race and racialized experiences inform Black men's sustained participation in STEM? Scholarship tends to frame the issue of Black male participation as helping society, helping to improve the economy and America's declining infrastructure. In the current study, participants also provided these rationales for their participation, almost as if repeating what they were told should be their reason for majoring in engineering. However, many Black men also chose science and engineering because of their strong desire to develop the tools needed to give back to their communities (both domestically and internationally). As expressed as recommendations for practice by participants in this study, selling STEM participation as an opportunity to "get rich" or "save the U.S. economy" should not be the only rationales used to convince Black men to enter—or remain in—STEM. Finally, my analyses suggest that race and racism affect all participants but that there are nuanced perceptions of and experiences with race and racism based on participants' citizenship status and ethnicity. That is, participants who were born and raised outside the United States, and/or those who identified as other than African American, perceived race differently and therefore negotiated and navigated their engineering educational differently. From a Sankofan perspective, capturing the experiences of Black men and their experiences with racism allows for a greater understanding of the ways that institutional racism emerges today. This study also emphasizes how racism is experienced differently and connected to a person's history. According to Jones and Leitner (2015), "for Blacks, when race becomes salient and is attached to injustice and racial hierarchy, its interpretations hinge to some extent on retrieving the past, 'going back and getting it' " (p. 202). Using CRT, these findings further highlight that when focusing on race and racism, all Black men are not the same. While they may share common experiences, their experiences may have subtle differences that affect individuals in distinct ways.

Men and Masculinity. The intersectional nature of the study of Black men in engineering requires deep interrogations of how race intersects with gender and STEM. Better understanding Black men's conceptions of gender and gender performance (Dancy, 2011) within the context of STEM, might be of the greatest interest. For example, in the current study, several men attempted to describe how they navigated and coped with the challenges of being in engineering (e.g., being strong, not being emotional, seeing the positive aspects in challenges). However, in their attempts, they often described needing to be strong "for" or "in the presence of" their Black women counterparts. These racial and gendered conceptions of what it means to be Black "and" male "and" in engineering present a quandary.

Questions that should be asked in future empirical work include: How is Black masculinity performed and displayed in engineering (and STEM broadly)? How do traditional forms of masculinity (i.e., White and male) in STEM influence how Black men assume they, too, need to perform in STEM to be successful? How do traditional models of STEM success (i.e., White and male, and increasingly Asian and male) inform how Black men adopt and incorporate practices of competition, individualism, and capitalism (i.e., the focus on money)?

Through this section related to theoretical frameworks, I am not suggesting that one perspective is better than another. Nor am I suggesting that these theories should be used individually. It is quite possible that where one theory falls short, combinations of multiple theories—or extensions of theories—might provide more rigorous and useful applications. Using new and underused theoretical frameworks in the study of Black men in engineering will further develop the body of work in this area.

FOREGROUNDING STUDENTS' DEMOGRAPHICS

There is a pervasive assumption that all Black students are "at-risk," from the "hood" or ghetto, living with one parent or guardian, and participated in remedial courses throughout their educational journey (Jackson & Moore, 2006). I am not suggesting by any means that these characteristics are bad. Rather, I am arguing that there are other narratives that are rarely presented in research because of a lack of attention paid to participants' demographics. Further, demographics are treated as "background" information; that is, scholars include demographic information as a required section in a research study, rather than as useful data to help scholars and readers fully understand who the study participants really are. From a sociocultural perspective, understanding students' demographics (e.g., race and ethnicity, nationality, gender, origin of baccalaureate degree, parents' educational and socioeconomic status) is vital to making sense of their learning and identity development (both personal and professional). Without a more nuanced investigation of students' demographic information and social identities, there is an underlying assumption that the Black men being studied are all the same. Instead, future research should shift to "foregrounding" students' demographic information (Dancy & Brown, 2008).

The majority of students reported on in this chapter come from two-parent, middle- to upper-income families, where both parents not only have a baccalaureate degree but some parents hold advanced degrees (e.g., PhD). In fact, all but one participant reported growing up in a middle-class, two-parent home; the remaining student classified his single-parent home as low-income. Of the 11 participants, three students' mothers had master's degrees, and two had doctorates. Similarly, all but one father had postsecondary education; two of the fathers had master's degrees, and three held doctorates.

In addition, most participants indicated that they lived in White-dominated or mixed-race educational environments. Specifically, five participants attended majority-White high schools, four attended high schools with racially and ethnically mixed populations, and two attended high schools where a majority of the students were classified as Black. At the collegiate level, all but one participant attended a predominantly White college or university for undergraduate studies. Thus, most of them—even those who attended historically Black colleges and universities (HBCUs) for undergraduate studies—had experience interacting with, and thriving in, academic spaces where they were not the racial majority.

In addition to parental level of education and family socioeconomic status, students' nationality is important to consider. In this chapter's data set, five participants self-reported being native born (i.e., born in the United States), whereas six self-reported being foreign born (i.e., born outside the United States). New scholarship on within-group similarities and differences with regard to students' nationalities (Fries-Britt, George Mwangi, & Peralta, 2014; George Mwangi et al., 2016) illustrates the need for greater focus on students' nationalities. For example, in George Mwangi et al.'s (2016) comparative study of Black native-born and foreign-born students' intraracial interactions, they found that the two populations have different perspectives on what it means to feel or be isolated in their predominantly White classrooms. Although all study participants were in STEM (physics), they viewed the concept of underrepresentation differently. The native-born Black physics students regularly mentioned the need for more representational diversity in terms of native-born Black students in the classroom; the foreign-born Black students did not have the same concerns, as they viewed their classrooms as already composed of other international students (of various races, ethnicities, and nationalities).

From a research perspective, scholars should also take into consideration how students' demographics inform the data that are collected. Areas to further explore regarding Black men doctoral students in engineering could include socioeconomic status, reason for institution selection, parents' background and education level, and distinctions between native- and foreign-born Black students. Although unanswered here, these are the kinds of empirical questions that can be posed when foregrounding students' demographics.

BLACK MEN'S HEALTH AND WELLNESS

Graduate school is a challenging time for many students; the constant uncertainty of progress, the long hours working in the lab or on assignments, and the forfeiting of personal care for the demands of school are a few of the difficulties in graduate school (Okahana et al., 2016; Sowell, Allum, & Okahana, 2014). Additionally, for many Black students, there are larger pervasive social issues that exacerbate the challenges of being a graduate student. Specifically, racism and chronic racial discrimination plague Black individuals. The nuanced ways in which these societal ills are present in the academy and contribute to the health disparities of Black men in engineering graduate programs warrant further attention (McGee & Stovall, 2015).

The 11 Black men in this chapter described unhealthy and unsupportive educational contexts. They were clear that it was not only the college (i.e., the physical structure, with photographs of old White men hanging in departmental hallways) that served as a constant reminder of their underrepresentation and isolation, but that classrooms, research labs, exchanges with non-Black peers, and one-on-one interactions with advisors also contributed to their daily negotiations of what it meant to be Black and male and to be in engineering. Unfortunately, the men in this study routinely described their engineering educational experiences in alarming ways. For example, some students used words such as "abusive" and "violent" to describe their advisors. It then was not shocking when some students admitted to feeling depressed, unhappy, and feeling like failures. The challenge for these men is that racism and chronic discrimination are cumulative. Contextually, the men in this study described dealing with racial discrimination at school, and once they left campus they also had to deal with issues of race and racism (while at the grocery store, mall, driving, etc.).

While other scholars report that students often seek out and turn to faculty of color for mentoring (DeFour & Hirsch, 1990; Tuitt, 2012), that was not regularly reported by students in this study. Instead, although the majority of students perceived that racist acts were occurring, the majority of participants described using forms of avoidance to cope with their experiences, or they rationalized and normalized the racialized experiences they faced. While not explicitly stated, patterns from participants revealed that their approaches to coping with the ongoing stressors of racism were likely conscious efforts to help reduce the psychological stings of racism. As expressed throughout this chapter, how and why students deal with racism appears to be related to their demographic characteristics (e.g., nationality), as well as to how they display masculinity (e.g., there was a pattern of equating racism with just another challenge that one is supposed to overcome in graduate school).

Considering Black men's health and wellness provides ample opportunities for future investigation. On one hand, it is extremely important to isolate and better understand the numerous experiences that threaten Black men's health and wellness (McGee & Stovall, 2015). But it is also critical that research explore how Black men cope with the stressors that they face within their engineering educational contexts (Ellis, 2015; Pittman, 2011).

What is important to understand about this line of inquiry regarding the health and wellness of Black men in engineering graduate programs is why such inquiry is necessary. I am not making the argument that if Black men are not healthy, they will not be physically able to contribute to the engineering workforce for 30 years (i.e., this could potentially be an "interest convergence" argument analyzed using CRT). Rather, better understanding the causes and implications of Black men's health disparities is important for improving the human lives of Black men. This study focused on the population of engineers solely for the purpose of isolating one domain-specific context in which to begin improving the circumstances that cause some Black men stress-related ailments.

Concluding Thoughts and Implications for Professional Practice

This conceptual chapter provided several suggested avenues for future scholarly inquiry through the use of empirical data from a study of Black men in engineering doctoral programs. Complicating the monolithic

Black male mystique requires us to examine alternative and sociocultural frameworks that explicitly consider students' multiple demographic identities (e.g., race, gender, socioeconomic status) and the nested contexts in which they are embedded. Without new knowledge that incorporates these suggestions, professional practice will continue to be based on hunches and anecdotal information, likely interpreted using a "monolithic Black male" framework.

My ongoing work on the experiences of Black men in engineering graduate programs lends itself to several implications for professional practice. While presented separately for the purpose of clarity, it is possible to consider multiple points simultaneously.

1. Sociocultural perspectives on learning: Intentionally consider how learning and professional identity development are affected by *who* students interact with and *how* they interact with them. With this in mind, develop an expanded view of the teaching and learning environments that impact students' experiences (for example, students are not solely shaped by the curriculum and classroom experiences but also by their research labs, their college and university campuses, etc.). Improving students' interactions with their nested educational contexts may improve their educational experiences and positively influence their persistence in STEM.

2. CRT: Be cognizant of how institutional- and college-level policies inadvertently negatively impact Black male graduate students, and take action—on behalf of Black men—to dismantle unjust policies and practices. For example, a policy that allows students to matriculate into graduate school and shop for an advisor may seem like a good strategy to allow students to find a mutual advisor–advisee match. However, some students may not understand how to identify an advisor. Additionally, because "race and racism are real," some professors may hold preconceived notions about students based on students' race and the professors' conscious or unconscious racial biases. In these circumstances, a student may not be able to locate a professor to serve as his advisor. Thus, a policy where students are assigned a temporary advisor upon admission might be more appropriate.

3. Men and masculinity: Recognize that Black men—and more broadly, men of color—are generally underrepresented in most college spaces. Allow for spaces where these men can share experiences with each other. Additionally, intentionally diversify engineering faculties and staff. In the same way that men want to complete their degrees in efforts to be role models for the future generation, they need to see current models of success in the academy to aid in their current persistence.

4. Student demographics: All Black men are not the same. Aggregating students to inflate data points does not serve students well. When running statistical reports, intentionally disaggregate demographic data to be more precise. For more sophisticated analyses, calculate data correlations on students' intersections. These more refined data points will provide clues to within-group patterns often undiscoverable when Black men are treated as a monolithic whole.

5. Black men's health: The health of students should be as important as their degree completion. Routinely inform students of the various resources and support networks across campus that can assist with promoting wellness. In addition, implement programmatic efforts within the engineering college to model the significance of maintaining one's health in the field of engineering. Such programs will tailor the resources to engineers and their unique needs and provide better access to these resources.

I would be remiss if I did not offer one additional implication for practice based on the voices of participants in this study. Specifically, Black men are rarely—if ever—asked about how they are experiencing their educational environment. Thus, I encourage administrators, staff, and faculty to talk to Black men graduate students in engineering. But they should not just seek out the voices of those who appear to be engaged in leadership activities within the college, those who are native born (i.e., African Americans), or those likely to provide a positive response. Instead, they should get a cross-section of students' views on the college's climate; their experiences with faculty, administrators, and staff; and ideas about how to improve the educational experiences of others. However, asking their opinions must be done with care, confidentiality, and genuine intent to act on what one learns. It is important to recognize that, depending on one's position, a *request* to speak with students may be viewed as coming from a position of power; some students may be reluctant to fully express themselves for fear of retaliation. Conversations with students will be most useful if they are regular rather than a one-time occurrence. Further, if asked for their opinion, students will expect something to be done with the information they provide. Thus, administrators and others must be prepared to help make changes and advocate for the students' interests. Finally, anyone who asks about their experiences needs to be open to hearing their truth, their lived experiences. Their experiences may be painful to hear or might appear to be personal—given one's position. But it is necessary that those who are listening not take offense and try to hear the essence of what students are communicating. In addition to speaking with students, it may also be useful to gain demographic information on Black men students. This information will be useful in gaining more nuanced understandings of the Black men engineering graduate students in one's college. Programmatic efforts based on more precise data on who students are and their unique challenges and strengths (through interviews and demographic information) will help stakeholders improve the educational environments needed to ensure the success of Black men engineering graduate students.

Through the voices of 11 Black men in engineering doctoral programs, this conceptual chapter has identified thematic gaps within existing scholarship on Black men in graduate education. These unanswered gaps need to be filled in efforts to forge promising pathways into and through graduate education (Council of Graduate Schools and Educational Testing Service, 2010, 2012). Black men are important learners and participants in the university enterprise. Thus, better understanding their lived experiences is necessary. To better serve Black men collegians and ensure their continued success, scholars, administrators, and policy makers must see Black men's multiple strengths, their multiple dimensions, their unique challenges, and their unique opportunities for growth. This chapter's focus on establishing a research agenda for future exploration, and the scholarship and practice that is to come, will serve to demystify the monolithic Black male mystique.

Works Cited

Griffith, D. W. (Director). (1915). *Birth of a nation* [Motion picture]. United States: Epoch Producing Corporation.

Austin, A. E. (2002). Preparing the next generation of faculty: Graduate school as socialization to the academic career. *The Journal of Higher Education, 73*, 94–121.

Barker, M. J. (2011). Racial context, currency and connections: Black doctoral student and white advisor perspectives on cross-race advising. *Innovations in Educational and Teaching International, 48*(4), 387–400.

Bell, D. (2005). Brown v. Board of Education and the interest-convergence dilemma. In R. Delgado & J. Stefancic (Eds.), *The Derrick Bell reader* (pp. 33–39). New York, NY: New York University Press.

Bhattacharryya, G., & Bodner, G. M. (2014). Culturing reality: How organic chemistry graduate students develop into practitioners. *Journal of Research in Science Teaching, 51*(6), 694–713.

Brazziel, M. E., & Brazziel, W. F. (2001). Factors in decisions of underrepresented minorities to forego science and engineering doctoral study: A pilot study. *Journal of Science Education and Technology, 10*(3), 272–281.

Brown, A. L. (2011). Same old stories: The Black male in social science and educational literature, 1930s to the present. *Teachers College Record, 113*(9), 2047–2079.

Burt, B. A. (2014). The influence of doctoral research experiences on the pursuit of the engineering professoriate. Dissertation. University of Michigan.

Burt, B. A. (2010). Surviving and striving: African American doctoral candidates in engineering at a predominantly White institution. Association for the Study of Higher Education (ASHE) Conference proceeding.

Burt, B. A., McKen, A., Burkhart, J., Hormell, J., & Knight, A. (2016). Racial microaggressions within the advisor-advisee relationship: Implications for engineering research, policy, and practice. American Society for Engineering Education (ASEE) Conference proceeding.

Butler, Paul. 2013. Black male exceptionalism? The problems and potential of Black male focused interventions. *Du Bois Review, 10*(2), 485–511.

Chubin, D. E., May, G. S., & Babco, E. L. (2005). Diversifying the engineering workforce. *Journal of Engineering Education, 94*(1), 73–86.

Council of Graduate Schools and Educational Testing Service. (2010). *The path forward: The future of graduate education in the United States.* Report from the Commission on the Future of Graduate Education in the United States. Princeton, NJ: Educational Testing Service.

Council of Graduate Schools and Educational Testing Service. (2012). *Pathways through graduate school and into careers. Report from the Commission on Pathways Through Graduate School and Into Careers.* Princeton, NJ: Educational Testing Service.

Crede, E., & Borrego, M. (2012). Learning in graduate engineering research groups of various sizes. *Journal of Engineering Education, 101*(3), 565–589.

Dancy, T. E., II (2011). Colleges in the making of manhood and masculinity: Gendered perspectives on African American males. *Gender and Education, 23*(4), 477–495.

Dancy, T. E., II (2014). (Un)doing hegemony in education: Disrupting school-to-prison pipelines for Black males. *Equity & Excellence in Education, 47*(4), 476–493.

Dancy, T. E., II, & Brown, M. C., II. (2008). Unintended consequences: African American male educational attainment and collegiate perceptions after Brown v. Board of Education. *American Behavioral Scientist, 51*(7), 984–1003.

DeFour, D. C., & Hirsch, B. J. (1990). The adaptation of Black graduate students: A social network approach. *American Journal of Community Psychology, 18*(3), 487–503.

Delgado, R., & Stefancic, J. (2012). *Critical race theory: An introduction.* New York, NY: New York University Press.

Dumas, M. J. (2016). My brother as "problem": Neoliberal governmentality and interventions for Black young men and boys. *Educational Policy, 30*(1), 94–113.

Ellis, K. R., Griffith, D. M., Allen, J. O., Thorpe, R. J., & Bruce, M. A. (2015). "If you do nothing about stress, the next thing you know, you're shattered": Perspectives on African American men's stress, coping and health from African American men and key women in their lives. *Social Science & Medicine, 139*, 107–114

Felder, P. P., & Barker, M. J. (2013). Extending Bell's concept of interest convergence: A framework for understanding the African American doctoral student experience. *International Journal of Doctoral Studies, 8*, 1–20.

Felder, P. P., Stevenson, H. C., & Gasman, M. (2014). Understanding race in doctoral student socialization. *International Journal of Doctoral Studies, 9*, 21–42.

Fries-Britt, S. R., Mwangi, C. A., & Peralta, A. M. (2014). Learning race in a U.S. context: An emerging framework on the perceptions of race among foreign-born students of color. *Journal of Diversity in Higher Education, 7*(1), 1–13.

Gardner, S. K. (2008) Fitting the mold of graduate school: A qualitative study of socialization in doctoral education. *Innovative Higher Education, 7*, 1–21.

George Mwangi, C. A., Fries-Britt, S. R., Peralta, A. M., & Daoud, N. (2014). Examining intraracial dynamics and engagement between native-born and foreign-born Black collegians in STEM. *Journal of Black Studies, 47*(7), 773–794.

Harper, S. R. (2014). (Re)setting the agenda for college men of color: Lessons learned from a 15-year movement to improve Black male student success. In R. A. Williams & F. A. Hrabowski (Eds.), *Men of color in higher education: New foundations for developing models for success* (pp. 116–144). Sterling, VA: Stylus.

Harper, S. R., & Nichol, A. H. (2008). Are they not all the same? Racial heterogeneity among Black male undergraduates. *Journal of College Student Development, 49*(3), 247–269.

Hernstein, R. J., & Murray, C. (1994). *The bell curve: Intelligence and class structure in American life*. New York, NY: Free Press.

Herzig, A. H. (2004). Becoming mathematicians: Women and students of color choosing and leaving doctoral mathematics. *Review of Educational Research, 74*(2), 171–214.

Jackson, R. L., II. (2006). *Scripting the Black masculine body: Identity, discourse, and racial politics in popular media*. Albany, NY: State University of New York Press.

Jackson, J. F. L., & Moore, J. L., III. (2008). The African American male crisis in education: A popular media infatuation or needed public policy response. *American Behavioral Scientist, 51*(7), 847–853.

Jackson, J. F. L., & Moore, J. L., III. (2006). African American males in education endangered or ignored. *Teacher College Record, 108*(2), 201–205.

Jones, J. M., & Leitner, J. B. (2015). The Sankofa effect: Divergent effects of thinking about the past for Blacks and Whites. In M. Stolarski, N. Fieulaine, & W. van Beek (Eds.), *Time perspective theory; review, research, and application: Essays in honor of Philip G. Zimbardo* (pp. 197–211). New York: Springer Publishing.

Ladson-Billings, G. (1998). Just what is critical race theory and what's it doing in a nice field like education? *International Journal of Qualitative Studies in Education, 11*, 7–24.

Lave, J., & Wenger, E. (1991). *Situated learning: Legitimate peripheral participation*. New York, NY: Cambridge University Press.

Maton, K. I., & Hrabowski, F. A., III. (2004). Increasing the number of African American PhDs in the sciences and engineering. *American Psychologist, 59*(6), 547–556.

Maxwell, J. A. (2013). *Qualitative research design: An interactive approach* (3rd ed.). Thousand Oaks, CA: Sage Publications.

McGee, E. O., & Stovall, D. (2015). Reimagining critical race theory in education: Mental health, healing, and the pathway to liberatory praxis. *Educational Theory, 65*(5), 491–511.

Moore, J. L. (2006). A qualitative investigation of African American males' career trajectory in engineering: Implications for teachers, school counselors, and parents. *Teachers College Record, 108*(2), 246–266.

National Action Council for Minorities in Engineering. (2014). *Research & policy brief, 4*(1). White Plains, NY.

Okahana, H., Allum, J., Felder, P. P., & Tull, R. G. (2016). *Implications for practice and research from Doctoral Initiative on Minority Attrition and Completion* (CGS Data Sources PLUS #16-01). Washington, DC: Council of Graduate Schools.

Pittman, C. T. (2011). Getting mad but ending up sad: The mental health consequences for African Americans using anger to cope with racism. *Journal of Black Studies, 42*(7), 1106–1124.

Robinson, W. H., McGee, E. O., Bentley, L. C., Houston, S. L., & Botchway, P. K. (2016). Addressing negative racial and gendered experiences that discourage academic careers in engineering. *Computing in Science & Engineering, 18*(29), 29–39.

Solorzano, D., Ceja, M., & Yosso, T. (2000). Critical race theory, racial microaggressions, and campus racial climate: The experiences of African American college students. *Journal of Negro Education, 69*(1–2), 60–73.

Sowell, R., Allum, J., & Okahana, H. (2015). *Doctoral initiative on minority attrition and completion* (DIMAC Report). Washington, DC: Council of Graduate Schools.

Tate, W. F. (1997). Critical race theory and education: History, theory, and implications. *Review of Research in Education, 22*, 195–247.

Tedla, E. (1995). *Sankofa: African thought and education.* New York, NY: Lang Publishing.

Tuitt, F. (2012). Black like me: Graduate students' perceptions of their pedagogical experiences in classes taught by Black faculty in a predominantly White institution. *Journal of Black Studies, 43*(2), 186–206.

Vekkaila, J., Pyhältö, K, Hakkarainen, K., Keskinen, J., & Lonka, K. (2012). Doctoral students' key learning experiences in the natural sciences. *International Journal for Researcher Development, 3*(2), 154–183.

Villa, E. Q., Kephart, K., Gates, A. Q., Thiry, H., & Hug, S. (2013). Affinity research groups in practice: Apprenticing students in research. *Journal of Engineering Education, 102*(3), 444–466.

Weidman, J. C., & Stein, E. L. (2003). Socialization of doctoral students to academic norms. *Research in Higher Education 44*(6), 641–656.

Wertsch, J. V., del Rio, P., & Alvarez, A. (1995). Sociocultural studies: History, action, and mediation. In J. V. Wertsch, P. del Rio, & A. Alvarez, *Sociocultural studies of mind* (pp. 1–34). New York: Cambridge University Press.

Yoder, B. L. (2015). Engineering by the numbers. Washington: American Society for Engineering Education. Retrieved from https://www.asee.org/papers-and-publications/publications/college-profiles

Yosso, T. J. (2005). Whose culture has capital? A critical race theory discussion of community cultural wealth. *Race Ethnicity and Education, 8*(1), 69–91.

Chapter 5

Being One of Few

Examining Black Biomedical PhDs' Training Experiences and Career Development through a Campus Racial Climate Lens

KIMBERLY A. GRIFFIN, KENNETH D. GIBBS JR., AND SHELVIA ENGLISH

African Americans have made substantial gains in terms of their educational attainment and representation in undergraduate and graduate education in recent decades. However, despite comprising more than 13% of the U.S. population and 14% of all students enrolled in college, African Americans made up 6% of full-time faculty at postsecondary institutions in 2014 (NSF, 2015a). This underrepresentation is particularly visible in science. African Americans represented 4% of all faculty with science, engineering, or health doctorates in 2008 (NSF, 2011). In 2013, Black scientists made up 3.4% of all science and engineering PhDs employed as research or teaching faculty at four-year colleges and universities (NSF, 2013). And in 2015, Black scientists were 1.6% of all faculty in basic science departments at AAMC MD-granting medical schools (AAMC, 2015).

These data are particularly troubling given their persistence and an observed lack of progress in increasing the number and representation of Black professors. Black faculty have represented approximately 5% to 6% of the professoriate since the early 1990s, despite increases in the number of Black students graduating with doctoral degrees (Perna, Gerald, Baum, & Milem, 2007). According to the National Academies of Sciences (2011), increasing the representation of people of color in science has perhaps been the least successful of the science diversity initiatives. This lack of faculty diversity is due, in part, to fewer Black PhDs in the applicant pool (Patel, 2015; NSF, 2015b), and institutional leaders and policy makers have increasingly turned their attention to developing strategies to attract more African Americans to science doctoral programs and the science, technology, engineering, and math (STEM) workforce (e.g., CGS & ETS, 2012). However, increases in the number of Black science PhDs have not translated to increased representation in the faculty. A report from the Council of Graduate Schools and Educational Testing Services (2010) notes that the increases in graduate degrees awarded to Black students between 1998 and 2008 exceeds the progress made in diversifying the professoriate. Similarly, Gibbs and colleagues (2016) found that while the number of underrepresented minorities graduating from PhD programs in biomedical science grew nine times between 1980 and 2014 (from 93 to 868), the number of underrepresented minority (URM) assistant professors in medical schools grew more slowly, increasing 2.6 times over the same time frame (from 132 to 341).

To increase the number of Blacks in the professoriate, scholars and leaders must explicitly address whether students completing their doctoral programs are actually interested in becoming faculty. While researchers suggest doctoral students generally report lower levels of interest in faculty careers at research-intensive universities as their training progresses (Austin, 2002; Fuhrmann, Halme, O'Sullivan, & Lindstaedt, 2011; Golde & Dore, 2001; Sauermann & Roach, 2012), the interests of women and underrepresented minority men decline more significantly than those of White and Asian men (Gibbs, McGready, Bennett, & Griffin, 2014; Gibbs, McGready, & Griffin, 2015). In studies comparing the career interests of scientists from underrepresented minority populations with those of their well-represented peers (e.g., Gibbs et al., 2014; Gibbs et al., 2015), lower levels of interest in the professoriate were not explained by research productivity, mentoring relationships, research self-efficacy, or training pedigree. This leads to the key question guiding this work: What factors drive career decision making and interest (or lack thereof) in a faculty career for Black scientists?

Some researchers have considered the characteristics and personal interests of those who become faculty, such as an interest in and commitment to research, academic achievement, and a preference for working autonomously in positions that allow for creative expression (e.g., Fox & Stephan, 2001; Lindholm, 2004; Schenkein & Best, 2001; Stephen, Barber,

& Cole, 2009); however, much of this work does not consider how racism or marginalization experienced during graduate training can shape that process. Scholars have increasingly examined how values and identity may influence the career development and aspirations of populations underrepresented in science (e.g., Gibbs & Griffin, 2013; Griffin, Gibbs, Bennett, Staples, & Robinson, 2015; Jaeger, Haley, Apaw, & Levin, 2013), as well as documenting racism and the challenges students of color face as they navigate graduate education (e.g., Carlone & Johnson, 2007; Felder, 2015; Felder & Barker, 2013; Gasman, Hirschfeld, & Vultaggio, 2008; Gildersleeve, Croom, & Vasquez, 2011). However, few studies critically consider how these experiences translate to not only retention to degree completion, but also career development and aspirations.

In recognition of the Sankofa theme, it is important to not accept traditional views of why students may not pursue faculty careers when examining how students might define their professional identities and aspirations. Instead, it is essential that research on career choice be engaged through a cultural lens that values and makes salient the voices and experiences of Black biomedical doctoral students. Thus, this study examines the relationship between racial climate, student experiences, and career development in STEM for recent Black doctoral degree graduates. We address the following research questions:

1. How do Black science PhDs describe and navigate the racial climate in their laboratories, graduate programs, and the broader scientific community?

2. How do climate-related experiences shape Black scientists' career development and commitments to pursuing faculty careers?

Background

Campus climate is defined as the current patterns of behavior in a campus community, as well as how those behaviors are perceived (Peterson & Spencer, 1990). In relation to issues of race and racism, campus climate can be understood as attitudes, beliefs, behaviors, and perceptions of community members around issues of racial and ethnic difference (Hurtado, Milem, Clayton-Pederson, & Allen, 1999). Several scholars have advanced conceptual frameworks to assess and better understand how students, faculty, and staff experience campus climate, and how climate may be related to educational experiences and outcomes. The multicontextual model of diverse learning environments (DLE) guides this work, and it is the most current version of a campus climate framework initially developed by Hurtado, Milem, Clayton-Pederson, and Allen. The DLE is unique in that it explicitly links climate-related experiences to three forms of student outcomes: habits of mind and lifelong learning, the competencies necessary to navigate in a multicultural world, and retention and achievement (Hurtado, Alvarez, Guillermo-Wann, Cuellar, & Arellano, 2012).

Hurtado and colleagues (2012) conceptualize climate as a multidimensional phenomenon, uniquely constructed on each campus through a convergence of external forces (governmental policy and sociohistorical factors) and institutional forces. Students' learning experiences in curricular and co-curricular contexts lie at the center of the model and are linked to their social identities, the identities of the faculty and staff they engage, and course and programmatic content. The model suggests that these learning experiences are also shaped by five interrelated institutional factors, which are referred to as the dimensions of climate: (1) compositional diversity; (2) historical legacy of inclusion or exclusion; (3) psychological climate; (4) behavioral climate; and (5) organizational diversity (Hurtado et al., 2012; Milem, Chang, & antonio, 2005).

Colleges and universities are often most aware of compositional diversity, or the numerical representation of people of color on campus (Hurtado et al., 1999; Milem et al., 2005), and may implement comprehensive strategies to increase the number of students from underrepresented populations on their campuses. While these strategies may result in campuses that appear diverse, representation is only one part of creating an inclusive environment. The other dimensions of climate must also be addressed to support students' learning experiences and promote belonging in campus communities, particularly for students from underrepresented populations.

Four additional dimensions are included in the DLE, which, along with compositional diversity, relate to the ways students experience campus contexts. An institution's legacy of inclusion or exclusion captures whether past treatment of marginalized groups is acknowledged and perceived as worthy of continued focus and attention. The psychological dimension reflects how students feel in an environment and includes sense of belonging as well as the perceived hostility, racism, and racial tension among community members. The behavioral dimension captures both frequency and quality of interaction between peers from diverse backgrounds. Organizational diversity represents how institutions can support equity or maintain disparities through structures, policies, and procedures that often unintentionally benefit dominant groups (Hurtado et al., 2012; Milem et al., 2005).

The five dimensions of the DLE do not function in isolation. They individually and collectively shape attitudes, beliefs, behaviors, and perceptions about race and diversity in a campus community, as well as student experiences and outcomes. They also can influence each other. For example, underrepresentation (a lack of compositional diversity) can be related to whether students feel isolated, feel a sense of belonging, or feel like the climate is welcoming and inclusive (psychological climate). Research documenting the experiences of Black graduate students (e.g., Gildersleeve, Croom, & Vasquez, 2011; Hunn, 2008; Johnson-Bailey, Valentine, Cervero, & Bowles, 2009) and African Americans in science (e.g., Kulis, Chong, & Shaw, 1999; Williams, Thakore, & McGee, 2016) shows that being one of few persons of color or the only person of color in their departments and programs translates to feelings of isolation, a perceived lack of fit with others in the department or field, and a lack of belonging. Scholars suggest that relationships with students and scholars of color can mitigate some of this isolation, creating communities of support that affirm students' abilities, provide access to information, and remind them that success in the field is possible (Gildersleeve, Croom, & Vasquez, 2011; Johnson-Bailey et al., 2008). Interestingly, participants in Williams, Thakore, and McGee's (2016) study of underrepresented minority scientists found that not having the opportunity to see or interact with other underrepresented scientists, particularly faculty, left trainees wondering about whether they had the skills necessary to be successful in the field as faculty themselves.

In addition, small numbers of African Americans in graduate programs and in the sciences can leave students feeling highly visible and more subject to marginalizing experiences with peers and faculty, which can be understood as part of the behavioral climate. Research suggests Black students are highly aware of stereotypes about their academic abilities (e.g., Fries-Britt, Younger, & Hall, 2010; McGee & Martin, 2011; Robinson, McGee, Bentley, Houston, & Botchway, 2016; Sanchez, Liu, Leathers, Goins, & Vilain, 2011; Williams, Thakore, McGee, & 2016). These stereotypes can manifest in their relationships in the form of microaggressions, subtle and often unintentional actions that marginalize individuals based on their identities (Sue, 2010), or other more overt and intentional acts of racism and oppression.

Black graduate students and scientists similarly report facing questions about their academic ability and low expectations of their performance, which can strain relationships with faculty and peers as students work hard to "prove" their worth as students (Fries-Britt, Younger, & Hall, 2010; McGee & Martin, 2011; Sanchez et al., 2011). For example, female doctoral students of color who participated in Zeligman, Prescod, and Green's (2015) study described themselves as highly visible because of their small numbers, and felt the need to work doubly hard to not only prove their worth, but also ensure that future underrepresented scholars would not be perceived as less able or intelligent. These interactions across difference can also be related to sense of belonging and the degree to which students feel welcome in their programs and the scientific community. For example, Clark and colleagues (2012) found that while graduate students of color reported similar levels of autonomy as their peers, they reported more exposure to microaggressions and less belonging, and underrepresented minority scientists in Williams and colleagues' (2016) study felt they were not perceived as fitting the mold as scientists, particularly when working with White advisors who viewed students through the lenses of their unconscious biases.

While this literature provides key insights into how climate-related factors may negatively influence the quality of Black graduate students' experiences in science, few scholars have used a climate model to frame their research, nor have they explored the relationship between climate and students' career decision making. Rather than climate, scholars have more often attended to how the nature of faculty work and life may influence interest in the professoriate. For example, Golde and Dore (2001) found that many graduate students across the arts, humanities, and sciences did not desire the ambiguities and challenges often associated with faculty life. Similarly, 91% of the graduate students participating in Fuhrmann, Halme, O'Sullivan, and Lindstaedt's (2011) study who lost interest in becoming academic principal investigators were influenced by negative perceptions of career path, and raised concerns about the lack of funding for research and heavy competition for a declining number of academic positions. Many graduate students perceive faculty work as all consuming, leaving little room for a personal life that includes family and personal interests (Griffin et al., 2015; Mason, Goulden, & Frasch, 2009). Further, trainees express concerns about the length of the academic training process, which may include several years of postdoctoral work before securing a faculty position (Fuhrmann et al., 2011; MacLachlan, 2006). The low salaries associated with postdoctoral training can discourage some from pursuing faculty careers, as they compare their financial resources and stability with peers who are their age but have spent less time in school (Gibbs & Griffin, 2013; Stephan, 2012). While several of these factors may be consistent across various identity groups (e.g., students from all racial backgrounds may be similarly frustrated with low postdoctoral pay or the all-consuming nature of faculty work and life), our work also considers whether some of the factors dissuading interest in the academy are amplified or experienced in a unique way by Black trainees and whether the demands of science can be considered as part of the climate.

Methods

This study examines the relationships between dimensions of climate, curricular, and co-curricular learning processes relevant to graduate education in science (e.g., classes, laboratory research, social engagement with peers and faculty) and how a group of Black scientists think about pursuing careers in the academy and the field of academic research. We use the climate model to illustrate both the individual level and systemic issues that can influence efforts to recruit and retain diverse talent in STEM. Specifically, we consider how the dimensions of climate function individually and collectively across participants' experiences, and whether and how climate can impact career development and aspirations.

Sample and Data Sources

Data were drawn from a larger, mixed-method study of career development and aspirations in the biomedical sciences. This study follows a sequential explanatory design (Creswell & Plano Clark, 2007), where data were collected in two phases. Quantitative data were collected in Phase 1. A total of 1,890 U.S. citizens and permanent residents who completed their doctoral degrees in STEM disciplines between 2007 and 2012 participated in an online survey examining career aspirations, training experiences, and perceptions of relationships with advisors, faculty, and peers. Our sample included 1,500 participants who completed degrees in biomedical science, including genetics, neuroscience, microbiology and immunology, psychology, bioinformatics, and biological sciences. Of particular interest, participants were asked to rate their level of interest in various career paths (faculty at a research institution, faculty at a teaching institution, non-academic researcher, position outside of research and the academy), reflecting on their interest at three different points in time: before beginning graduate school, after completing graduate school, and currently (at the time of survey completion).

The survey data were used to generate a group of scientists with varying career interests to interview in Phase 2, which created an opportunity for deeper understanding of the trends observed during Phase 1. We recruited a group of 69 scientists, diverse in terms of race, gender, and career aspirations, to participate in semistructured interviews on their training experiences and career development. This research presents quantitative and qualitative data collected from the 21 (9 female, 12 male) Black biomedical scientists who participated in Phase 1 and 2 of this study. Participant information can be found in Table 5.1. All participants are U.S. citizens, and they attended predominantly White institutions for their graduate programs; 15 different institutions are represented in the sample. Sixteen participants completed or were currently in postdoctoral traineeships, and three did not do a postdoc.

Data Collection and Procedures

Given our interest in understanding the experiences and career development of those for whom faculty careers were a viable option and narratives that suggest individuals do not become faculty because they are not qualified or academically capable, we selected participants who demonstrated high levels of achievement in their graduate programs who had first-authored Pubmed-indexed paper, and who completed a PhD from a Top-50 research university (as defined by NSF Science and Engineering Indicators, 2012: http://www.nsf.gov/statistics/seind12/append/c5/at05-10.pdf). Eligible participants were then categorized by data collected from their survey responses during Phase 1: race, gender, level of interest in a faculty career at a research university before and after graduate school, and current roles and aspirations.

All identified Black participants who met the selection criteria were contacted by email and invited to participate in Phase 2. Those responding to the email were assigned a pseudonym and participated by phone or Skype in a semistructured interview (60–120 minutes). Each interview

Table 5.1. Participants' Background Information

Pseudonym	Gender	Current/Completed Postdoctoral Training	Change in Interest in Research Faculty Position during Graduate School	Interest in Being Any Kind of Faculty Member	Position at Interview
Christina	Female	Yes	Decreased (high to little interest)	No	Science policy
Damien	Male	No	Decreased (high to little interest)	Yes	Tenure-track faculty
Denise	Female	Yes	Increased (no to little interest)	Yes	Tenure-track faculty
Elias	Male	Yes	Consistent (interest)	No	Postdoc
Harris	Male	Yes	Decreased (some to little interest)	No	Industry scientist
Helene	Female	Yes	Decreased (high to no interest)	No	Science policy
Isaac	Male	Yes	Decreased (interest to little interest)	No	Industry scientist
Jayden	Male	Yes	Decreased (interest to no interest)	No	Postdoc
Joan	Female	Yes	Decreased (some to no interest)	No	Postdoc
Joi	Female	Yes	Consistent (little interest)	Yes	Tenure-track faculty
Layla	Female	Yes	Consistent (high interest)	Yes	Postdoc
Luke	Male	Yes	Consistent (high interest)	Yes	Research scientist—academia
Ralph	Male	Yes	Consistent (some interest)	No	Industry scientist
Ryan	Male	Yes	Decreased (little to no interest)	Yes	Postdoc
Sarai	Female	No	Decreased (little to no interest)	No	Science policy
Tamara	Female	Yes	Decreased (interest to little interest)	No	Science policy
Tyrone	Male	Yes	Consistent (high interest)	Yes	Postdoc
Wanda	Female	Yes	Decreased (interest to little interest)	Yes	Postdoc
Wesley	Male	Yes	Decreased (interest to little interest)	No	Research scientist—academia
Will	Male	Yes	Decreased (some to little interest)	No	Postdoc
Zachary	Male	No	Consistent (no interest)	No	Business

addressed life before graduate school, the emergence of educational and career aspirations, graduate school experiences, postdoctoral experiences (if relevant), and current interests and perceptions of career options. Throughout the interview, participants were asked to reflect on the quality of their relationships with faculty and peers, their sense of belonging in their programs and laboratories, and the role of their identity and background in their training experiences.

Analysis

Survey data collected during Phase 1 were used to track participants' interests in faculty careers, particularly at research universities. These data were used to frame our analysis of the qualitative data collected during Phase 2, deepening our understanding of each scientist's career interests and providing a framework for how they changed over time. The qualitative data were analyzed based on methods used in team-based studies conducted by the Centers for Disease Control and Prevention (see MacQueen, McLellan, Kay, & Milstein, 1998, for details), integrating deductive and inductive strategies. Three members of the research team met to develop the codebook through an iterative process. The deductive process led to the development of structural codes, which enabled identification of students' narratives associated with specific research questions, the DLE, and alignment with research on the experiences of students of color in STEM graduate programs. Then a list of inductive codes was developed based on emerging themes. The deductive and inductive lists were combined into one codebook, assigning each code a definition, rules for usage, and an example of coded data to facilitate consistency in coding across members of the research team. Consistent with methods outlined by Bogdan and Biklen (1998) and Merriam (1998), the codes were then applied to the data. Data were then sorted by codes and clustered into themes to examine how Black students describe and experience various dimensions of climate and examine relationships between climate and retention in academe.

Findings

Data presented in Table 5.1 suggest that while many participants started graduate school with some interest in pursuing a career at a research university, that interest declined over time, with few participants reporting increases in their interest in being professors. At the time of their interviews, eight participants had some level of interest in a faculty career, with three of those individuals already in faculty positions. Thirteen participants reported that their interest in becoming faculty at research universities declined from the beginning to the end of graduate school. One participant reported that their interest increased from "none" to "little," and two participants reported that they maintained little or no interest in a research faculty career over time.

Participants' narratives collected during Phase 2 of the study suggest that their career decision-making processes were complex, and they weighed multiple factors as they considered multiple career options. When asked about the core factors in their career decision making, some participants acknowledged the difficulty in finding a faculty position and low pay given the extent of their training. For example, Will called the low pay given the number of years in training "a huge turn off," and Harris shared that he did not think that there was an academic job that could pay him what he was worth. However, these factors were rarely the sole or main reason for a decline in interest in pursuing a faculty career. Instead, participants spoke more holistically about their experiences in the academy and the ways these experiences shaped their perceptions, their sense of membership in the academic community, and their confidence and efficacy. Specifically, the challenges they encountered while navigating academia as one of few Black scientists shaped their relationships and the ways they perceived science as a field, and appeared to influence their interest in pursuing faculty careers, particularly at research universities.

BEHAVIORAL AND PSYCHOLOGICAL CLIMATE: EXPERIENCES WITH SUBTLE AND OVERT RACISM IN THE LAB

Some participants described the behavioral climate in their laboratories as uncomfortable, focusing largely on how they were treated by their principal investigators (PIs) or the senior faculty who ran their research labs. Eleven trainees described occasions when they perceived differences between how they and their peers were treated, offering insights into how their race may have influenced their experiences. For example, when asked about the memorable (both positive and negative) aspects of graduate school, Sarai recalled the difficult interactions with her PI (who is White), whom she described as "verbally abusive." There was a moment when he "lashed out" and tried to kick her out of the lab, telling her "most PI's don't accept minorities like myself."

Often, the experiences participants had with stereotypes and marginalization were subtle. Racial slurs or stereotypical images were rarely openly invoked; instead, participants observed unexplained differences between the level of support, kindness, or latitude they and their peers received. For example, Denise explained that her PI chastised her and critiqued her work ethic. She had a White male colleague whom she felt did not work as much and sometimes made more significant mistakes, but was not treated harshly. She shared that she "could see the contrast, and I think that's what started to bother me after a while; that he [the PI] was treating us differently and I couldn't figure out why." Similarly, Luke believed his co-advisor had more of a mentoring and "buddy like" relationship with other students than he observed in their own. Harris noted a difference in how other students were treated in terms of support for their research. As he described his frustration at not being able to publish his thesis research, he said, "But you know what? The Taiwanese girl who was in the lab, oh, she got support. She got her paper published . . . she was the same year as me . . . she got her work published but I didn't get to publish mine. I don't know, you tell me what that is." While it was not explicit, Harris saw little difference between himself and his peer except for that she and his PI were both Asian and he was not. As a consequence, Harris attributed his PI's lack of support to his own racial identity.

Compositional Diversity Shapes Behavioral and Psychological Climate: Underrepresentation in Their Programs and the Field

Participants frequently spoke to a lack of compositional diversity in science and noted that there were few to no Black graduate students, faculty, and administrators in their graduate programs. Will recalled attending his first class, when he immediately recognized the lack of diversity in his program. "I remember looking around the room . . . I was the only black man in a room of two hundred people . . . [It] almost throws you off a bit." Similarly, Joan felt "awkward" when she first started graduate school because she was one of few people of color, and she believed her peers looked at her differently. Jayden's comments aptly capture the feelings many participants shared about their underrepresentation and visibility: "being an African American in science, I mean, that was definitely like a thing that influenced my science career . . . you can't help but feel like you're the only one in the room. I mean when there's just very few black people in sciences in general, and it's true with science. I mean that if I go to a conference with ten thousand people, there might be a handful of us around. I mean it's just, you feel that difference."

Noticing the lack of Black scientists in both their departments and their larger disciplines had multiple implications. First, not seeing or not being able to engage with Black students and faculty influenced how they experienced the psychological and behavioral dimensions of climate, leaving some participants feeling isolated and feeling as if they did not fully belong. While ultimately he was able to open up and develop relationships with his classmates, Will's immediate response to being the only Black students in his class was, "you're kind of like immediately an outsider in a way." Joan also noted that being one of few Black students made the early stages of relationship development with her peers more difficult. "[W]hen you're the only one, it's weird because a lot of students would come from places across the U.S. where they haven't been exposed to people of color, and so they would, you know, just kinds of size you up and look at you and not really speak to you. So it was very awkward in the very beginning." Joan perceived a distance between herself and her classmates based on their lack of exposure to and preconceived notions about Black people. These narratives suggest that low representation influenced the behavioral climate as well, making it more difficult for them to interact with their peers. While Joan and Will acknowledge that they became more integrated in their communities over time, they also were among the participants who noted that they were no longer interested in staying in the academy by the end of their graduate programs. Thus, the early isolation they felt as Black students may have contributed to their diminished interest in staying in the academy as faculty.

In addition to isolation and a lack of belonging, some participants described how being one of few or the only Black scientist in their areas influenced their self-confidence and efficacy. Jayden explained the challenges associated with being an African American in science and how always feeling highly underrepresented "can play on you psychologically after a while." Damien also shared that being a member of a population underrepresented in science could "lead to a lot of pressures that can get a person to question if they're up to standard or not." Thus, the lack of compositional diversity was palpable for some participants and also had a psychological impact on how they viewed themselves and their place at the institution, leading them to have doubts about their own abilities and wonder whether they were able to succeed where other Black students had not.

Luke's narrative demonstrated both how underrepresentation and isolation could undermine one's confidence, as well as how a critical mass and connections to community could affirm one's identity as a scientist. When speaking about his training experiences, he explained, "one of the things that was always tough for me was, again, that sense of isolation because sometimes I didn't have someone who looked like me that I could talk to." He went on to share that he felt he could not let his guard down or ask questions about his research because he was afraid of making a bad impression:

> I didn't feel like I could be ignorant in front of my advisor or in front of other students in my laboratory. Of course it's like one of those things, you make the situation what it is based on your own, inner perceptions of your own reality, but it was one of those things where I didn't have a cohort of individuals that I could completely identify with and that could identify with me.

Ultimately, he was able to connect with a faculty member who regularly hosted African American male scientists at his home, which created a unique space in which he found support. According to Luke,

> . . . these were all just other African American men in science, and some were in medicine, and you know, it was a relatively small group when it started. And we would meet once a month and sometimes we would meet individually as we saw fit to kind of talk to one another. But it was just kind of a social thing where we would meet at [the senior scientist's] house; he would barbeque to kick off the year every year, and we would talk about "What's going on in your lab? How are your classes going? Your research going?" And it was kind of different; it was like being at the barber shop, but we're talking about science and careers.

While the underrepresentation of Black scientists continued to be unsettling for Luke, exposure to a group of peers who shared his professional and personal identities created new opportunities for engagement and a sense of belonging, which translated into greater comfort and confidence.

ORGANIZATIONAL DIMENSION: ASSESSING COMMITMENT TO THE NORMS AND VALUES OF SCIENCE

We consider the norms, values, and reward structures in science and academic research as part of the campus climate, particularly reflecting the organizational dimension. While norms, values, policies, and procedures can be perceived as value neutral, they may have differential impacts on underrepresented and marginalized populations, negatively influencing perceptions of the campus climate and student outcomes (Milem et al., 2005).

Participants described the messages they received about what a scientist does, the values of science, and what is rewarded in academia, which shaped their perceptions of what meant to be successful. Several participants believed being an academic scientist required an almost all-consuming love and commitment to science and research. Ralph explained that his PI told new lab members, "expect to work . . . between fifty and sixty hours a week," and told them that publishing as much as possible was a high priority. Sarai similarly shared that in her lab, there was "such a heavy focus on, you know, get the work done, get the work done." Being a scientist was connected to hard work in the laboratory that would consume large amounts of time.

The pressures and expectations throughout their training led some to believe that academia may not be the right fit because they don't "love" science in the same ways their colleagues do. For example, Jayden does not consider himself a "true scientist" and expressed little interest in an academic career. He explained that while he likes science, he saw his professors and peers display a different level of commitment, noting they "live it, eat it, breathe it . . . I don't think I'm as consumed by my science as I probably should be to be successful in this game." Ryan was also discouraged by what he referred to as the "publish or perish paradigm," where assistant professors faced expectations that, in his mind, were unrealistic:

> The pressure on assistant professors to be super productive while still maintaining this whole thing about teaching and service to the department. It seems like they want you to apply 300% of your time when you only have 100% of it.

Helene similarly shared that she was not willing to devote her life to science in the ways necessary to be successful as a faculty member. She observed professors' lack of work/life balance and several Black women faculty getting what she perceived as stress-related illnesses and she noted how that factored into her own decision to leave academia. She shared, "I don't care about the number of publications and the number of grants . . . I wanted to have a life." Thus, in addition to requiring a significant time commitment, being a professor was also perceived as requiring a commitment to research that supersedes other responsibilities and interest in having a life outside one's work.

In addition to requiring passion and all-consuming commitment, participants often described academic research as narrow and as disconnected from addressing practical issues and solving problems. In several cases, participants saw the value placed on certain kinds of scientific discovery as divergent from their own commitments to making an impact. Ralph shared his opinion that "the emphasis [in academic science] is placed on doing research that has the highest novelty value because that's what's going to get you into journals and into conferences . . . But there's not enough emphasis on the practicality and the ability to implement that research." Similarly, Isaac was initially drawn to science by his desire to make an impact, but he realized that in academic research, "if there's an impact it's very tiny and it's incremental and it's just too slow." He described this as the most important part of his decision to pursue careers outside academia. Ryan also shared, "I feel like I just need to be doing something that helps more people. And you know, I love, like I said I love science for science but I don't necessarily love it as a career and especially in this environment." Thus, while Ryan loved science, he did not see it as a way to meet his core need to help people, making an academic career a less interesting option. In the process of completing her graduate training and dissertation, Helen realized, "I didn't want my energy to be focused on creating tools creating solutions for things that would never be translated to really improve biomedical research . . . it's more than just publications and grants for me . . . they're multiple careers outside of academia that will provide meaningful work." Academia was not perceived as a space from which they could have a significant impact or help people, and participants sought opportunities outside the academy where they felt they could contribute in more meaningful ways.

Part of participants' focus on practicality and solving problems appeared in their commitments to working closely with students. Wanda described her PI as a "good role model overall for someone who wanted to be tenure track faculty" but went on to say, "I think that my relationship with her kind of helped me see that I didn't want that anymore," based on Wanda's desire to mentor and work closely with students. For her, academic science was very "lab focused," with little time for the form of mentorship in which she wanted to engage. Joan also described her conflicted thoughts about whether she wanted to stay in the academy:

> I feel like that's why I'm like so torn about what I want to do because I really want to like mentor and work with students. I want to teach. I like teaching, I like being in front of a group of students and talking to them about research, but I don't love research. But I really like doing the research. I like thinking about questions, but I also like talking with students. I really enjoy talking with students. Not even a like, I really love it, you know, and just having an impact on people.

While there are certainly teaching expectations associated with faculty work, participants largely perceived teaching as less valued in the academy and as secondary to research. Thus, those whose love for teaching superseded their love of research did not necessarily perceive a faculty career, particularly at a research institution, as a good fit.

Finally, participants shared a commitment to increasing diversity in the sciences, although they varied in their perception of whether this could be best accomplished through an academic career. Jayden developed an interest in more practical applications of his work and science knowledge over time, explaining,

> My focus now is trying to take my understanding of science and use it for something that's more, I guess, immediately gratifying and immediately applicable. So instead of having some esoteric paper be cited by someone twenty years from now and maybe used for something that will lead to more science, I want to use it for things like you know science education or you know let's say an increase in the number of underrepresented students in the sciences.

Thus, for Jayden, faculty work was not well suited for making the most significant impact on increasing diversity in science. Damien wanted to stay in the academy, but wanted to reach out to underrepresented students, explaining, "I would have goals of increasing access because I think that a lot of times especially underrepresented students just don't know what their options are, and so they don't pursue things just because they don't know they can . . . That would be an important thing to me—that a program that I was part of would increase access." Luke also wanted to stay in the academy, and prioritized providing underrepresented minority students with access to science training, ensuring that they were exposed to rigorous coursework and research experiences that would instill the skills and confidence necessary to compete at the highest levels in graduate school.

Discussion

While much attention has been focused on increasing the number of Black scientists through increased access to and retention in doctoral programs, less attention has been focused on how these scholars' training experiences are shaped by their identities and how these experiences are linked to their interest in becoming faculty. Recent research suggests that underrepresented minority scientists report lower levels of interest in faculty careers than their more well-represented peers, even when accounting for scholarly productivity, training pedigree, advisor relationships, and research self-efficacy (Gibbs & Griffin, 2013; Gibbs et al., 2014). This work makes a unique contribution to understanding the whys behind these trends, providing insights into how the unique ways Black students experience graduate education and various dimensions of campus climate relate to interest in remaining in the academy, and how Black trainees think about their careers.

This study adds nuance to this conceptualization of career development, reminding faculty, institutional leaders, and policy makers about the importance of remembering the role that affirmed identity, sense of belonging and inclusion, socioemotional connections, and climate can play in the career development process. While participants described managing microaggressions and marginalizing experiences, particularly with their faculty members, they spoke perhaps more often about how lack of representation of people who shared their identities made them feel, and the challenges associated with being one of few African Americans in their respective fields. They often began their graduate training experiences feeling like they were isolated and were outside key social networks, wondered about their advisors' belief in and commitments to their success, and questioned whether they had what it took to be successful given that there were few other Black scientists in their fields.

Viewing our findings through the lens of a campus climate framework highlights the relationships between these experiences, offering an integrated way to understand how underrepresentation, marginalizing experiences, and climate can be related to interest in remaining in academia as a professor in complex, indirect ways. The connections between sense of belonging (psychological climate), underrepresentation (compositional diversity), and interactions with faculty and peers (behavioral climate) must be addressed directly as institutional leaders develop strategies to support Black scientists. It is easy, in some ways, to get into a circular argument: Students of color feel isolated because there are not any other students of color; there are not any students of color who want to be faculty because there are not any faculty of color. However, the findings of this study emphasize the importance of providing students with support and a sense of community membership, rather than focusing solely on efforts to bring in more students and faculty of color. Rather than leaving the development of relationships and close connections to chance, we recommend the implementation of intentional strategies designed to build community and encourage strong, supportive relationships between trainees and faculty within academic departments and programs. Intentional outreach and the development of structured study groups, mentoring programs, and social events that create opportunities for peers to connect and bond outside the laboratory can help foster these connections, creating a greater sense of fit and belonging.

Our findings also suggest that it is important to affirm trainees' identities by facilitating opportunities to meet and connect with other Black graduate students generally, and scientists specifically. Previous work suggests that campus-wide events that create opportunities for students of color to connect can mitigate isolation, reminding students that they are part of a larger community beyond their laboratories and academic programs (e.g., Griffin, Muniz, & Smith, 2016). Further, cross-institutional collaborations like the PROMISE AGEP program in the University of Maryland system (see Tull, Rutledge, Carter, & Warnick, 2012) can also create opportunities to generate a critical mass of Black scientists, allowing students to connect with others who share their identities.

This work also offers an integrated understanding of how structural issues may also be related to campus climate, sense of belonging, and interest in pursuing a career in academia. Participants perhaps made the most explicit connections between climate and career aspirations when speaking about the perceived misalignment between their values and what is rewarded in academic spaces. Similar to past research on doctoral career aspirations (Antony & Taylor, 2002; Austin, 2002; Mason, Goulden, & Frasch, 2009), participants described low-paying postdoc positions, a competitive job market, and an overemphasis on academic productivity as deterrents from pursuing a faculty career. However, participants spoke more directly to how endorsed values and the goals and outcomes rewarded in science may relate to trainees' identities and create a climate in which they do not feel they fit.

These findings are consistent with previous research, which suggests that trainees often receive messages that suggest that scientists devote their lives to the laboratory and do little else (Fuhrmann, et al., 2011; Griffin et al., 2015; Mason, Goulden, & Frasch, 2009). The value placed on productivity, total investment in science, and discoveries that privilege intellectual rather than practical significance were not always perceived as congruent with the values of participants who expressed less or decreasing levels of interest in faculty careers. These individuals emphasized their commitments to solving problems, teaching, meeting community needs, and increasing diversity in the STEM fields.

When commitments to practical problem solving, teaching, and increasing diversity in underrepresented communities are written off as being outside "real science," Black scientists may feel that faculty life and work may not be a good fit. In many ways, these goals are consistent with Sankofa's emphasis on contributing to the community and commitment to work that does not only serve the self (Tedla, 1995). Furthermore, it is important to note that the Black scientist, as opposed to the White scientist, may come to understand modern-day racism differently when considering the role of sociohistorical context and how individuals use the past to form their "sense of self" and their individual and collective identities (Jones & Leitner, 2015, p. 202). Institutional leaders must reconsider the role and importance of teaching and training the next generation of diverse scientists as they craft job descriptions and tenure and promotion criteria, demonstrating a genuine commitment to these critical components of faculty work. We also encourage institutional leaders to embrace a broader understanding of "scientific contribution," assessing the impact of a scholar's work not only by citation count or the quality of the journal in which it is published, but also whether it is being used to solve pressing problems or develop interventions that support underserved communities, which may create new opportunities for many Black scientists to contribute to the field in ways that align with their cultural commitments and identities.

Conclusion

Examining Black biomedical scientists' perceptions, training experiences, interactions with faculty, and outcomes through a climate framework responds to national conversations and commitments regarding faculty diversity. Funding agencies and campuses across the nation are grappling with the state of diversity in the professoriate, particularly as students protesting the hostility, marginalization, and underrepresentation they experience in their campus communities demand increased representation of faculty of color generally, and Black faculty in particular (Flaherty, 2015). *The Pathways Through Graduate School and Into Careers* report (CGS & ETS, 2012) proposes a model documenting the multiple factors and forces shaping students' career pathways. This model describes the process as multidimensional, and highlights the importance of access to information and opportunities, preparation, relationships with peers and faculty, and content knowledge.

As policy makers and institutional leaders aim to support the career development of Black scientists and potentially increase their representation in the academy, we recommend privileging two key ideas emerging from these data. First, career development initiatives must consider whether Black scientists feel a sense of belonging and inclusion in their specific programs, and science more generally. Participants' narratives suggest that, in addition to considering whether or not Black scientists are being intentionally excluded or marginalized, departments and programs must consider whether and how students are being included. Intentional rather than accidental community development and cultivation of Black graduate students' sense of belonging may translate to better relationships and greater perceived fit in science, and ultimately with an academic career. Second, it is important that faculty members, institutional leaders, and search committees continue to reconsider the messages they send about what it means to be a "good scientist," leaving (and in some cases creating) room for scholars who prioritize teaching, cultivating a diverse science workforce, and addressing community needs.

We urge institutional leaders, faculty, and policy makers to reflect on the Sankofa principles of identity and community, develop inclusion-based interventions that validate students' experiences, and actively promote Black trainees' sense of belonging in science. These efforts must move beyond traditional strategies focused on increasing the number of Black scholars completing PhDs. While addressing issues related to access to graduate education are important, focusing on entry alone misses the importance of encouraging talent to consider how they can contribute to the field by becoming faculty.

Acknowledgments

The authors thank the Burroughs Wellcome Fund (Carr Thompson; Grant Number 1011798) for resource support of this work. The research that is the basis of this manuscript was conducted prior to Kenneth D. Gibbs starting at the National Institute of General Medical Sciences. Thank you to Domonic Rollins, Maya Graham, and Jessica Bennett for your contributions to this research. All questions can be directed to the lead author at kgriff29@umd.edu, University of Maryland, Counseling, Higher Education, Special Education Department, 3214 Benjamin Building, College Park, Maryland, 20742. The ideas expressed in this manuscript are the opinions of the authors and do not represent the organizations with which they are affiliated.

References

Antony, J. S., & Taylor, E. (2004). Theories and strategies of academic career socialization: Improving paths to the professoriate for Black graduate students. In D. H. Wulff and A. E. Austin (Eds.), *Paths to the professoriate: Strategies for enriching the preparation of future faculty* (pp. 92–114). San Francisco, CA: Jossey-Bass.

Association of American Medical Colleges. *Reports: U.S. Medical School Faculty 2015.* Retrieved from https://www.aamc.org/data/facultyroster/reports/453490/usmsf15.html

Austin, A. E. (2002). Preparing the next generation of faculty: Graduate school as socialization to the academic career. *The Journal of Higher Education, 73*(1), 94–122.

Bogdan, R. C., & Biklen, S. K. (1998). *Qualitative research in education: An introduction to theory and methods* (3rd ed.). Boston, MA: Allyn & Bacon.

Cabrera, A. F., Nora, A., Terenzini, P. T., Pascarella, E., & Hagedorn, L. S. (1999). Campus racial climate and the adjustment of students to college: A comparison between White students and African-American students. *Journal of Higher Education, 70*(2), 134–160.

Carlone, H. B., & Johnson, A. (2007). Understanding the science experiences of successful women of color: Science identity as an analytic lens. *Journal of Research in Science Teaching, 44*, 1187–1218.

Clark, C. R., Mercer, S. H., Zeigler-Hill, V., & Dufrene, B. A. (2012). Barriers to the success of ethnic minority students in school psychology graduate programs. *School Psychology Review, 41*(2), 176.

Council of Graduate Schools and Educational Testing Service. (2010). *The path forward: The future of graduate education in the United States.* Report from the Commission on the Future of Graduate Education in the United States. Princeton, NJ: Educational Testing Service.

Council of Graduate Schools and Educational Testing Service. (2012). *Pathways through graduate school and into careers. Report from the Commission on Pathways through Graduate School and Into Careers.* Princeton, NJ: Educational Testing Service.

Creswell, J. W., & Clark, V. L. P. (2007). *Designing and conducting mixed methods research.* Thousand Oaks, CA: Sage Publications.

Felder, P. P. (2015). Edward A. Bouchet: A model for understanding African Americans and their doctoral experience. *Journal of African American Studies, 19*(1), 3–17.

Felder, P. P., & Barker, M. J. (2013). Extending Bell's concept of interest convergence: A framework for understanding the African American doctoral student experience. *International Journal of Doctoral Studies, 8*, 1–20.

Flaherty, C. (2015, November 30). Demanding 10 percent. *Inside Higher Ed.* Retrieved from https://www.insidehighered.com/news/2015/11/30/student-activists-want-more-black-faculty-members-how-realistic-are-some-their-goals

Fox, M. F., & Stephan, P. E. (2001). Careers of young scientists: Preferences, prospects and realities by gender and field. *Social Studies of Science, 31*(1), 109–122.

Fries-Britt, S. L., Younger, T. K., & Hall, W. D. (2010). Lessons from high-achieving students of color in physics. *New Directions for Institutional Research*, 75–83.

Fuhrmann, C. N., Halme, D. G., O'Sullivan, P. S., & Lindstaedt, B. (2011). Improving graduate education to support a branching career pipeline: Recommendations based on a survey of doctoral students in the basic biomedical sciences. *CBE Life Sciences Education, 10*(3), 239–249.

Gasman, M. B., Hirschfeld, A., & Vultaggio, J. (2008). Difficult yet rewarding: The experiences of African American graduate students in education at an Ivy League institution. *Journal of Diversity in Higher Education, 1*(2), 126–138.

Gibbs, K. D., Basson, J., Xierali, I. M., & Broniatowski, D. A. (2016). Decoupling of the minority PhD talent pool and assistant professor hiring in medical school basic science departments in the US. *eLife, 5*, e21393. http://doi.org/10.7554/eLife.21393

Gibbs, K. D., Jr., & Griffin, K. A. (2013). What do I want to be with my Ph.D.? The roles of personal values and structural dynamics in shaping the career interests of recent biomedical science Ph.D. graduates. *CBE Life Sciences Education, 12*(4), 711–723.

Gibbs, K. D., Jr., McGready, J., Bennett, J. C., & Griffin, K. A. (2014). Biomedical science Ph.D. career interest patterns by race/ethnicity and gender. *PLOS One, 9*(12), 1–18.

Gibbs, K. D., Jr., McGready, J., & Griffin, K. A. (2015). Career development among American biomedical postdocs. *CBE Life Sciences Education, 14*(4), 1–12.

Gildersleeve, R. E., Croom, N. N., & Vasquez, P. L. (2011). "Am I going crazy?!": A critical race analysis of doctoral education. *Equity & Excellence in Education, 44*(1), 93–114.

Golde C. M., & Dore, T. M. (2001). *At cross purposes: What the experiences of today's doctoral students reveal about doctoral education.* Philadelphia, PA: Pew Charitable Trusts.

Griffin, K. A., Gibbs, K. D., Jr., Bennett, J. C., Staples, C., & Robinson, T. (2015). "Respect me for my science": A Bourdieuan analysis of women scientists' interactions with faculty and socialization into science. *Journal of Women and Minorities in Science and Engineering, 21*(2), 159–179.

Griffin, K. A., Muniz, M., & Smith, E. J. (2016). Graduate diversity officers and efforts to retain students of color. *Journal of Student Affairs Research and Practice, 53*(1), 26–38.

Hunn, L. R. (2008). Proof in the pudding: Does Guiffrida's cultural advancement of Tinto's theory apply to African American graduate students? *Journal of Ethnographic and Qualitative Research, 2*(4), 255–263.

Hurtado, S., Alvarez, C. L., Guillermo-Wann, C., Cuellar, M., & Arellano, L. (2012). A model for diverse learning environments. In J. C. Smart & M. B. Paulsen (Eds.), *Higher education: Handbook of theory and research* (pp. 41–122). New York, NY: Springer.

Hurtado, S., Milem, J. F., Clayton-Pederson, A. R., & Allen, W. R. (1999). Enacting diverse learning environments: Improving the campus climate for racial/ethnic diversity in higher education. *ASHE-ERIC Higher Education Reports Series, 26*(8). San Francisco, CA: Jossey Bass Publishers.

Jaeger, A. J., Haley, K. J., Ampaw, F., & Levin, J. S. (2013). Understanding the career choice for underrepresented minority doctoral students in science and engineering. *Journal of Women and Minorities in Science and Engineering, 19*(1), 1–16.

Johnson-Bailey, J., Valentine, T., Cervero, R. M., & Bowles, T. A. (2009). Rooted in the soil: The social experiences of Black graduate students at a southern research university. *The Journal of Higher Education, 80*(2), 178–203.

Jones, J. M., & Leitner, J. B. (2015). The Sankofa effect: Divergent effects of thinking about the past for Blacks and Whites. In M. Stolarski, N. Fieulaine, & W. van Beek (Eds.), *Time perspective theory; review, research, and application: Essays in honor of Philip G. Zimbardo* (pp. 197–211). New York: Springer Publishing.

Kulis, S., Chong, Y., & Shaw, H. (1999). Discriminatory organizational contexts and Black scientists on postsecondary faculties. *Research in Higher Education, 40*(2), 115–148.

Lindholm, J. A. (2004). Pathways to the professoriate: The role of self, others, and environment in shaping academic career aspirations. *The Journal of Higher Education, 75*(6), 603–635.

MacLachlan, A. J. (2006). Developing graduate students of color for the professoriate in science, technology, engineering, and mathematics (STEM). *Center for Studies in Higher Education.* UC Berkeley: Center for Studies in Higher Education. Retrieved from http://escholarship.org/uc/item/3892k4rm

MacQueen, K. M., McLellan, E., Kay, K., & Milstein, B. (1998). Codebook development for team based qualitative analysis. *Cultural Anthropology Methods, 10*(2), 31–36.

Mason, M. A., Goulden, M., & Frasch, K. (2009). Why graduate students reject the fast track. *Academe, 95*(1), 1–8.

McGee, E. O., & Martin, D. B. (2011). "You would not believe what I have to go through to prove my intellectual value!" Stereotype management among academically successful Black mathematics and engineering students. *American Educational Research Journal, 48*(6), 1347–1389.

Merriam, S. B. (1998). *Qualitative research and case study applications in education.* San Francisco, CA: Jossey-Bass.

Milem, J. F., Chang, M. J., & antonio, a.l. (2005). *Making diversity work on campus: A research-based perspective.* Washington, DC: Association of American Colleges & Universities.

Museus, S. D., Nichols, A. H., & Lambert, A. D. (2008). Racial differences in the effects of campus racial climate on degree completion: A structural equation model. *The Review of Higher Education, 32*(1), 107–134.

National Academy of Sciences. (2011). *Expanding underrepresented minority participation.* Washington, DC: National Academies Press.

National Science Foundation. (2012). Science and engineering indicators. Retrieved from http://www.nsf.gov/statistics/seind12/append/c5/at05-10.pdf

National Science Foundation/National Center for Science and Engineering Statistics. (2013). Science, engineering, and health doctorate holders employed in universities and 4-year colleges, by type of academic position, sex, race, ethnicity, and disability status: 2013. Retrieved from https://www.nsf.gov/statistics/2015/nsf15311/tables/pdf/tab9-22.pdf

National Science Foundation/National Center for Science and Engineering Statistics. (2011). Survey of Doctorate Recipients. Retrieved from http://www.nsf.gov/statistics/infbrief/nsf11320/

National Science Foundation. (2015). U.S. citizen and permanent resident doctorate recipients, by ethnicity, race, and broad field of study: Selected years, 1994–2014. Retrieved from http://www.nsf.gov/statistics/2016/nsf16300/data/tab23.pdf

Patel, V. (2015, December 4). Dearth of Black Ph.D. recipients will complicate efforts to diversify faculty. *The Chronicle of Higher Education*. Retrieved from http://chronicle.com/article/Dearth-of-Black-PhD/234469

Perna, L. W., Gerald, D., Baum, E., & Milem, J. (2007). The status of equity for black faculty and administrators in public higher education in the South. *Research in Higher Education, 48*(2), 193–228.

Peterson, M. W., & Spencer, M. G. (1990). Understanding academic culture and climate. In W. Tierney (Ed.), *New Directions for Institutional Research* (pp. 3–18), Hoboken, NJ: Wiley.

Rankin, S. R., & Reason, R. D. (2005). Differing perceptions: How students of color and White students perceive campus climate for underrepresented groups. *Journal of College Student Development, 46*(1), 43–61.

Robinson, W. H., McGee, E. O., Bentley, L. C., Houston, S. L., & Botchway, P. K. (2016). Addressing negative racial and gendered experiences that discourage academic careers in engineering. *Computing in Science & Engineering, 18*(2), 29–39.

Sánchez, F. J., Liu, W. M., Leathers, L., Goins, J., & Vilain, E. (2011). The subjective experience of social class and upward mobility among African American men in graduate school. *Psychology of Men & Masculinity, 12*(4), 368.

Sauermann, H., & Roach, M. (2012). Science PhD career preferences: levels, changes, and advisor encouragement. *PLoS One, 7*(5), e36307.

Schenkein, H. A., & Best, A. M. (2001). Factors considered by new faculty in their decision to choose careers in academic dentistry. *Journal of Dental Education, 65*(9), 832–840.

Stephan, P. E. (2012). *How economics shapes science* (Vol. 1). Cambridge, MA: Harvard University Press.

Stephen, C., Barber, E. G., & Cole, S. (2009). *Increasing faculty diversity: The occupational choices of high-achieving minority students*. Cambridge, MA: Harvard University Press.

Sue, D. W. (2010). *Microaggressions in everyday life: Race, gender, and sexual orientation*. Hoboken, NJ: John Wiley & Sons.

Tedla, E. (1995). *Sankofa: African thought and education.* New York: Lang Publishing.

Tull, R. G., Rutledge, J. C., Carter, F. D., & Warnick, J. E. (2012). PROMISE: Maryland's Alliance for Graduate Education and the Professoriate enhances recruitment and retention of underrepresented minority graduate students. *Academic Medicine, 87*(11), 1562–1569.

Williams, S. N., Thakore, B. K., & McGee, R. (2016). Career coaches as a source of vicarious learning for racial and ethnic minority PhD students in the biomedical sciences: A qualitative study. *PloS One, 11*(7), e0160038.

Zeligman, M. R., Prescod, D. J., & Greene, J. H. (2015). Journey toward becoming a counselor education doctoral student: Perspectives of women of color. *Journal of Negro Education, 84*(1), 66–79.

Chapter 6

From Firm Foundations to Where?

Understanding the Role of HBCUs in African American PhD Student Commitment

PAMELA FELDER SMALL AND CARMEN M. MCCALLUM

Historically Black colleges and universities (HBCUs) have made significant contributions to the nation's educated citizenry (Allen, Jewel,
Griffin, & Wolf, 2007; Brown & Davis, 2001; Gasman, 2013; Gasman,
Wagner-Lundy, Ransom, & Bowman, 2010; Palmer & Gasman, 2008; Palmer
& Wood, 2012). In response to a historical legacy of exclusion of African
Americans, HBCUs were created to facilitate pathways to educational
attainment and success amid strained resources and challenges associated
with ingrained systemic institutionalized racism and discrimination. Their
institutional mission was, and still is, to provide educational opportunities
that would lead to equality, dignity, and racial uplift of the Black community.
Similar in the African Akan culture, from which Sankofa derives, HBCU
culture might be linked to ofie or house (Tedla, 1995). The notion of an
ofie (house) in Akan is rooted to the feeling of togetherness, which is
linked to one's identity (Van der Geest, 1998). In other words, there exists
a relationship between identity, context, and community that is exhibited at
HBCUs. Thus, HBCUs were purposefully designed to empower individuals
to change lives and their community and to evoke societal justice.

HBCUs strive to (1) maintain Black historical and cultural traditions;
(2) cultivate leadership in the Black community, especially among college
administrators, scholars, and students involved in community affairs; (3)
contribute to the economic growth of the Black community; (4) create

role models to demonstrate how one should interact with social, political, and economic dynamics that impact Black people; (5) produce college graduates with the knowledge needed to address issues between minority and majority populations; and (6) develop Black leaders proficient in specialized research, institutional training, and information dissemination pertinent to Black and other minority communities (Allen, 1992; Brown & Davis, 2001). These educational tenets provide the foundation for the mission and vision of HBCUs (Abelman & Dalessandro, 2009), allowing them to create pathways to success for African Americans during and after their undergraduate and graduate degree programs.

The role of these pathways in facilitating academic success and doctoral degree completion for African Americans is notable (Palmer, Hilton, & Fountaine, 2012). Though knowledge about the role of HBCUs is emerging, more research is needed to understand the ways these pathways impact students' commitment to pursue the doctorate. We know the majority of African Americans who earn their PhD complete their undergraduate degree at an HBCU and that HBCUs are the largest producer of African American PhDs (Sibulkin & Butler, 2011), but the impact these institutions have on students' commitment to pursue their degrees is underdeveloped. To understand the impact HBCUs have on African American students' commitment to pursue the doctorate, we must explore the role of HBCUs' institutional mission in the decision-making process. We must also examine students' interactions with HBCUs' environments. Both can provide valuable insights about students' doctoral degree commitment.

Understanding how HBCUs contribute to PhD student commitment is important for several reasons. First, U.S. graduate education is considered a strategic national asset (Wendler et al., 2010; Commission for the Future of Graduate Education, 2012). Therefore, it is important that we continue to develop a robust pool of qualified applicants. One way of achieving this goal is to put effort into diversifying the pool of qualified applicants. Thus, identifying efforts that single out and attract diverse talented students can be useful. These efforts may also reveal ways to improve completion rates and prepare future faculty invested in strengthening the role of U.S. higher education in a global competitive market (Wendler et al., 2010). Second, identifying strategies that facilitate students' interest in graduate school prior to matriculation into doctoral programs can inform programs and policies geared toward minimizing student isolation and attrition while in graduate school (Ali, 2007), increasing the number of diverse students who complete their degree programs.

Third, there continues to be a grave underrepresentation of African American doctoral degree attainment compared with their White counterparts. While there has been an 87% increase in doctoral degrees between 1992 and 2012, African Americans represent approximately 7% of all doctorates attained in 2015 (National Science Foundation, 2016). Fourth, an underrepresentation of African Americans with doctoral degrees limits the production of scholars prepared to move into faculty ranks, contributing to a systemic imbalance in creating future diverse leaders in the academy and along the educational pipeline. The number of African Americans in the professoriate remains stagnant and is historically marginalized compared to White faculty (National Center of Education Statistics, 2016).

Fifth, there has been a significant amount of research examining the statistical trends of doctoral degree attainment (Bowen & Rudenstine, 1992; Nettles & Millett, 2006), but emerging literature about students' commitment to pursue doctoral study is limited. Often this commitment involves an aspiration to uplift and/or give back to the Black community—an African American cultural phenomenon that has not been thoroughly explored within the context of graduate education (Hinton, Grim, & Howard-Hamilton, 2009; McCallum, 2017; Williams, Brewley, Reed, White, & Davis-Haley, 2005). Perhaps this is indicated by the large number of African Americans attaining doctoral degrees in the field of education, representing approximately 10% of about 5,100 education doctorates earned in 2015 and the largest percentage of earned doctorates by field of study for African Americans (National Science Foundation, 2016).

Finally, understanding the role of HBCUs in supporting the commitment of African Americans who choose to pursue their doctorate can increase awareness about students' PhD decision-making process and the ways their HBCU academic environment influenced that process. Thus, this study aims to increase the understanding of HBCUs' impact on the ways African Americans reach a commitment to pursue doctoral study and how that commitment is connected to social justice and uplift of their community.

Literature Review

HBCUs and Student Transition toward the Doctoral Process

HBCUs play in important role in the preparation of Black graduate students. Black students who attend HBCUs are more likely to pursue the doctorate than Black students who attend predominantly White selective institutions (Allen & Jewell, 1991; Brazziel, 1983, Brown & Davis, 2001; Pascerella et al., 2004, Perna, 2001; Solorzano, 1995; Wenglinsky, 1996). In fact, between 1980 and 1990, 76% of Black females and 57% of Black males who earned the doctorate received their bachelor's degrees from an HBCU (Solorzano, 1995). This is quite significant given that HBCUs represent only 3% of the nation's colleges and universities (Allen & Jewell, 2002).

The majority of previous research that has explored the connection between HBCUs and pursuit of doctoral study has been quantitative in nature, contributing to a greater awareness of large-scale trends associated with African Americans and the doctoral experience. This previous work provides important guidance for understanding the large contextual factors shaping the development and progress of African Americans pursuing and attaining doctoral degrees. For example, in his work "Baccalaureate College of Origin of Black Doctorate Recipients," Brazziel (1983) found that HBCUs have had notable success in preparing their graduates for doctoral study. This study was largely a statistical portrait of HBCUs and their productivity of doctoral degree holders.

Similarly, in a study on support for Black doctorate recipients, Brazziel and Brazziel (1987) found that out of their subsample of 52 recipients, 20% reported that they had attained their baccalaureate degree from a Black college. Both of these studies, although relevant, are inconclusive with regard to the experiential characteristics of individuals who attend these institutions. They attribute the desire to attend graduate school and the successful completion of the degree to the history and tradition of HBCUs encouraging students to pursue graduate education, but the specific mechanism utilized remains unknown. The authors assert that with many Ivy League colleges and universities, familial legacy seems to be a tie that binds success within the culture of many HBCUs.

Likewise, Wolf-Wendel's (1998) analysis of the baccalaureate origins of successful women (1998) emphasized that historically Black women's colleges produced the largest proportion of successful African American women. This study continues to affirm the existence of HBCUs, as the productivity ratios for these institutions showed that HBCU graduates were 47 times more likely than were PWI graduates to receive their undergraduate degrees from these institutions. Comparatively, the ratios were 6 times greater for Black women's colleges than for historically Black coeducational institutions. Wolf-Wendel (1998) further explained that the baccalaureate origin studies are powerful, especially when considering ethnicity.

There are several institutional factors that contribute to students' decisions to pursue and enroll in doctoral degree programs. Smaller class sizes, accessibility to faculty, and pathways into enriched social networks have all been found to influence students' enrollment decisions (e.g., Palmer, Hilton, & Fountaine, 2012). These institutional characteristics are embedded in the culture of HBCUs. For example, Black women who were successful at pursuing science, technology, engineering, and mathematics (STEM) careers at Spelman College attributed their success, which included developing graduate school aspirations, to faculty and peer support they received during their undergraduate years (Perna et al., 2009); they believed this support was only provided to them because they attended an HBCU. Likewise, Palmer and Gasman (2008) posit that HBCUs uniquely function as a purveyor of social capital for Black students, providing opportunities and networks that would otherwise be unavailable. In general, HBCUs are committed to students' success in ways that (research has proven) positively influences students to pursue the doctorate (Anchor & Morales, 1990; Brown & Davis, 2001; King & Chepyator-Thomson, 1996; Perna, 2001).

MOTIVATING FACTORS TO ENROLL IN DOCTORAL STUDY FOR AFRICAN AMERICAN STUDENTS

There are several factors that motivate students to pursue and enroll in doctoral degree programs. For example, faculty support, parental educational background, and student academic achievement have all been found to be influential on the doctoral decision (McCallum, 2014). However, research suggests that there are two factors that are culturally specific that influence Black students: (1) a desire to give back to the community and (2) racial uplift (McCallum, 2017). This is not surprising, considering that the majority of Black students who pursue the doctorate have attended an HBCU (Solorzano, 1995). By educating oneself, Black students believe they will gain the knowledge and the abilities to help other African Americans in the educational pipeline—a guiding principle of HBCUs (Louque, 1999; Schwartz et al., 2003; Williams, et al., 2005). What is less known is the process through which students embrace HBCUs' institutional values and how those values promote advanced degree attainment.

Conceptual Framework

The Diverse Learning Environment (DLE) multicontextual model provides conceptual guidance for exploring how HBCUs contribute to African American PhD student commitment (Hurtado, Alvarez, Guillermo-Wann, Cuellar, & Areallano, 2012). The Hurtado et al. (2012) perspective builds on the work focused on the racial and cultural experiences of students in relation to understanding key elements of campus climate in an effort to increase awareness about the role of diversity on college campuses (Hurtado, Clayton-Pedersen, Allen, & Milem (1999). Drawing on social identity theory, the DLE model considers student, instructor, and staff identity at the center of diverse student learning experiences and as key processes of campus climate, emphasizing interaction among these experiences. A centralized perspective of interactions among African American students and their HBCU environments lends insightful meaning to how these interactions influence African Americans to engage in decision making relevant to developing a commitment to pursue the doctorate.

The DLE model also considers the historical context as a race-sensitive aspect of campus climate, and the model is flexible in regard to addressing the broad nature of diversity and what diversity means within specific institutional contexts. This race-sensitive focus aligns with the Sankofa principle by honoring the role and value of race regarding institutional legacy. Because of the racial homogeneity often associated with HBCUs, the role of diversity may be overlooked within HBCU environments and, when discussed, may emphasize the international student experience. Yet, with the growing nature of globalization, the broad nature of the DLE model allows for understanding how non-racial/ethnic diversity may influence student commitments.

The non-racial/-ethnic aspect of this model lends unique implications to the role of African American PhD students as a national investment. Moreover, the DLE model embraces institutional structure, the role of mission, and pedagogy in considering the student learning experience—features that create the unique character of the HBCU campus culture. Overall, the primary function of the DLE model is to assist educational leaders with assessing educational outcomes. This model's emphasis on the role of interactions within the campus environment to increase an awareness of how institutional characteristics influence student experience makes it a natural guide for exploring HBCUs' mission and African American PhD student commitment. In applying this framework, we ask: How do student, faculty, and staff interactions shape commitment toward pursuit of the doctoral degree? How do these interactions provide a foundation for students as they transition toward doctoral study?

Data Sources or Evidence

The data for this study come from a larger investigation of relationships and experiences that contribute to African Americans enrolling in graduate study. From within the larger sample of 40 currently enrolled doctoral students, we withdrew all students who attended an HBCU for undergraduate study. All 12 self-identified as "African American" or "Black." Individuals with multiple racial identities claimed "African American" or "Black" as their primary racial classification, with White, Asian, and Native American as secondary affiliations. All but two participants were female. Half were first-generation college students. The majority majored in psychology and self-identified as middle-class. Students pursuing professional degrees (e.g., law, social work, business) were excluded from the study, as research suggests their experiences may be different from those enrolling in PhD programs (Mullen et al., 2003).

All students were U.S. citizens and attended one of two research-intensive institutions for graduate study—one public, one private (Carnegie Foundation, n.d.). One institution is located in a large city on the East Coast. The other resides in a large city in the Midwest. The Carnegie Foundation classifies both as comprehensive doctoral institutions that are highly residential. Both were among the top institutions in the United States to award the doctorate to African Americans (Borden, 2009). Additional information about participants can be found in Table 6.1 on page 146.

Methods

We use phenomenology and the concept of Sankofa to guide and shape our approach in this study. Phenomenology embraces the philosophy that realities are rooted in day-to-day lived experiences (Creswell, 1998). In this study, we focused on the lived experiences of African American students within the context of HBCUs. The concept allowed us to explore students' PhD aspirations and the meaning they ascribe to the role of HBCUs in

Table 6.1. African American PhD Student Data

Pseudonym	Gender	First-generation	Graduate Institution	SES	Field of Study
Alexa	F	N	HBCU	Upper Middle	Psychology
Ava	F	N	HBCU	Middle	Sociology
Carl	M	Y	HBCU	Middle	Psychology
Dawn	F	Y	HBCU	Middle	Psychology
Donna	F	N	HBCU	Middle	Psychology
Elva	F	Y	HBCU	Middle	Psychology
Fawn	F	N	PWI	Middle	Biopsychology
Joann	F	Y	HBCU	Working	Mathematics
Krissy	F	N	HBCU	Middle	Sociology
Makayla	F	Y	HBCU	Middle	Psychology
Michael	M	Y	HBCU	Poor	Economics
Stacey	F	N	HBCU	Poor	Communications

developing and supporting their interest in enrolling in doctoral study. Sankofa is a word found in the Twi language of Ghana. In translation, it means "go back and fetch it," "return to your past," and "it is not taboo to go back and retrieve what you have forgotten or lost" (Temple, 2010, p. 27). According to Quarcoo (1971), it is a constant reminder that the past for African Americans is not all shameful, and the future for oneself and others should be built on aspects of the past. Thus, it is important that all African Americans learn from the past and use that knowledge to solidify their future. This concept provided us a culturally grounded way to understand students' lived experiences within the context of HBCUs.

Using criterion and network sampling, participants were solicited to participate in a semistructured interview via email or through referral. Interviews lasted between 45 and 90 minutes and were audio recorded. Questions elicited information about participants' relationships and experiences that led to their decision to enroll in doctoral study. Experiences with family members, peers, community, and their undergraduate institution were discussed. Attempts to ask clarifying questions were made only after participants finished their narrative, synchronizing their voice with the research process (Corbin & Strauss, 2008). After each interview, notes were recorded in a journal to document thoughts and observations of the participants. Journal notes were incorporated into the analysis of the data. All interviews were conducted by one of the authors; audiotapes were transcribed verbatim by one of the authors (25%) or a professional transcriptionist. To ensure accuracy, each transcribed file was compared with its audiotape, and any discrepancies were noted.

The data were analyzed using a multistep process (Creswell, 2003). First, all transcripts were read line by line to identify statements that revealed how students perceived their undergraduate experience influenced their doctoral enrollment decision. Next, those statements were analyzed and clustered into discrete categories using matrices and schematic displays (Miles & Huberman, 1994). Taken-for-granted assumptions were then explored while paying special attention to student statements as well as how they experienced the phenomena they discussed (Sparks & Trinidad, 2007). Statements were then categorized into codes. All transcripts were reread and coded with the newly created codes. Codes were reexamined, and similar codes were collapsed. Finally, the transcripts were reread using the newly formed codes that determined our presented findings.

Findings

The findings provide insight into the ways participants perceived attending an HBCU influenced their commitment to earn a PhD. All embraced the institutions' educational values and strived to operationalize those values in their everyday lives. Commitment to academic excellence, giving back to the community, engagement in professional networks, and appreciation for African American history were all discussed as key values they learned from their HBCU, and that value fueled their commitment to earn an advanced degree. This commitment represents the significant potential of Sankofa as a tool for operationalizing togetherness related to building networks of students committed to HBCU institutions. In fact, all but one participant chose to attend an HBCU for graduate study in the hope of replicating the camaraderie and support they found during their undergraduate years.

COMMITMENT TO EXCELLENCE

Several participants indicated that faculty and other members of the college community held them to very high standards. There was an expectation of excellence, meaning students were expected to always present their best work and their best selves all the time. Fawn recalled how a particular instructor demanded excellence and would not accept any work that she envisioned to be below her standards:

> . . . when she wants something, she wants it then. If you don't deliver it properly she will tell you, and if you do it wrong, she will tell you it's wrong and to redo it. If it looks like you did it really quickly, or if it looks like she knows that it is wrong and you brought it to her knowing that it was wrong . . . she would say, "*why would you bring me something like this*." . . . She is probably one of those teachers that you wanted to come to correct. You wanted to make sure that whatever you are bringing to her, it was done correctly and [to] your utmost ability.

Witnessing occurrences like this inspired Fawn to hold herself to high standards. She wanted to be the best, and being the best meant earning her PhD.

> I kind of feel like a PhD is a terminal degree—so if that is as high as I can go, then why not? The sky is the limit, so why not try to touch it? That's the reason I wanted to try and pursue the Doctoral degree. In the event I don't finish (god forbid), at least I tried.

Joann had a similar experience. She had always been good at math until she reached calculus. For the first time in her life, she didn't know how to solve a math problem, so she considered giving up her dream of being a math teacher to pursue an alternative career. Her math professor would not allow her to quit. She encouraged her to strive for excellence and eventually introduced her to more complex mathematics. Joann stated that these experiences, though challenging, taught her to never give up, and that concept of excellence influenced her commitment to pursue her PhD. Joann explained,

> . . . [my professor] introduced me to a new world of math. I'd seen different ways [to solve a problem], but I had never proved [a math problem] in my life . . . It actually pushed me

more to go to graduate school. I want to go to school and tell her all about and say thank you for taking care of me . . .

Joann hopes to be a professor one day and give back by helping other students who, like her, struggle but have great potential. In addition to supporting academic excellence, faculty and staff pushed students to strive for excellence in their daily lives. Fawn said,

> I feel like they expected a lot from us, we weren't allowed to just wear pajamas at school; no we can't do that. You can't even walk into the cafeteria with a scarf on your head; I feel like they expected us to act in a certain way too. I feel like that was also part of self-esteem building.

Academic excellence and pride in oneself and one's community are institutional values ingrained in the fabric of HBCUs. These values promoted self-esteem and provided participants with the confidence needed to take a leap of faith and apply to PhD programs.

Commitment to Better Oneself and One's Community

Participants also discussed how they were motivated to pursue a graduate degree as a means to better themselves and the African American community. Individually, they envisioned that the PhD would provide them the means to earn a large salary, acquire prestige, and gain specialized knowledge and job security within their given field. For example, Elva said, "I wanted to make a lot of money, I wanted to have letters behind my name, I wanted someone to call me Dr. so and so—so, that is what I wanted." Alexa agreed, but her commitment to pursuing the degree was directly tied to her career goals. As a psychology major, she recognized that the only way to reach her goals and better herself was to pursue the PhD. Alexa explained,

> . . . psychology is one of those degrees that you can't use a bachelors [degree], so to be honest, unless you are Clinical, a Master's degree doesn't do you much good either. So when I decided, "psychology is what I need to do," I knew that I

needed a PhD and I did want to teach and do research; I love doing research, so that is really what drove me to a doctoral degree.

Elva's and Alexa's commitment to pursue their PhD were tied to their commitment to do better for themselves, as well as a desire to do better than their family members had done before them so that they could have an opportunity to give back. They also wanted an opportunity to reach back and better the African American community. Tedla (1995) emphasizes that community in Sankofa-centered education was key to individuals understanding themselves. Giving back to the community was a foundational value espoused at their HBCU as well as a deciding factor in their decision to pursue their doctorate. Participants stated that faculty, administrators, and staff frequently informed them that they were part of the "talented tenth," and as such it was their obligation to succeed and give back. Participants embodied this ideology and stated they would give back by increasing the number of PhD recipients, financially contributing to HBCUs and the African American community, and making those who came before them and behind them proud to be African American. When reflecting on the notion of giving back, Makayla said,

> . . . when I leave [HBCU] I am going to be working in my community and hopefully I will be making some very serious and real changes and hopefully my [grandparents] live to see those changes come to fruition and they [will] know that their granddaughter heard about their struggle and was able to make it better for those who came after her.

Dawn concurred:

> I know the state of my community, not only here but com- munities across the country and the world, [for people] who look like me, people of color, and I know it's not a good look overall . . . as opposed to getting discouraged by watching the news about someone else got shot, someone else got murdered, this person was bullied and committed suicide, all these things and being like, "What do I do, woe is me in my community," I am like, ok, given this, this motivates me to move forward and do research that gets at the root of these issues to prevent

stuff like this from happening more and more. I feel like my story [of successfully enrolling in a PhD program] has been a testimony to all of the people in my community, that I am beneficial. . . . That's something that keeps me going [toward earning the degree].

COMMITMENT TO PROFESSIONAL NETWORKS

Participants repeatedly discussed the importance of developing professional networks with African Americans who have similar interests, especially those interested in pursuing their PhD. The importance of making such connections was frequently discussed in formal and informal settings at their undergraduate institutions. Observing faculty engage in such networks, especially on their behalf, motivated participants to commit to pursue their doctorates. For example, Elva stated that she was discouraged from pursuing the degree when her research advisor told her she would never be accepted into any PhD programs because of her writing skills. She was devastated and considered an alternative career path. Her commitment to pursuing the degree was renewed when a faculty member said she had faith in her and believed she could successfully earn the degree. This faculty member also used her professional network to help facilitate Elva's application process. Elva stated, "[S]he was emailing people for me, looking over my personal statements and CV, and she was the one that really helped me. She was the one that said, 'that's not true, you can write' and she was like, 'and you should get a PhD.'" It is Elva's hope to be able to use her professional network as a faculty member to do the same for other African Americans considering pursuing the degree.

The importance of networking was something several participants mentioned as being a core value that they learned from their HBCU. Operationalizing that value into networking skills allowed participants to navigate the application process with confidence and persistence. Although some ran into challenges, they never took no for an answer. They understood that the process of being admitted and successfully persisting in doctoral programs often went beyond academics. Thus, they used their networking skills to build connections and successfully enroll in their programs. Christy explained,

[The institution] has made me such a go-getter . . . you were kind of trained to [think] "if you want it go and get it" and kind of schooled in how to make no's become yes's and how to talk to people and interact with people and network and all of those kind of things. As far as doing my PhD . . . [the institution] has definitely prepared me for everything that it entails beyond this academic setting.

Discussion

HBCUs provide enriching environments where students are encouraged to explore their historical, collective, Diaspora experience in their daily lives. This connection is a foundation to develop a frame of reference for the meaning of community historically and presently. Similar to other studies that explore the role of HBCUs in African Americans' pursuit and obtainment of the PhD (e.g., Felder, 2010; Fountaine, 2012; Hall & Closson, 2005), this study has found that HBCUs contribute to students' commitment to pursue the degree. What makes this study unique is that it provides empirical evidence illustrating how the values embedded in the mission of HBCUs directly influence students' doctoral enrollment decision. Specifically, participants discussed three core values: academic excellence, bettering oneself as a means to give back to the African American community, and professional networking. Participants witnessed all three values operationalizing in practice by faculty and staff at their institutions. In turn, they desired to model that behavior in their own professional lives. Pursuing the doctorate was the means they choose to fulfill that goal.

Students' decisions to pursue PhD programs is not made in isolation. It is an accumulation of educational experiences that they have throughout their academic careers. For those who attend HBCUs, those experiences are grounded in an institution that recognizes that racism, discrimination and injustices exist, yet they do not allow students to use those experiences as a reason not to excel. Participants' commitment to pursue the PhD occurred in spite of the challenges they encountered during their undergraduate study. Their desire to succeed and help others in the pipeline succeed contributed to their commitment to pursue the degree.

The concept of Sankofa was found to be useful when analyzing the data. Phenomenology allowed us to conceptualize students' lived experiences, but Sankofa provided a cultural lens to help us understand how reaching back to help others was a cultural phenomenon embedded in

African American culture. According to Quarcoo (1972), ". . . there must be movement with the time but as the forward march proceeds, the gems must be picked up from behind and carried forward" (p. 17). Our findings show that the values operationalized by faculty and staff at HBCUs are gems and move forward our participants' desire to use those gems to help themselves and others in the pipeline be successful. Previous work documents the critical importance of HBCUs (Perna, 2001), and our study adds to that body of literature.

As new demands are placed on higher education that call for rethinking doctoral degree production as a national investment (Wendler et al., 2010), the relevance of HBCUs to producing doctoral degrees for historically marginalized students is valuable and relevant. Historically, these institutions have made great strides in serving and educating African Americans, both racially/culturally and academically, whom other institutions have not. As HBCUs continue to make important strides in developing African American leadership, their significant involvement in producing doctoral degree recipients can serve as a model for student success for all races and levels of education.

Limitations

There are several limitations to this study. First, the data presented here are from a larger study that specifically looked at the relationships and experiences that contributed to Black students pursuing doctoral degree programs. The interviews focused primarily on relationships and did not inquire about the uniqueness of the undergraduate institution, causing the data related to this study to be limited. Second, our sample contained only two male students. There may be ways Black males experience HBCUs differently from Black females. Those nuances may have appeared less important because of the composition of the sample. Finally, participants were currently-enrolled PhD students who were asked to reflect back on their undergraduate years. Thus, they were required to use their memory to recall past experiences that influenced their commitment. Because they used memory to reconstruct original complex experiences, including their perceptions of those experiences, that can be considered a limitation to the study. Participants' recollections of past experiences may not accurately reflect the actual experiences they had.

Conclusion

Based on the findings of this study, it is important to note that there are several key issues to consider for future research. First, it is clear that participants in this study value the role of community within HBCU environments and highly value it in their academic and social decision making. Community is valued when considering commitment to pursue the doctorate and when considering how this commitment might relate to specific disciplines. Focusing on the role of community networks related to the HBCU campus both internally and externally could be beneficial to supporting doctoral student success and degree completion.

Participants were not only discussing their commitment to the pursuit of the doctorate and interest in their discipline, and to some degree this commitment facilitated resilience and empowerment through the process of giving back to enhance community. More research on post-degree completion activities would be helpful in understanding how commitment is translated in terms of investing in community. This investment might involve participation in community by way of specific disciplinary interests or through social activism.

The role of HBCU structure, pedagogy, and mission was evident in perceptions of advisement, mentoring, and learning experiences. Findings indicate that participants highly valued and respected student–faculty relationships where faculty promoted students' learning and empowered them to pursue the doctoral degree. However, as research indicates that HBCU faculty workloads are demanding, future research might consider how faculty workload hinders and/or promotes support for students and their interest in doctoral study. Finally, more research must be conducted to understand the role of HBCUs' mission in supporting academic success toward doctoral study. This is especially critical given the increasingly complex demands of a higher education system that is becoming more globalized.

This study used a phenomenological approach and the concept of Sankofa to explore student perceptions related to the HBCU student experience as it relates to pursuing the PhD. Commitment to pursuing the PhD was often characterized as an interest in giving back to the community or related to larger social justice goals in their respective disciplines. Global demands have resulted in US colleges and universities embracing strategies to remain viable and competitive. This includes strengthening institutional capacity to support historically marginalized students' academic success and degree completion. HBCUs have traditionally served marginalized students (especially those with limited resources) in ways that have been remarkable. Findings in this study demonstrate the HBCU contribution as a vital national asset in strengthening student commitment to the pursuit of the doctoral degree.

Works Cited

Adam, M. (2007). Doctoral programs: Enrollment, completion, and minorities. *The Hispanic Outlook in Higher Education, 17*(19), 24–26.

Allen, W. R. (1992). The color of success: African American college student outcomes at predominantly White and historically Black public colleges and universities. *Harvard Educational Review, 62*(1), 26–44.

Allen, W. R., Epps, E. G., & Haniff, N. Z. (Eds.). (1991). *College in Black and White: African American students in predominantly White and in historically Black public universities.* Albany, NY: State University of New York Press.

Arce, C. H., & Manning, W. H. (1984). *Minorities in academic careers: The experiences of Ford Foundation fellows.* New York, NY: Ford Foundation.

Baird, L. L. (1993). Increasing graduate student retention and degree attainment. *New Directions for Institutional Research, 80*, 3–12.

Ballard, H. E., & Cintron, R. (2011). Critical race theory as an analytical tool: African American male success in doctoral education. *Journal of College Teaching & Learning, 7*(10), 11–23.

Blackwell, J. E. (1987). *Mainstreaming outsiders: The production of Black professionals* (2nd ed.). Dix Hills, NY: General Hall.

Brown, C. M., Davis, G. L., & McClendon, S. A. (1999). Mentoring graduate students of color: Myths, models, and modes. *Peabody Journal of Education, 74*(2), 105–118.

Carter, D. J., & Wilson, R. (1993). *Minorities in higher education.* Washington, DC: American Council on Education.

Council of Graduate Schools and Educational Testing Service. (2012). *Pathways through graduate school and into careers.* Report from the Commission on Pathways Through Graduate School and Into Careers. Princeton, NJ: Educational Testing Service.

DeCoster, J. (1998). *Overview of factor analysis.* Retrieved from http://stat-help.com/factor.pdf

DeSousa, D. J., & Kuh, G. (1996). Does institutional racial composition make a difference in what Black students gain from college? *Journal of Student Development, 37*(3), 257–267.

Eimers, M. T., & Pike, G. R. (1997). Minority and non-minority adjustment to college: Differences or similarities? *Research in Higher Education, 38*(1), 77–97.

Ellis, E. M. (2000). *Race, gender, and the graduate student experience: Recent research.* Retrieved February 10, 2007, from http://www.diversityweb.org/Digest/F00/graduate.html

Felder, P. (2010). On doctoral student development: Exploring faculty mentoring in the shaping of African American doctoral student success. *The Qualitative Report, 15*(3), 455–474. Retrieved from http://nsuworks.nova.edu/tqr/vol15/iss3/1

Felder, P. P., & Barker, M. J. (2013). Extending Bell's concept of interest convergence: A framework for understanding the African American doctoral student experience. *International Journal of Doctoral Studies, 8,* 1–20.

Felder, P. P., & Freeman, S., Jr. (2016). Editors' introduction: Exploring doctoral student socialization and the African American experience. *The Western Journal of Black Studies, 40*(2), 77–79.

Felder, P. P., Stevenson, H. C., & Gasman, M. (2014). Understanding race in doctoral student socialization. *International Journal of Doctoral Studies, 9,* 21–42. Retrieved from http://ijds.org/Volume9/IJDSv9p021-042Felder0323.pdf

Fountaine, T. P. (2012). The impact of faculty–student interaction on Black doctoral students attending historically Black institutions. *Journal of Negro Education, 81*(2), 136–147.

Gildersleeve, R. E., Croom, N. N., & Vasquez, P. L. (2011). Am I going crazy?!": A critical race analysis of doctoral education, *Equity & Excellence in Education, 44*(1), 93–114.

Golde, C. M., & Dore, T. M. (2001). *At cross purposes: What the experiences of today's graduate students reveal about doctoral education.* Philadelphia, PA: The Pew Charitable Trusts. Retrieved from http://www.phd-survey.org/report%20fi-nal.pdf

Golde, C., & Walker, G. (2006). *Envisioning the future of doctoral education: Preparing stewards of the discipline.* San Francisco, CA: Jossey-Bass.

Hall, B., & Closson, R. B. (2005). When the majority is the minority: White graduate students' social adjustment at a historically Black university. *Journal of College Student Development, 46*(1), 28–42.

Hinkle, D. E., Wiersma, W., & Jurs, S. G. (2003). *Applied statistics for the behavioral sciences.* Boston, MA: Houghton Mifflin Company.

Hirt, J. B., Strayhorn, T. L., Amelink, C. T., & Bennett, B. R. (2006). The nature of student affairs work at historically Black colleges and universities. *Journal of College and Student Development, 47*(6), 661–676.

Hurte, V. J. (2003). Mentoring: The forgotten retention tool. *Black Issues in Higher Education, 19*(18), 49–50.

Jackson, J. F. L. (2001, November). *Retention of African American administrators at predominantly White institutions: Using professional growth factors to inform the discussion.* Paper presented at the Annual Meeting of the Association for the Study of Higher Education, Richmond, VA (ERIC Document Reproduction Service No. ED 457 818).

Jones, T. B., Wilder, A., & Osborne-Lampkin, L. (2013). The race against time: Preparing Black students for the changing landscape of higher education. *The Journal of Negro Education, 82*(3), 326–338.

Kuh, G. D. (2009). The National Survey of Student Engagement: Conceptual and empirical foundations. *New Directions for Institutional Research, 141,* 5–20.

Kuh, G. D., Kinzie, J., Schuh J. H., Whitt, E. J., & Associates. (2005). *Student success in college: Creating conditions that matter.* San Francisco, CA: Jossey-Bass.

Latiker, T. T. (2003, April). *A qualitative study of African American student persistence in a private Black college.* Paper presented at the Annual Meeting of the American Educational Research Association, Chicago, IL.

Lott, J. L. (2013). Racial identity and Black students' perceptions of community outreach: Implications for bonding social capital. *The Journal of Negro Education, 77*(1), 3–14.

Lovitts, B. E. (2005). Being a good course-taker is not enough: A theoretical perspective on the transition to independent research. *Studies in Higher Education, 30*(2), 137–154.

Lundy-Wagner, V., Vultaggio, J., & Gasman, M. (2013). Preparing underrepresented students of color for doctoral success: The role of undergraduate institutions. *International Journal of Doctoral Studies, 8,* 151–172. Retrieved from http://ijds.org/Volume8/IJDSv8p151-172Lundy-Wagner0381.pdf

Maton, K. I., & Hrabrowski, F. A., III. (2014). Increasing the number of African American PhDs in the sciences and engineering: A strengths-based approach. *American Psychologist, 59*(6), 547–556.

McGlynn, A. P. (2006). Mentoring and the STEM gender gap: AWIS and MentorNet confront the divide. *The Hispanic Outlook in Higher Education, 16,* 31.

Means, D. R., Beatty, C. C., Blockett, R. A., Bumbrey, M., Canida, R. L., & Cawthorn, T. W. (2016). Resilient scholars: Reflections from Black gay men on the doctoral journey. *Journal of Student Affairs, Research and Practice.* Retrieved from http://dx.doi.org/10.1080/19496591.2016.1219265

National Center for Education Statistics. (2012). *The condition of education 2012.* Washington, DC: US Department of Education. Retrieved from https://nces.ed.gov/fastfacts/display.asp?id=72

National Center for Education Statistics. (2005). *Doctor's degrees conferred by degree-granting institutions, by sex, racial/ethnic group, and major field of study: 2003–04.* Washington, DC: US Department of Education. Retrieved from http://nces.ed.gov/programs/digest/d05/tables/xls/tabn268.xls

National Center for Education Statistics. (2015). *Selected statistics on degree-granting historically Black colleges and universities, by control and level of institution: Selected years, 1990 through 2013.* Washington, DC: US Department of Education. Retrieved from http://nces.ed.gov/programs/digest/d14/tables/dt14_313.30.asp?current=yes

National Opinion Research Center. (2006). *Survey of earned doctorates: Summary report 2005.* Washington, DC: National Academy Press. Retrieved from http://www.norc.org/NR/rdonlyres/2E87F80C-82F6-4E26-9F78-CA4C6E0B79C6/0/sed2005.pdf

National Opinion Research Center. (2007). *Survey of earned doctorates: Summary report 2006.* Washington, DC: National Academy Press. Retrieved from http://www.norc.org/NR/rdonlyres/C22A3F40-0BA2-4993-A6D3-5E65939EEDC3/0/06SRFinalVersion.pdf

National Science Foundation (2014). Doctorate recipients from US universities: 2014. Retrieved from https://www.nsf.gov/statistics/2016/nsf16300/digest/theme1.cfm

Nerad, M., & Miller, D. S. (1996). Increasing student retention in graduate and professional programs. *New Directions in Institutional Research, 92,* 61–76.

Nettles, M. T., & Millet, C. M. (2006). *Three magic letters: Getting to Ph.D.* Baltimore, MD: Johns Hopkins University Press.

Okahana, H., Allum, J., Felder, P. P., & Tull, R. G. (2016). Implications for practice and research from Doctoral Initiative on Minority Attrition and Completion (CGS Data Sources PLUS #16-01). Washington, DC: Council of Graduate Schools.

O'Meara, K., Knudsen, K., & Jones, J. (2010). The role of emotional competencies in faculty–doctoral student relationships. *The Review of Higher Education, 36*(3), 315–347.

Ottinger, C., Sikula, R., & Washington, C. (1993). *Production of minority doctorates* (Research Briefs, Vol. 4, No. 8). Washington, DC: American Council on Education.

Palmer, R. T., & Gasman, M. (2008). "It takes a village to raise a child": The role of social capital in promoting academic success of African American men at a Black college. *Journal of College Student Development, 49*(1), 52–70.

Palmer, R. T., Hilton, A. A., & Fountaine, T. P. (Eds.). (2012). *Black graduate education at historically Black colleges and universities: Trends, experiences, and outcomes.* New York, NY: Information Age Press.

Pascarella, E. T., & Terenzini, P. T. (2005). *How college affects students: A third decade of research.* San Francisco, CA: Jossey-Bass.

Patterson-Stewart, K., Richie, M. H., & Sanders, E. T. W. (1997). Interpersonal dynamics of African American persistence in doctoral programs at predominantly White universities. *Journal of College Student Development, 38*(5), 489–498.

Pontius, J., & Harper, S. (2006). Principles for good practice in graduate and professional student engagement. *New Directions for Student Services, 115,* 47–58.

Quarcoo, A. K. (1972). *The language of Adinkra symbols.* Legon, Ghana: Sebewie Ventures.

Reeder, M. C., & Schmitt, N. (2013). Motivational and judgment predictors of African American academic achievement at PWIs and HBCUs. *Journal of College Student Development, 54*(1), 29–42.

Roach, R. (1997, July). Clouded optimism: Graduate and professional degree rate among minorities outpaces that of whites, but experts predict surge will end if affirmative action backlash continues. *Black Issues in Higher Education, 14*(11), 17.

Santos, S. J., & Reigadas, E. T. (2005). Understanding the student–faculty mentoring process: Its effects on at-risk university students. *Journal of College Student Retention, 6*(3), 337–358.

Spaulding, L. S., & Rockinson-Szapkiw, A. J. (2012). Hearing their voices: Factors doctoral candidates attribute to their persistence. *International Journal of Doctoral Studies, 7,* 199–219. Retrieved from http://ijds.org/Volume7/IJDSv7 p199-219Spaulding334.pdf

St. John, E. (2000, July 6). More doctorates in the house—More African American students are receiving doctorates. *Black Issues in Higher Education.* Retrieved from http://findarticles.com/p/articles/mi_m0DXK/is_10_17/ai_63817017

Tedla, E. (1995). *Sankofa: African thought and education.* New York, NY: Lang Publishing.

Terenzini, P. T., Yaeger, P. M., Bohr, L., Pascarella, E. T., & Nora, A. (1997). *African American college students' experiences in HBCUs and PWIs and learning outcomes.* University Park, PA: National Center on Postsecondary Teaching, Learning, and Assessment.

Thompson, G. L. (1999). What the numbers really mean: African American underrepresentation at the doctoral level. *Journal of College Student Retention, 1*(1), 23–40.

Tinto, V. (1993). *Leaving college: Rethinking the causes and cures of student attrition* (2nd ed.). Chicago, IL: University of Chicago Press.

Turner, C. S. V., & Thompson, J. R. (1993). Socializing women doctoral students: Minority and majority experiences. *Review of Higher Education, 16*(3), 355–370.

Van der Gest, S. (1998). Yebisa Wo Fie: Growing old and building a house in the Akan culture of Ghana. *Journal of Cross-Cultural Gerontology, 13,* 333–359.

Watson, L. W., & Kuh, G. D. (1996). The influence of dominant race environments on students' involvement, perception and educational gains: A look at historically Black and predominantly White liberal arts institutions. *Journal of College Student Development, 37*(3), 415–424.

Willie, C. V., Grady, M. K., & Hope, R. O. (1991). *African Americans and the doctoral experience: Implications for policy.* New York, NY: Teachers College Press.

Wilson, V. W., Andrews, M., & Leners, D. W. (2006). Mentoring as a strategy for retaining racial and ethnically diverse students on nursing programs. *Journal of Multicultural Nursing & Health, 12*(3), 17–24.

Chapter 7

Rethinking Engagement

Examining the Role of Faculty–Student Interactions and
Black Doctoral Student Success at HBCUs

Tiffany Fountaine Boykin

Over the last two decades, scholars have learned a considerable amount
about the socialization experiences and graduation outcomes of Black
students who attend historically Black colleges and universities (HBCUs).
In general, HBCUs have been credited with cultivating supportive and
engaging environments (Hall & Closson, 2005) where Black students have
a strengthened self-esteem and stronger sense of racial pride (Hirt, Strayhorn, Amelink, & Bennett, 2006; Palmer & Gasman, 2008). Further, the
literature is clear that Black students who attend HBCUs perform better
academically, build more meaningful relationships with faculty and staff,
are more engaged in the campus environment, and have a better sense of
belonging and connection than Black students who attend predominantly
White institutions (PWIs) (Jackson, 2001; Palmer & Gasman, 2008; Terenzini, Yaeger, Bohr, Pascarella, & Nora, 1997). Simply put, HBCUs have
been cited as being able to provide Black students, at both undergraduate
and graduate levels, with an exceptional educational experience, often
unachievable at PWIs (Allen, 1992; Fountaine, 2012).

Recent trends in higher education have shown indicators for con-
tinual and impressive progress for the future of Black doctoral students
(Golde & Walker, 2006; National Opinion Research Center [NORC], 2007;
Roach, 1997; Survey of Earned Doctorates, 2014; Thompson, 1999). In

fact, there has been a 70% increase in the number of doctorates awarded to Blacks over the past 20 years (Survey of Earned Doctorates, 2014). The literature has offered a variety of factors that may have contributed to this increase, including strengthening the pipeline of aspiring Black doctorates, particularly in STEM, at the undergraduate level (Maton & Hrabrowski, 2004); employing a Black feminist approach to doctoral advising (Jones, Wilder, & Lampkin, 2013); and providing comprehensive support for doctoral students who are at the intersection of identities, especially gay men (Means, Beatty, Blockett, Bumbry, Canida, & Cawthorn, 2016). Moreover, research has confirmed that institutional characteristics such as type, racial and ethnic composition, selectivity, and geographic location also matter in terms of producing successful minority doctoral students (Lundy-Wagner, Vultaggio, & Gasman, 2013). In fact, it has been suggested that earlier aspects of a doctoral student's educational pipeline, specifically attending an HBCU, also play a significant role in preparing Black students for doctoral success (Lundy-Wagner, Vultaggio, & Gasman, 2013).

While HBCUs represent just 3% of U.S. higher education institutions, and despite relatively smaller endowments and lower institutional resources, HBCUs have been a critical force in the production of Black advanced degree recipients. The National Center for Education Statistics (NCES) (2005) reported that HBCUs produced 6,900 master's degree recipients (5,034 for Blacks), accounting for roughly 10% of master's degrees awarded to Black students that year. HBCUs have also been a principal producer of Black doctorates; between 1992–1993 and 1997–1998, HBCUs increased their number of doctoral graduates by 15.2% (St. John, 2000). By 2012–2013, the percentage of Black doctoral recipients who received their degrees from HBCUs was approximately 12% (NCES, 2015). Although HBCUs have made considerable strides in the production of Black doctorates over the last 30 years, progress has been slow. Blacks' total share of doctoral recipients increased from 3.8% in 1977 to only 4.8% in 2000 (Nettles & Millett, 2006). And, as of 2010, Blacks' share had increased to just 7.4% (NCES, 2012), considerably lagging behind that of White students (Adam, 2007; Carter & Wilson, 1993; Lundy-Wagner, Vultaggio, & Gasman, 2013; Ottinger, Sikula, & Washington, 1993). In fact, in 2010, Blacks earned 10,417, or 7.4%, of all doctorates conferred; Whites earned 104,426 doctorates, or 74.3% (NCES. 2012). This chapter examines how faculty interactions impact HBCU students' perceived perceptions of doctoral program persistence and the doctoral experience. It fits within the Sankofa tradition of this volume because of its attention to both the history and contributions of HBCUs and the ways that faculty, an important aspect of the HBCU community, influence the future of student experiences in doctoral programs. Tedla (1995) captured the spirit of Sankofa and the interconnectedness of one's context and future outcomes in this way: "the meaning of becoming a person and the meaning of work are derived from the community," which Tedla described as the "very core of African life" (p. 18). With a focus on community, one may consider how African traditions, values, and principles found its way to HBCU culture and in the development of Black students.

Examining Black Doctoral Student Experiences

While national data on doctoral degree attainment are generally available, few large-scale research studies have examined key dimensions of a student's prior educational and cultural backgrounds, financial supports, or perceptions and experiences regarding their development and progress in a program (Nettles & Millett, 2006). In addition, when examining the literature as a whole, relatively few studies have concentrated on specific factors influencing the experiences and persistence for Black doctoral students, despite continuing evidence of growth in Black doctoral program enrollment and attainment (Survey of Earned Doctorates, 2014). Notwithstanding, there is a recent growing body of literature examining experiences and factors that impact the success of Black doctoral students (Gildersleeve, Croom, & Vasquez, 2011; Felder & Barker, 2013; Felder, Stevenson, & Gasman, 2014; Okahana, Allum, Felder, & Tull, 2016). However, much of the research that actually has examined Black doctoral students has not necessarily investigated the implications of an HBCU setting (Ellis, 2000; Palmer, Hilton, & Fountaine, 2012; Nerad & Miller, 1996; Nettles & Millett, 2006; Turner & Thompson, 1993).

These gaps in the literature fail to expand the knowledge base of Black student experiences at HBCUs that could prove critical to matriculation and completion of the doctorate for these students. In addition, the literature offers minimal understanding for current and prospective Black students to deal with the personal and professional challenges of doctoral study. The problem in this investigation centered on the fact that, in general, little is known about the factors that impact the academic and social experiences or the perceived persistence of Black doctoral students attending HBCUs. This study did not attempt to uncover or identify a disparity between doctoral student achievements at HBCUs versus PWIs, nor is it designed to compare the experiences of doctoral students at one institution over another. Independent of comparisons, the influences that promote (or challenge) success among HBCU Black doctoral students are independently important. The purpose of this study was to determine if faculty–student engagement was predictive of Black doctoral students' overall experiences and if it influenced students' belief that they would persist to completion. This chapter discusses the variance within and impact of faculty–student engagement on HBCU doctoral students' positive academic experiences and perceived persistence. Recommendations for future research and practice are offered.

Theoretical Framework

Student experience serves as an invaluable resource from which scholars have learned about the significance of the faculty–student relationship on doctoral degree attainment (Felder, 2010). The present inquiry uses a synthesis of Baird's (1993) integrated model of student development and Tinto's (1993) model of doctoral student attrition. Constructs of Lovitts's (2005) theoretical perspective on doctoral students' transition to independent researchers are also considered.

Baird's (1993) integrated model for student development was an appropriate guide for this inquiry, as it incorporated a new subgroup not mentioned in previous persistence paradigms—doctoral students. This model described the doctoral experience as a process of socialization to an ultimate professional role. This role, according to Baird (1993), involved learning the specialized knowledge, skills, attitudes, values, norms, and interests of the profession. In this model, the graduate faculty was considered a critical agent for conducting doctoral student socialization, because faculty members defined knowledge and disciplinary values. Faculty members model the roles of academics in the discipline and provide practical help and advice. The goal for Baird (1993) was to help doctoral students become closer to faculty as they navigated through their academic careers. From his perspective, there was a correlation between attrition and inadequate faculty support.

Likewise, Tinto's (1993) sociologically oriented model of doctoral student attrition also served as an appropriate guide for this inquiry. The model described three general stages after program admission: (1) transition to membership into the graduate community in the first year,

(2) the attaining of candidacy through development of competence, and (3) active research. In the first stage, attrition and slower progress were linked with low levels of social and academic interactions with the doctoral program community and a low commitment to degree and career goals. Later, attrition was linked to inadequate interactions concerning the student's academic competence. In the last stage, the actions of a specific faculty member were determining factors. Both Baird's and Tinto's models contributed to the development of the independent variable in this study: faculty agency. In this investigation, faculty agency related to student–faculty engagement through academic and social interactions, faculty mentorship, and faculty advising practices.

A critical question in doctoral education, particularly Black doctoral education, is why students who succeed in the coursework (dependent) phase of their doctoral studies have different fates in the dissertation (independent) research phase of their education. That is, the literature tells us that Black doctoral students are accessing and participating in doctoral programs at increased rates (Felder & Freeman, 2016; NCES, 2015). Yet Black students' completion of doctoral programs in which completion of the dissertation is absolutely necessary, has not enjoyed similar outcomes. Lovitts (2005) postulated a theoretical perspective on factors that facilitate or impede a doctoral student's transition to conducting and producing independent research—a task necessary for doctoral study completion. Those factors included (1) individual resources (e.g., intelligence, motivation, learning styles and personality); (2) microenvironment (e.g., location, department, peers and other faculty, and advisor); and (3) macroenvironment (e.g., culture of graduate education and culture of the discipline). Constructs of Lovitts's (2005) perspective, along with the extant literature and research questions, were critical in constructing the dependent variables: (a) doctoral experience and (b) perceived persistence. Doctoral experience accounted for those experiences, positive or negative, acquired through student–faculty interaction. Perceived persistence pertained to the degree to which a student believed he or she would complete a doctoral program within the time period in accordance with time-to-degree consistencies at selected HBCUs.

While none of the aforementioned models or theoretical perspectives has been applied specifically to Black doctoral student populations, together they served as an appropriate lens for this inquiry, as they consistently align with many of the assumptions of this investigation and the general doctoral student population under study. Using this framework, the researcher identified one independent variable (faculty agency) and two dependent variables (doctoral experience and perceived persistence), as well as the overarching research question: What is the relationship between faculty agency, and doctoral experience and perceived persistence for Black students attending an HBCU?

Method

A nonexperimental, correlational survey design was used to examine a nonprobability purposive sample of Black doctoral students ($N = 190$) attending thirteen doctorate degree-granting private and public HBCUs. These institutions were identified through data collected by the National Center for Education Statistics (NCES) and its Integrated Postsecondary Education Data Set (IPEDS). Participants completed a web-based survey with questions relating to the independent variable—faculty–student engagement—as well as questions designed to measure participants' satisfaction with their doctoral experience and expectations for completing their doctoral studies. Participants were invited to complete a web-based survey.

Instrument

A questionnaire was developed through the extraction of a battery of items from the Survey of Doctoral Student Finances, Experiences and Achievement (Nettles & Millett, 2006), the Survey on Doctoral Education and Career Preparation (Golde & Dore, 2001), and the Survey of Earned Doctorates (NORC, 2006). Because the current study's final instrument consisted of multiple items extracted from multiple instruments and because some items were modified and others were deleted, Cronbach's alpha was calculated for each set of items measuring the independent and dependent variable to test reliability. A reliability coefficient of .70 or higher was regarded as satisfactory for the reliability scores for this instrument.

Independent Variable

Faculty Agency (FACAGE) contained items concerning the amount and quality of time spent between the student and the faculty advisor, and faculty feedback on writing and progress toward degree completion. Responses to FACAGE items were scored on a four-point Likert scale such that 1 = strongly disagree, 2 = disagree, 3 = agree, and 4 = strongly agree. Respondents could also select not applicable.

DEPENDENT VARIABLES

Doctoral experience (DOCEXP) referred to the degree to which participants had a positive experience during their doctoral studies and the satisfaction they had for the overall doctoral process. Responses were scored on a four-point Likert scale such that 1 = strongly disagree or very dissatisfied, 2 = disagree or dissatisfied, 3 = agree or satisfied, and 4 = strongly agree or very satisfied. Perceived persistence (PERPER) contained items related to program progress, degree completion expectations, and program progress inhibitors. Responses were scored on a four-point Likert scale such that 1 = strongly disagree, 2 = disagree, 3 = agree, and 4 = strongly agree. Respondents could also select not applicable for all items measuring the dependent variables.

ANALYTICAL PROCEDURES

A factor analysis was calculated to statistically reduce the 41-item FACAGE variable to determine if there were underlying constructs and to allow for a more manageable data set for inferential analysis. Factor analysis is a statistical approach used to examine interrelationships among a large number of variables and to explain these variables in terms of their common underlying dimensions (Hinkle, Wiersma, & Jurs, 2003). The goal is to find a way to condense the information included in a number of original variables into a smaller set of dimensions or factors with a minimum loss of information. In general, when conducting factor analyses, the researcher is examining the pattern of correlations between the observed measures. Measures that are highly correlated are likely influenced by the same (common) factors, while those that are relatively uncorrelated are likely influenced by different factors (DeCoster, 1998).

In this study, post-reduction analysis for the FACAGE variable yielded seven engagement components: (1) Selection Engagement (SELENG), or the interaction between a student and a faculty member during the time the student selected a particular faculty member as his or her advisor; (2) Internal Engagement (INTENG), or the level of involvement between a student and an advisor with regard to academic program progress and research practices; (3) External Engagement (EXTENG), or the social components for student success that were external to a student's program and research practices; (4) Interpersonal Engagement (ITRENG), or the level of interpersonal interaction between the student and faculty advisor; (5) Advisor Engagement (ADVENG), or the overall interaction between the student and the advisor; (6) Resource Engagement (RESENG), or the contact between a student and a faculty member in terms of skill building and resources, such as faculty assistance with securing funding for research and with writing grant and contract proposals; and (7) Negative Engagement (NEGENG), or any negative interaction between the student and faculty.

Results

Correlation and multiple linear regression were used to better explain the relationship between FACAGE, DOCEXP and PERPER. Significance was determined at $\alpha = .05$. The findings concluded that significant correlation existed between the independent variable and the dependent variables. Table 7.1 displays the regression analysis for all components of the FACAGE variable. INTENG ($b = .478$, $t = 2.539$, $p = .012$), EXTENG ($b = .517$, $t = 3.192$, $p = .002$), and ADVENG ($b = .789$, $t = 3.520$, $p = .001$) were predictive of DOCEXP. SELENG, ITRENG, RESENG, and NEGENG were not associated with DOCEXP.

Table 7.2 illustrates that INTENG ($b = .153$, $t = 2.177$, $p = .031$), EXTENG ($b = .193$, $t = 3.183$, $p = .002$), ITRENG ($b = -.201$, $t = -2.615$, $p = .010$), and ADVENG ($b = .195$, $t = 2.325$, $p = .021$) were predictive of PERPER. SELENG, RESENG, and NEGENG were not predictive factors of PERPER.

The researcher desired to determine if the variance in doctoral experience and perceived persistence could best be explained by any single independent variable component. A stepwise method of multiple linear regression was calculated to address this inquiry. The stepwise regression findings indicated that EXTENG was the best predictor of both DOCEXP ($R^2 = .351$, $b = .971$, $t = 10.167$, $p < .001$) and PERPER ($R^2 = .300$, $b = .298$, $t = 9.054$, $p < .001$).

Discussion

The findings in this investigation revealed that faculty agency, characterized as faculty–student engagement, is indeed a critical factor for the experiences

Table 7.1. Multiple Linear Regression Analysis: Faculty Agency, Doctoral Experience

Independent Variable	Unstandardized Coefficients		Standardized Coefficients		
	B	**Std. Error**	**Beta**	**T**	**P**
Constant	9.480	4.408		2.151	.033
Selection Engagement	−.056	.055	−.068	−1.020	.309
Internal Engagement	.478	.188	.197	2.539	.012
External Engagement	.517	.162	.317	3.192	.002
Interpersonal Engagement	−.146	.205	−.060	−.712	.478
Advisor Engagement	.789	.224	.241	3.520	.001
Resource Engagement	−.238	.248	−.057	−.960	.338
Negative Engagement	−.696	.378	−.111	−1.842	.067

Table 7.2. Multiple Linear Regression Analysis: Faculty Agency, Perceived Persistence

Independent Variable	Unstandardized Coefficients		Standardized Coefficients		
	B	**Std. Error**	**Beta**	**T**	**P**
Constant	2.538	1.647		1.541	.125
Selection Engagement	.021	.020	.077	1.023	.307
Internal Engagement	.153	.070	.190	2.177	.031
External Engagement	.193	.061	.356	3.183	.002
Interpersonal Engagement	−.201	.077	−.248	−2.615	.010
Advisor Engagement	.195	.084	.179	2.325	.021
Resource Engagement	.065	.093	.047	.706	.481
Negative Engagement	−.168	.141	−.081	−1.189	.236

and perceived persistence of Black doctoral students attending HBCUs. The findings in this inquiry validated the notion that Black doctoral students at HBCUs who are highly involved with faculty members regarding program progress and who interact regularly with a faculty advisor have better doctoral experiences. Results showed a significant association between three of the seven faculty agency variable constructs—internal engagement, external engagement, and advisor engagement—and positive doctoral experience. It was suggested, then, that level of involvement between Black participants in this study at selected HBCUs and faculty members regarding program progress (INTENG) and level of interaction with a faculty advisor (ADVENG) were predictive of their positive doctoral experiences. This investigation also concluded that this sample of Black doctoral students who attend HBCUs are more likely to have a positive doctoral experience when they engage with faculty about social components external to the academic program (EXTENG).

These findings were consistent with past research studies and literature pertaining to the impact of faculty on students' doctoral experience. For example, in Baird's (1993) integrated model for student development, the doctoral experience was described as a process of socialization to an ultimate professional role. In this model, the graduate faculty was considered a critical agent for conducting doctoral student socialization, and the graduate faculty provided practical help and advice. Latiker (2003) also found that one of the major socializing agents of graduate students on private Black campuses was the faculty and staff. Lovitts (2005), although not examining Black doctoral students exclusively, posited that faculty do indeed exert power over micro- and macroenvironments and are able to influence student persistence by aligning their structure with actions that positively affect student persistence. For instance, in the microenvironment, Lovitts (2005) found that faculty can engage students into the department and into scholarly discourse with peers and other faculty. Similarly, in the macroenvironment, faculty can promote relationships with students where students are encouraged to express their ideas and concerns, develop relationships with faculty, and have meaningful discussions with faculty about their research interests and endeavors. Essentially, the micro- and macroenvironments represent the community of the doctoral student; the more faculty promote a community conductive to supporting student goals and needs, the less likely the student is to leave the program prior to completion.

The findings in the current inquiry were also relevant to the literature concerning the impact of faculty on persistence. There was a significant association found between four of the seven faculty agency variables—internal engagement, external engagement, interpersonal engagement, and advisor engagement—and perceived program persistence. Other researchers (Eimers & Pike, 1997) have pointed out these significant relationships as well, maintaining that faculty–student interaction is a consistent predictor of persistence. Pascarella and Terenzini (2005) suggested that out-of-classroom interaction between faculty and students was also linked to persistence and degree completion. Furthermore, researchers (Arce & Manning, 1984; Ballard & Cintron, 2010; Blackwell, 1987; Felder, 2010; O'Meara, Knudsen, & Jones, 2013) have consistently found that graduate students perceived the relationships with faculty and mentors as critical to their satisfaction and successful completion of graduate programs. Other researchers (Spaulding & Rockinson-Szapkiw, 2012; Willie, Grady, & Hope, 1991) have also concluded that the kinds of relationships students develop with faculty members strongly impact students' persistence in completing their degrees.

Conclusions and Recommendations

In general, the positive findings in this study suggested that the HBCU, particularly its faculty, serves as a positive model for other higher education institutions for supporting Black doctoral education. Doctoral education is critical, as students see the doctorate as a prerequisite for entry into leadership professions, and as more and more graduate schools promote institutional research. The findings of this study suggested that HBCUs provide learning environments where Black doctoral students encounter purposeful interaction with faculty to sustain a successful doctoral experience and hold high expectations to persist to graduation. With those factors in place, HBCUs have a unique opportunity to become even more of a powerhouse in the production of Black doctorates, thus adding to the success of higher education, the economy, and the civic and social order of future generations in the United States. Student development programming and persistence strategies designed to meet the needs of today's Black doctoral learner at the HBCU are essential in sustaining the legacy of the HBCU and further reaffirming its viability and important role in the production of the Black doctorate, and are essential in the higher education landscape overall. HBCUs serve as culturally rich and affirming environments where the Sankofan principles of community, sharing, and helping others is core to the building of the *munthu* or the person (Tedla, 1995, p. 38).

Directions for Future Research

It is important to note that no single characteristic determines whether an individual will complete doctoral study. Different characteristics can and do combine in different ways to yield successful outcomes for Black doctoral students; thus, this issue remains ripe for further investigation. Despite the valuable contributions of this study, there remains limited research available pertaining to Black doctoral student experiences and persistence, particularly at HBCUs. This inadequate knowledge base, coupled with the correlational design of the current inquiry, warrants a future study constructed from a qualitative lens, or at minimum a future inquiry that includes a qualitative component. Not only would a qualitative approach allow for a richer description of the data, but it would provide additional opportunities to further explore the voices of Black doctoral students and foster ways to determine the impact of additional factors. Future studies might also include an expanded sample to include recent Black doctorate degree completers as well as non-completers who attended HBCUs.

The existing literature, including the current investigation, lacks empirical evidence pertaining to gender differences in Black doctoral education, particularly at HBCUs. While there is some research that suggests there are no significant gender differences in time to completion, a previous study revealed that men were in fact more satisfied with their doctoral education and the quality of interaction with faculty than were women (Seagram, Gold, & Pike, 1998). Furthermore, other research has shown that male PhD candidates submit and publish papers at much higher rates than women, even at the same institution (Lubienski, Miller, & Saclarides, 2017). Given these outcomes, and the existing void in the knowledge base concerning gender differences in Black doctoral education, a future exploration specific to gender differences for experiences and perceived persistence among Black doctoral students at HBCUs is recommended.

An additional recommendation for future research would be to further examine external engagement, as this variable was shown to be the best predictor for both doctoral experience and perceived persistence. Faculty and administrators in any higher education context might benefit from further research that focuses on this concept and its specific impact on Black students during the doctoral process.

Directions for Practice

Although graduate and professional students comprise a substantial percentage of all students enrolled in American colleges and universities, the literature and efforts to achieve educational excellence regarding student engagement have remained focused almost exclusively on undergraduates (Pontius & Harper, 2006). Traditional notions of engagement have focused heavily, and validly so, on engagement as an indicator of institutional quality. Kuh, Kinzie, Whitt, and Associates (2005) defined student engagement as a twofold construct of collegiate quality. First, student engagement represents the amount of time and effort students put into their studies and other educationally purposeful activities. Secondly, student engagement considers how an institution deploys its resources and organizes the curriculum and other learning opportunities to get students to participate in activities that decades of research studies show are linked to student learning. Benchmarks for assessing faculty's role in student engagement have focused on the amount of time students practice and get feedback on their writing and collaborative problem solving (Kuh, 2009).

While Kuh et al.'s (2005) traditional notions of engagement were also validated in this study, the historical focus on undergraduate student experiences, and the fact that the external engagement factor was so influential in this investigation, may warrant a rethinking of student engagement, particularly at the doctoral level for Black students attending an HCBU. In this study, faculty agency, conceptualized as faculty–student engagement, was not only positively associated with doctoral experience and perceived persistence, but it also incorporated the external engagement construct, which was identified as the best predictor of both. Faculty's interaction with students went beyond and much deeper than providing feedback on papers and discussing progress in a program. In fact, external engagement referred to the social components for student success that were external to a student's program and research practices. Essentially, this study revealed that faculty who took an interest in students' lives outside the classroom and consistently inquired about their general well-being were most influential in students' having a positive experience and believing they would graduate.

Given this finding, it is suggested that faculty members, in their roles as advisors, teachers, and mentors, remain open and supportive to the various ways of encouraging, engaging, and nurturing Black students. One strategy to encourage such support is for HBCUs to create faculty mentor programs in which doctoral students are paired with faculty members to develop meaningful mentor/mentee relationships. These relationships might include assistance in navigating the program and networking with other faculty, help with early exploration of dissertation topics, review of manuscripts and identification of publishing opportunities, support with identifying funding sources, and advice for professional development and involvement with professional and scholarly organizations. Scholars

(Brown, Davis, & McClendon, 1999; Hurte, 2003; Mc-Glynn, 2006; Santos & Reigadas, 2005; Wilson, Andrews, & Leners, 2006) have cited the success of similar programs, many with minority focus, in other higher education programs and contexts. In addition, such mentoring programs might also look at expanding the focus of graduate education to include development of professional skills, such as oral communication, writing, analysis and synthesis of data, presentation skills, and planning and organization. These competencies are especially important for doctoral students and have substantial implications for success beyond completion (Council of Graduate Schools & Educational Testing Service, 2012).

Another recommendation is for doctoral program administrators to partner with student affairs professionals to create culturally relevant engagement plans for students. Pontius and Harper (2006) have noted that cooperation, meaningful dialogue, and strategic planning between faculty and student affairs professionals typify good practice. As pointed out by Pontius and Harper (2006), "engagement could, and should, be at the core of these conversations" (p. 54). The extent to which doctoral students are engaged in educationally purposeful experiences should not occur by chance. Therefore, faculty and student affairs professionals have an opportunity to develop plans and strategies for connecting students to the larger campus community and positively affecting learning and outcomes beyond the classroom.

In summary, the results of this study have made important contributions to the knowledge base surrounding Black doctoral education, specifically at HBCUs. Its intent was to examine the impact of faculty agency on doctoral students' experiences and perceived persistence. The findings in this study suggest that the HBCU has served and continues to serve as a positive model for higher education institutions. Therefore, the proposed recommendations for practice and future research support the success of Black doctoral students at HBCUs, but may also have implications for students in programs in other institutional settings. The current study provides a modest, but worthwhile, platform for Black students and their stake in pursuing the doctorate degree. It is hoped that the findings from this investigation have contributed to a framework for faculty and administrators to provide additional outlets for informing practice and developing programs, in the interest of improving the educational experiences and perceived persistence for Black doctoral students attending HBCUs.

Works Cited

Adam, M. (2007). Doctoral programs: Enrollment, completion, and minorities. *The Hispanic Outlook in Higher Education, 17*(19), 24–26.

Allen, W. R. (1992). The color of success: African American college student outcomes at predominantly White and historically Black public colleges and universities. *Harvard Educational Review, 62*(1), 26–44.

Allen, W. R., Epps, E. G., & Haniff, N. Z. (Eds.). (1991). *College in Black and White: African American students in predominantly White and in historically Black public universities.* Albany, NY: State University of New York Press.

Arce, C. H., & Manning, W. H. (1984). *Minorities in academic careers: The experiences of Ford Foundation fellows.* New York: Ford Foundation.

Baird, L. L. (1993). Increasing graduate student retention and degree attainment. *New Directions for Institutional Research, 80*, 3–12.

Ballard, H. E., & Cintron, R. (2011). Critical race theory as an analytical tool: African American male success in doctoral education. *Journal of College Teaching & Learning, 7*(10), 11–23.

Blackwell, J. E. (1987). *Mainstreaming outsiders: The production of Black professionals.* (2nd ed.). Dix Hills, NY: General Hall.

Brown, C. M., Davis, G. L., & McClendon, S. A. (1999). Mentoring graduate students of color: Myths, models, and modes. *Peabody Journal of Education, 74*(2), 105–118.

Carter, D. J., & Wilson, R. (1993). *Minorities in higher education.* Washington, DC: American Council on Education.

Council of Graduate Schools and Educational Testing Service. (2012). *Pathways through graduate school and into careers.* Report from the Commission on Pathways Through Graduate School and Into Careers. Princeton, NJ: Educational Testing Service.

DeCoster, J. (1998). *Overview of factor analysis.* Retrieved from http://stat-help.com/factor.pdf

DeSousa, D. J., & Kuh, G. (1996). Does institutional racial composition make a difference in what Black students gain from college? *Journal of Student Development, 37*(3), 257–267.

Eimers, M. T., & Pike, G. R. (1997). Minority and non-minority adjustment to college: Differences or similarities? *Research in Higher Education, 38*(1), 77–97.

Ellis, E. M. (2000). *Race, gender, and the graduate student experience: Recent research.* Retrieved February 10, 2007, from http://www.diversityweb.org/Digest/F00/graduate.html

Felder, P. (2010). On doctoral student development: Exploring faculty mentoring in the shaping of African American doctoral student success. *The*

Qualitative Report, 15(3), 455–474. Retrieved from http://nsuworks.nova.edu/tqr/vol15/iss3/1

Felder, P. P., & Barker, M. J. (2013). Extending Bell's concept of interest convergence: A framework for understanding the African American doctoral student experience. *International Journal of Doctoral Studies, 8,* 1–20.

Felder, P. P., & Freeman, S., Jr. (2016). Editors' introduction: Exploring doctoral student socialization and the African American experience. *The Western Journal of Black Studies, 40*(2), 77–79.

Felder, P. P., Stevenson, H. C., & Gasman, M. (2014). Understanding race in doctoral student socialization. *International Journal of Doctoral Studies, 9,* 21–42. Retrieved from http://ijds.org/Volume9/IJDSv9p021-042Felder0323.pdf

Fountaine, T. P. (2012). The impact of faculty–student interaction on Black doctoral students attending historically Black institutions. *Journal of Negro Education, 81*(2), 136–147.

Gildersleeve, R. E., Croom, N. N., & Vasquez, P. L. (2011). "Am I going crazy?!": A critical race analysis of doctoral education. *Equity & Excellence in Education, 44*(1), 93–114.

Golde, C. M., & Dore, T. M. (2001). *At cross purposes: What the experiences of today's graduate students reveal about doctoral education.* Philadelphia, PA: The Pew Charitable Trusts. Retrieved from http://www.phd-survey.org/report%20fi-nal.pdf

Golde, C., & Walker, G. (2006). *Envisioning the future of doctoral education: Preparing stewards of the discipline.* San Francisco, CA: Jossey-Bass.

Hall, B., & Closson, R. B. (2005). When the majority is the minority: White graduate students' social adjustment at a historically Black university. *Journal of College Student Development, 46*(1), 28–42.

Hinkle, D. E., Wiersma, W., & Jurs, S. G. (2003). *Applied statistics for the behavioral sciences.* Boston, MA: Houghton Mifflin Company.

Hirt, J. B., Strayhorn, T. L., Amelink, C. T., & Bennett, B. R. (2006). The nature of student affairs work at historically Black colleges and universities. *Journal of College and Student Development, 47*(6), 661–676.

Hurte, V. J. (2003). Mentoring: The forgotten retention tool. *Black Issues in Higher Education, 19*(18), 49–50.

Jackson, J. F. L. (2001, November). *Retention of African American administrators at predominantly White institutions: Using professional growth factors to inform the discussion.* Paper presented at the Annual Meeting of the Association for the Study of Higher Education, Richmond, VA. (ERIC Document Reproduction Service No. ED 457 818).

Jones, T. B., Wilder, A., & Osborne-Lampkin, L. (2013). The race against time: Preparing Black students for the changing landscape of higher education. *The Journal of Negro Education, 82*(3), 326–338.

Kuh, G. D. (2009). The National Survey of Student Engagement: Conceptual and empirical foundations. *New Directions for Institutional Research, 141,* 5–20.

Kuh, G. D., Kinzie, J., Schuh J. H., Whitt, E. J., & Associates. (2005). *Student success in college: Creating conditions that matter.* San Francisco, CA: Jossey-Bass.

Latiker, T. T. (2003, April). *A qualitative study of African American student persistence in a private Black college.* Paper presented at the Annual Meeting of the American Educational Research Association, Chicago, IL. (ERIC Document No. ED 477 444).

Lott, J. L. (2013). Racial identity and Black students' perceptions of community outreach: Implications for bonding social capital. *The Journal of Negro Education, 77*(1), 3–14.

Lovitts, B. E. (2005). Being a good course-taker is not enough: A theoretical perspective on the transition to independent research. *Studies in Higher Education, 30*(2), 137–154.

Lubienski, S. T., Miller, E. K., & Saclarides, E. K. (2017). Sex differences in doctoral student publication rates. *Educational Researcher, 47*(1), 76–81.

Lundy-Wagner, V., Vultaggio, J., & Gasman, M. (2013). Preparing underrepresented students of color for doctoral success: The role of undergraduate institutions. *International Journal of Doctoral Studies, 8,* 151–172. Retrieved from http://ijds.org/Volume8/IJDSv8p151-172Lundy-Wagner0381.pdf

Maton, K. I., & Hrabrowski, F. A., III. (2014). Increasing the number of African American PhDs in the sciences and engineering: A strengths-based approach. *American Psychologist, 59*(6), 547–556.

McGlynn, A. P. (2006). Mentoring and the STEM gender gap: AWIS and MentorNet confront the divide. *The Hispanic Outlook in Higher Education, 16,* 31.

Means, D. R., Beatty, C. C., Blockett, R. A., Bumbrey, M., Canida, R. L., & Cawthorn, T. W. (2016). Resilient scholars: Reflections from Black gay men on the doctoral journey. *Journal of Student Affairs, Research and Practice, 54,* 109–120.

National Center for Education Statistics. (2012). *The condition of education 2012.* Washington, DC: US Department of Education. Retrieved from https://nces.ed.gov/fastfacts/display.asp?id=72

National Center for Education Statistics. (2005). *Doctor's degrees conferred by degree-granting institutions, by sex, racial/ethnic group, and major field of study: 2003–04.* Washington, DC: US Department of Education. Retrieved from http://nces.ed.gov/programs/digest/d05/tables/xls/tabn268.xls

National Center for Education Statistics. (2015). *Selected statistics on degree-granting historically Black colleges and universities, by control and level of institution: Selected years, 1990 through 2013.* Washington, DC: US Department of Education. Retrieved from http://nces.ed.gov/programs/digest/d14/tables/dt14_313.30.asp?current=yes

National Opinion Research Center. (2006). *Survey of earned doctorates: Summary report 2005.* Washington, DC: National Academy Press. Retrieved from http://www.norc.org/NR/rdonlyres/2E87F80C-82F6-4E26-9F78-CA4C6E0B79C6/0/sed2005.pdf

National Opinion Research Center. (2007). *Survey of earned doctorates: Summary report 2006*. Washington, DC: National Academy Press. Retrieved from http://www.norc.org/NR/rdonlyres/C22A3F40-0BA2-4993-A6D3-5E659 39EEDC3/0/ 06SRFinalVersion.pdf

National Science Foundation (2014). *Doctorate recipients from US universities: 2014*. Retrieved from https://www.nsf.gov/statistics/2016/nsf16300/digest/ theme1.cfm

Nerad, M., & Miller, D. S. (1996). Increasing student retention in graduate and professional programs. *New Directions in Institutional Research, 92*, 61–76.

Nettles, M. T., & Millet, C. M. (2006). *Three magic letters: Getting to Ph.D.* Baltimore, MD: Johns Hopkins University Press.

Okahana, H., Allum, J., Felder, P. P., & Tull, R. G. (2016). Implications for practice and research from Doctoral Initiative on Minority Attrition and Completion (CGS Data Sources PLUS #16-01). Washington, DC: Council of Graduate Schools.

O'Meara, K., Knudsen, K., & Jones, J. (2010). The role of emotional competencies in faculty–doctoral student relationships. *The Review of Higher Education, 36*(3), 315–347.

Ottinger, C., Sikula, R., & Washington, C. (1993). *Production of minority doctorates* (Research Briefs, Vol. 4, No. 8). Washington, DC: American Council on Education.

Palmer, R. T., & Gasman, M. (2008). "It takes a village to raise a child": The role of social capital in promoting academic success of African American men at a Black college. *Journal of College Student Development, 49*(1), 52–70.

Palmer, R. T., Hilton, A. A., & Fountaine, T. P. (Eds.). (2012). *Black graduate education at historically Black colleges and universities: Trends, experiences, and outcomes*. New York: Information Age Press.

Pascarella, E. T., & Terenzini, P. T. (2005). *How college affects students: A third decade of research*. San Francisco, CA: Jossey-Bass.

Patterson-Stewart, K., Richie, M. H., & Sanders, E. T. W. (1997). Interpersonal dynamics of African American persistence in doctoral programs at predominantly white universities. *Journal of College Student Development, 38*(5), 489–498.

Pontius, J., & Harper, S. (2006). Principles for good practice in graduate and professional student engagement. *New Directions for Student Services, 115*, 47–58.

Reeder, M. C., & Schmitt, N. (2013). Motivational and judgment predictors of African American academic achievement at PWIs and HBCUs. *Journal of College Student Development, 54*(1), 29–42.

Roach, R. (1997, July). Clouded optimism: Graduate and professional degree rate among minorities outpaces that of whites, but experts predict surge will end if affirmative action backlash continues. *Black Issues in Higher Education, 14*(11), 17.

Santos, S. J., & Reigadas, E. T. (2005). Understanding the student-faculty mentoring process: Its effects on at-risk university students. *Journal of College Student Retention, 6*(3), 337–358.

Seagram, B. C., Gould, J., & Pike, S. W. (1998). An investigation of gender and other variables on time to completion of doctoral degrees. *Research in Higher Education, 39*(3), 319–335.

Spaulding, L. S., & Rockinson-Szapkiw, A. J. (2012). Hearing their voices: Factors doctoral candidates attribute to their persistence. *International Journal of Doctoral Studies, 7*, 199–219. Retrieved from http://ijds.org/Volume7/IJD Sv7p199-219Spaulding334.pdf

St. John, E. (2000, July 6). More doctorates in the house—More African American students are receiving doctorates. *Black Issues in Higher Education.* Retrieved from http://findarticles.com/p/articles/mi_m0DXK/is_10_17/ai_63817017

Tedla, E. (1995). *Sankofa: African thought and education.* New York: Lang Publishing.

Terenzini, P. T., Yaeger, P. M., Bohr, L., Pascarella, E. T., & Nora, A. (1997). *African American college students' experiences in HBCUs and PWIs and learning outcomes.* University Park, PA: National Center on Postsecondary Teaching, Learning, and Assessment.

Thompson, G. L. (1999). What the numbers really mean: African American underrepresentation at the doctoral level. *Journal of College Student Retention, 1*(1), 23–40.

Tinto, V. (1993). *Leaving college: Rethinking the causes and cures of student attrition* (2nd ed.). Chicago, IL: University of Chicago Press.

Turner, C. S. V., & Thompson, J. R. (1993). Socializing women doctoral students: Minority and majority experiences. *Review of Higher Education, 16*(3), 355–370.

Watson, L. W., & Kuh, G. D. (1996). The influence of dominant race environments on students' involvement, perception and educational gains: A look at historically Black and predominantly White liberal arts institutions. *Journal of College Student Development, 37*(3), 415–424.

Willie, C. V., Grady, M. K., & Hope, R. O. (1991). *African Americans and the doctoral experience: Implications for policy.* New York, NY: Teachers College Press.

Wilson, V. W., Andrews, M., & Leners, D. W. (2006). Mentoring as a strategy for retaining racial and ethnically diverse students on nursing programs. *Journal of Multicultural Nursing & Health, 12*(3), 17–24.

Chapter 8

Double Consciousness

Exploring Black and Doctoral Student Identity within Cross-Race Advising Relationships

Marco J. Barker and C. Ellen Washington

Introduction

African American or Black doctoral students in predominantly white institutions (PWIs) often face the reality of navigating spaces where they are underrepresented while also developing their scholarly or doctoral identities within their respective fields (M. Barker, 2012; P. P. Felder, Stevenson, & Gasman, 2014). This is compounded by the already small percentage of U.S. citizens with doctoral degrees. According to the U.S. Census Bureau (2017), 1.1% percent of Blacks 25 years and older hold doctoral degrees. In comparison to all U.S. citizens, Black doctoral degree holders comprise only 0.1% of those 25 years and older. Blacks are also underrepresented at the doctoral level. Table 8.1 on page 182 indicates that among doctoral degrees conferred between fall 2012 and fall 2013, Blacks received 6.9% of doctoral degrees conferred, while Asian Americans, Whites, and international students comprised 10.5%, 63.3%, and 11.6% of doctoral degree holders, respectively (DOE, 2014).

Additionally, these data provide implications for the presence of Black faculty among the faculty ranks. Not surprisingly, Blacks comprise only 6% of full-time instructional faculty (NCES, 2003). These and prior data indicate that Black doctoral students are in a world where there are

Table 8.1. Degrees Conferred by Sex and Race, 2012–2013

Type of Degree	Total	% American Indian and Alaska Native	% Asian American and Pacific Islander	% Black	% Latina/o	% Two or more races	% White	% International
Associate's degrees	1,006,961	1.0	4.9	13.5	15.7	1.9	61.3	1.7
Bachelor's degrees	1,840,164	0.6	7.1	10.4	10.1	1.9	66.4	3.5
Master's degrees	751,751	0.5	6.0	11.7	7.0	1.6	60.6	12.6
Doctoral degrees	175,038	0.5	10.5	6.9	5.8	1.4	63.3	11.6
Professional degrees	100,356	0.5	13.7	7.2	6.6	1.7	67.9	2.4

not many who share their distinct experiences of being Black and holding an academic doctoral degree.

The concept of existing in two worlds is not a new concept. Du Bois (1903) recognized the psychological and socially complexity of Blacks at the beginning of the 20th century. He stated,

> It is a peculiar sensation, this double-consciousness, this sense of always looking at one's self through the eyes of others, of measuring one's soul by the tape of a world that looks on in amused contempt and pity. One ever feels his two-ness—an American, a Negro; two souls, two thoughts, two unreconciled strivings; two warring ideals in one dark body, whose dogged strength alone keeps it from being torn asunder. (p. 9)

Du Bois eloquently captured this concept of this two-ness, and it is consistent in how Blacks experience their doctoral programs. Research on the Black doctoral experience already indicates how Black doctoral students, and in some instances other students of color (Winkle-Wagner, Johnson, Morelon-Quainoo, & Santiague, 2010), are left to not only move through a doctoral program but to do so while having racialized experiences—being marginalized, experiencing racism, being underestimated, and feeling isolated because of their race (M. Barker, 2012; M. J. Barker, 2014; P. P. Felder & Barker, 2013; P. P. Felder et al., 2014; Gasman, Gerstl-Pepin, Anderson-Thompkins, Rasheed, & Hathaway, 2004; Green & Kim, 2005; Milner, 2004; Patterson-Stewart, Ritchie, & Sanders, 1997).

While student interactions in doctoral programs have been understood generally, this volume calls for an understanding of experiences through a more Afrocentric lens—Sankofa. Therefore, this chapter applies the Sankofa element by exploring the dynamics of identity and student–faculty interactions and its connection to race and the "two-ness" that DuBois addressed. In the African culture, community is important to understanding one's own identity, duties, obligations, and relatedness to others (Tedla, 1995). The concept of community is rooted in the Sankofa tradition known as "Mahbereseb" (Tedla, 1995, p. 56), which emphasizes that it is through community by which an individual comes to understand self. To compare with doctoral student identity, doctoral students undergo a process of socialization within their professional or disciplinary community with the intent of developing their scholar identity in their respective field (Gardner, 2009). For Black doctoral students, the doctoral experience calls for them to navigate both their doctoral identity and racial identity. This experience is further complicated by the fact that individuals of African culture face processes reflective Western ways of thinking (Tedla, 1995) and institutions embedded with racism (Harper, Patton, & Wooden, 2009). The utilization of W. E. B Dubois's double consciousness aims to support the *Sankofan* theme of this volume. As "*Sankofan* education promotes understanding and appreciation of sensibilities, experiences and creations of continental and diasporan Africans" (Temple, 2010), this chapter exposes how Black doctoral students in cross-race doctoral advising relationships experience doctoral education. Additionally, it supports the Sankofa tradition (Jones & Leitner, 2015) through recognizing the historical context of race and oppression through the contemporary narratives of the study participants. To explore this "two-ness" or how double consciousness may manifest in the lives of Black doctoral students, this chapter provides empirical evidence on the lived of experiences of Black students and how these students fully live the Nkyinkyim principle of playing many parts to be versatile and resilient (Tedla, 1995). We address the research question: How do Black doctoral students in cross-race advising relationships with White faculty advisors navigate their doctoral experience and how race plays a role in this process?

Literature Review

To further explore the phenomenon of how Black doctoral students come to understand and manage their racial and doctoral experiences and identities, this constructed literature review addresses two areas of literature: a) the development of doctoral identity and b) the racial experiences and racial identity of doctoral students.

Development of Doctoral Identity

Scholars describe the development of a doctoral identity as undergoing a form of socialization and as being developmental (Gardner & Barnes, 2007; Golde, 2005; Lovitts, 2001; Tinto, 1975) along with definitive milestones—course taking, comprehensive exams, approval of the dissertation prospectus, the research and writing of the dissertation, and the final oral defense (Walker, Golde, Jones, Bueschel, & Hutchings, 2008, p. 10). Specific to socialization, Weidman, Twale, and Stein (2001) identified two central components of socialization: The process is developmental, and there are core elements related to "role identity" and "commitment" (p. 11). The authors posited that developing an identity or role acquisition was at the cornerstone of acclimating to the profession.

While socialization provides a framework for how students come to develop their identity within the profession, Gardner (2010) found it to be limiting in capturing the personal developmental process that occurs during the doctoral student experience. According to Gardner (2010), doctoral students undergo development in three key areas while navigating the doctorate: psychosocial development, social identity development, and cognitive-structural development. We focus on social identity in this literature review given the focus of this chapter. Within social identity development, Gardner emphasizes the importance of recognizing and understanding that doctoral students enter their programs with diverse backgrounds, including race, gender, and other forms of sociocultural identities. Gardner and Barker concluded that while graduate and professional students go through the socialization process and navigate these milestones, they may also begin to "reconcile their identity as individuals, students, and professionals in their field" (p. 39). The concepts of identity and socialization are tightly woven together when exploring doctoral student identity development (Baker & Lattuca, 2010).

Furthermore, for students of color, engagement and identity development happens very differently, especially in predominantly White contexts, given that these students often do not have the same emotional and social support as their White peers and given that there are fewer opportunities for them to engage faculty who look like them or who have had similar intersecting cultural and doctoral experiences (P. P. Felder et al., 2014; Winkle-Wagner et al., 2010). Therefore, it is important to explore the experiences of students of color and, in this particular chapter, the experiences of Black students, to better understand how racial experiences further shape Black doctoral students' doctoral process.

Racial Experiences and Racial Identity of Black Doctoral Students

Black doctoral students experience a range of experiences during the doctoral process that may influence their perceptions of departmental climate, sense of affirmation and support, and ability to form connections within their department and profession (Anderson-Thompkins, Gasman, Gerstl-Pepin, Hathaway, & Rasheed, 2004; M. Barker, 2012; M. J. Barker,

2014; P. P. Felder & Barker, 2013; Gasman et al., 2004; Gildersleeve, Croom, & Vasquez, 2011; Jones, 2000; Mabokela & Green, 2000; Milner, 2004; Rogers & Molina, 2006). Black graduate and doctoral students have reported institutional climates that were unfriendly or that merely lacked diversity (P. Felder, 2010; Willie, Grady, & Hope, 1991), while others have reported issues of stereotype threat, tokenism, marginalization, and labeling (P. P. Felder & Barker, 2013; Taylor & Antony, 2000). Particularly in predominantly White contexts, Black doctoral students are often the target of microaggressions (Gildersleeve et al., 2011), or they become salient objects (M. Barker, 2012) as the only person of color or Black student in these spaces. In other instances, Black doctoral students' racial background and culture are not appreciated, which results in students feeling a sense of "social estrangement and sociocultural alienation" (Robinson, 1999, p. 124).

The racialized experiences that Black doctoral students have during their doctoral programs may impact how they come to understand and develop their own cultural, racial, and doctoral identities. Davidson and Foster-Johnson (2001) forwarded that many graduate programs approach socialization from the perspective of assimilation as opposed to cultural pluralism or recognizing each person's background and either cultural contribution. Additionally, scholars contend that Black doctoral students are more successful when they are able to connect with their racial identity and with the Black community (Acosta, Duggins, Moore, Adams, & Johnson, 2015; M. Barker, 2012; M. J. Barker, 2014; P. P. Felder et al., 2014; Sulé, 2009; Winkle-Wagner et al., 2010). While Black doctoral students carry this higher social responsibility to their race and in some cases find community among other Black doctoral students, faculty, and staff, Barker (2012) found that they still struggled with whether and how to bring their race into their doctoral experience. And while Barker's (2012) study of Black doctoral students explicitly examined students' racial identity, it did not capture the full extent to which those doctoral students wrestled with developing both a doctoral and racial identity. To better understand the unique experience of Black doctoral students and their ability to reconcile their doctoral socialization and racial identity, we use Du Bois's concept of double consciousness.

Conceptual Framework: Double Consciousness

In *The Souls of Black Folk* (Du Bois, 1903), Du Bois wrote, "The history of the American Negro is the history of this strife,—this longing to attain self-conscious manhood, to merge his double self into a better and truer self." Du Bois's recognition of a "double consciousness" is that of a repressive culture that forced Blacks to see themselves through the eyes of the dominant White society (Rath, 1997). Having two antagonistic identities means time and energy negotiating and enduring conflicts between who one is as a person and how one deals with the misrepresentations of the outside world. Du Bois outlines double consciousness as having three issues: the real power of white stereotypes on Black life and thought, double consciousness as created by practical racism that excludes Black Americans from mainstream society, and the internal conflict between what is "African" and what is "American" (Du Bois, 1903).

According to E. Victor Wolfenstein (2007), "on a psychological level, the veil of 'double-consciousness' transforms the hyphen in African-American into the painful two-ness of self-alienation" (pp. 8–9). Du Bois believed that the true self-consciousness prevented by this condition may be a merging of two positive identities (Black and American) without the harmful ascription, contempt, and negation from the outside world. Du Bois (1965) writes,

> The history of the American Negro is the history of this strife—this longing to attain self-conscious manhood, to merge his double self into a better and truer self. In this merging, he wishes neither of the older selves to be lost. He would not Africanize America . . . He would not bleach his Negro soul . . . He simply wishes to make it possible for a man to be both a Negro and an American, without being cursed and spit upon by his fellow, without having the doors of Opportunity closed roughly in his face. This, then, is the end of his striving; to be a co-worker in the kingdom of culture. (p. 215)

This double consciousness framework speaks to the fact that two American cultures—(a) mainstream American and (b) African American ideas and practices—shape the daily lives of many African Americans (Brannon, Markus, & Taylor, 2015). This results in self-schemas, which are cognitive structures that direct and regulate self and behavioral processes that lead to individuals asking questions such as *Who am I?*, *What should I be doing?*, and *How do I relate to others?* (Banaji & Prentice, 1994; H. Markus, 1977; H. R. Markus & Kitayama, 2010).

Methodology

This study used a qualitative, phenomenological method to understand how Black doctoral students engaged in cross-race relationships managed and understood their own racial and doctoral identities during their doctoral program. Phenomenology allows the researcher to "focus on exploring how human beings make sense of experience and transform experience into consciousness, both individually and as shared meaning" (Patton, 2002, p. 104).

The study, which was originally conducted by Barker (2010), included doctoral students who self-identified as Black or African American, completed at least two years of coursework, and had a faculty advisor who self-identified as White. The researcher invited all Black doctoral students in social sciences, humanities, and business at one research-extensive PWI and accepted referrals from other doctoral students and faculty of the same institution. As a result, the final sample included seven Black doctoral students (see Table 8.2).

DATA COLLECTION

This study's data represent data from a larger study that examined cross-race advising relationships between White faculty advisors and Black doctoral student protégés. Interviews were 60 to 90 minutes, and they followed an open-ended interview protocol. In the study, Barker (2010) conducted one-on-one interviews with each student, and data were transcribed and

Table 8.2. Black Doctoral Student Participants

Student	Race	Gender	Age	Years in Program
Daphne	B	F	30–35	More than 3.5
James	B	M	25–30	Fewer than 3.5
Jordan	B	F	30–35	More than 3.5
Lionel	B	M	35–40	Fewer than 3.5
Marion	B	F	30–35	Fewer than 3.5
Terrie	B	F	30–35	More than 3.5
Walter	B	M	35–40	More than 3.5

Participants self-identified as Black = B, Female = F, or Male = M.

coded utilizing NVivo software. Some questions included "Are you able to discuss race-related issues (related or not related to your education) with your advisor/student? and "Have you faced any issues, obstacles, or experiences in your program, department, institution, or discipline that you attribute to your race?"

DATA ANALYSIS

A specific constant comparative method for dual pairs served as an analytical tool to compare responses of individuals, advising pairs, and racial groups (Boeije, 2002). This constant comparative method for dyads included 1) comparison within a single interview, 2) comparison between interviews within the same group, 3) comparison of interviews from different groups, 4) comparison in pairs at the level of the couple, and 5) comparing couples. In terms of research actions, Barker (2010) completed open coding through analysis of each individual, axial coding through analysis of the Black doctoral students alone, triangulation through comparing the Black doctoral perspective with that of their faculty members, thematic coding through comparing each faculty-study pair, and couple comparison through analysis of each cross-race pair with the other. The use of phenomenological reduction allowed for the identification of descriptions only related to the research topic and for the further reduction of descriptions into themes and subsequently "textual descriptions" (Moustakas, 1994, p. 97). Barker and Washington further analyzed descriptions within the Black doctoral student group from the 2010 study to identify themes reflective of the double consciousness theoretical framework.

TRUSTWORTHINESS AND LIMITATIONS

From the original study, Barker (2010) completed reflexivity through a process of "self-reflections" and identifying "biases" (Johnson & Christensen, 2004, p. 249) and conducted member checks through having study participants review the verbatim transcript and provide any necessary edits or clarifications. Additionally, the original study relied on theory triangulation using critical race theory (Ladson-Billings & Tate, 1995), research on faculty–doctoral student interaction (Lovitts, 2001), cross-cultural interaction (Goto, 1997), and the impact of race on college life and student development (Astin, 1993; Pascarella & Terenzini, 2005; Tinto, 1975).

This study's scope represents one institution in the American South, a region in the United States with a distinct and unique history (Anderson, 1988), which may make aspects of the participants' experience unique to a particular region. The study also includes participants who were in the social sciences, humanities, and business. At the doctoral level, disciplinary differences and nuances significantly impact the doctoral experience (Gardner, 2007, 2008), which may make the results of the study not applicable to science, technology, engineering, and mathematics (STEM) and professional programs. Last, the researcher's own level of subjectivity (Riley, Schouten, & Cahill, 2003) may exist in this culturally based research.

Findings

The doctoral students in this study described instances of how they managed and navigated their doctoral students in the context of race; or, in turn, how they managed and navigated their racial experiences in the context of a doctoral program. Both perspectives are valid approaches given the two-ness that Black doctoral students experience during their pursuit of the PhD. There were three themes that emerged from these students' narratives that illustrated both competing and intersecting identities: a) identifying individuals who share the experience, b) otherness and sense of belonging, and c) at the intersection of doctoral and racial identity.

Identifying Individuals Who Share the Experience

Within this theme, doctoral students shared the importance of connecting with other Black doctoral students, faculty, and staff. This need to connect with other members of the Black community speaks to how students searched for opportunities to relate to others. There is an African term, *yilougnta*, or community-mindedness, that emphasizes the importance of feeling connected to one's community (Tedla, 1995, p. 66). Because Black doctoral students are underrepresented in doctoral education, they may struggle to find community among others who share their unique teaching, learning, and racial experiences—impacting their own doctoral socialization (Felder, Stevenson, & Gasman, 2014). Given the role of community in African culture and its importance in navigating the doctoral process, it made it even more important for students to form connections. Furthermore, findings students who shared the experience addressed how being in these communities or spaces allowed students to be affirmed in their feelings and experiences of being Black doctoral students in predominantly White environments. One doctoral student, Daphne, reflected on the importance of her all-Black female support network of doctoral students:

> Well, first of all, they were African American and they were female. And I did not have that in my department at all. It was good to go and be around people who were like me and who understood what I was going through. Who understood I'm in a class with all these White men and old White male teachers that I'm speaking for the race and the gender. You know, still, it was just [that] they understood what I was going through at the time. They had experienced it you know. It was just a good support. And I did do social things with them. I went to one of their houses. One time we had dinner. Another time I went to one of the girls' houses and we had like wine and dinner and just talking and stuff like that.

Daphne continuously identified the clear distinction of what it meant to navigate between worlds—her fellow Black female doctoral student community and her predominantly white classroom. She later shared more explicitly about how a Black support network was different from the broader doctoral group:

> It was completely different because I was able to let my guard down because I felt they understood what I was going through, you know; it was just completely different. They were out of my department. They were in another department, so I just felt like I was able to let my guard down. They were like mothers. They were older than me. I felt I wasn't being challenged or intimidated. They were very accepting and they were really trying to genuinely help me and not hurt me in any kind of way.

Similarly, two additional students, Jordan and Terrie, found other Black doctoral students as a support system. Jordan had a Black female confidant in her program with whom to share feelings, thoughts, and issues. She commented,

> My colleagues in my department, one in particular, I mean, everything that has happened to me, she knows. Everything that has happened to her I know about. We just talk about everything. That feels good to have someone to vent to, but somebody who's in the same experience so she can identify and give me advice or whatever support.

Terrie also saw the value of a support system of Black doctoral students on campus. For Terrie, having same-race support provided her with other individuals "who understand what I'm going through and they can relate to the feelings that I have."

Last, James commented how he spent a great deal of time in the cultural office and McNair office because of the diversity of individuals in the offices. Forming racial-based connections is incredibly important for students given that doctoral programs can be developmental (Baker & Lattuca, 2010; Gardner, 2009) and that Black doctoral students may be experiencing their own racial identity development (M. Barker, 2012). Furthermore, studies (Brannon et al., 2015) have indicated that having a sense of double consciousness where African Americans connect with members of their community can have positive effects on the ability of college students to perform, which may translate well for doctoral students.

Otherness and Sense of Belonging

The theme of otherness and sense of belonging captures the notion that instances where Black doctoral students encounter racism, marginalization, and other forms of isolation can have a negative impact on their doctoral experience and ability to establish themselves in the discipline. This particular theme is consistent with Du Bois's double consciousness—emphasizing how the sense of two-ness is precipitated by negative experiences faced by Black doctoral students. In these moments, students feel the severity of being the other and truly having to navigate in two worlds.

Racial marginalization occurs when students feel objectified based on their race (Suarez-Balcazar, Orellana-Damacela, Portillo, Rowan, & Andrews-Guillen, 2003). Some doctoral students experienced marginalization through departmental events. One student, Daphne, often felt that she was invited to departmental events and social functions because she represented the "diversity" of the department. James also described his involvement in faculty recruitment activities and being asked to participate when there were minority faculty visiting the campus as opposed to all faculty visits. In the case of Walter, he felt that the attitude among the faculty was, " 'Well that's Walter, he's our affirmative action initiative.' Don't have any proof of that . . . I can [see] other students there were shown a little more consideration for going to conferences or whatever." Daphne, James, and Walter all recognized some form of objectification, which further created this figurative line where their doctoral identity was on one side and their racial identity (i.e., Blackness) was on the other.

Students also noted how they saw departmental practices as treating Black doctoral students differently. Lionel, a student who also had family obligations, perceived his department as indirectly and negatively impacting Black doctoral students by encouraging them not to work full-time in lieu of designing programs that would allow for other ways to complete the program:

> I learned about this residency requirement about going to school full-time for a year and I thought, "There's not a Black person I know who can just afford to go to school full time for a whole year." And, I blamed that directly to race. I think that was like this [legal] barrier to get, you know, more African Americans not being able to get through the program.

Jordan also felt that departmental racism was practiced through the ease with which White students finished the program compared to her. These two examples illustrate how Black doctoral students may experience the world different and apart from their White counterparts. However, students also experienced racism through their interactions with students and faculty. In their relationships with faculty, two students described how they were underestimated by their faculty members. Walter recalled an experience where he completed an exam and faculty members were surprised by how well he articulated his arguments. Marion had an experience where she was mistaken for a master's-level student in one encounter, and in another encounter, she received a grade lower than expected—she wondered if race was at the center of both experiences:

> I always kind of think about [race]. It's always kind of there. Did I really just get this B or did you just grade me even harder . . . you know, I have gotten that from one member of the faculty. It was kind of like, when I first met her, she

> was like, "Oh you're a master's student." I was like, "No I'm a doctoral student." Every time I see her, it's kind of like [her] nose up in the air, kind of thing. Like, "You didn't see me coming down the hall when we were the only two people?" So, from that, I've got to prove myself because I am the only [Black student] and so, I'm always working harder and stuff. So anytime something like that comes up, it always crosses your mind like, "You grade me harder because you feel I'm not supposed to be here," that kind of thing.

The racialized experiences or acts of racism that Black doctoral students face served to remind Black doctoral students that they were others. These experiences also suggested to students that they and other Black doctoral students may not belong. This feeling of the other perpetuates the notion of double consciousness as students must consider and determine how they are viewed by "others" while also navigating the program to be successful.

At the Intersection of Doctoral and Racial Identity

The students described instances where race and discussions of race emerged in their doctoral programs, which pointed to a greater interconnection between their culture and the doctoral program. It appeared that academic contexts (i.e., class topic, research project, dissertation topic) allowed for the best opportunity for faculty and students to discuss race. Five of the seven doctoral students mentioned that they gained insight into their advisor's perceptions and understandings of race through discussing research. The doctoral students in the study had either conducted research on a race-related topic or were in the process.

One student would discuss with her advisor the implications of her research on the political process. She provided an example:

> We've just been talking about how it's important for ethnic minorities to participate in the political process, be informed about the elections, and civic[ly] engage[d] . . . and how institutions of government have an obligation to help [ethnic minorities] be informed.

Another student shared his experience working with his faculty member and talking through the racial implications of the findings. He described the experience:

Looking at differences . . . 'cause with the family, we ask them a question about race—if they believed race influenced their current living conditions. Stemming from [this question], [we] talk about the differences and the stuff that we've noticed in different families, mainly between Whites and Blacks, because that's pretty much the dynamic in the city. There was another thing. We talked about, last week, the economic mobility and stuff. Like, how a lot of Black families have less mobility than White women and how the economic philosophies in social work are off . . . that kind of thing. And, [we discussed] different perceptions and how research has put stuff out there versus the actual reality and stuff. [For example], how African Americans are not as successful but that might not be the case. So, it kind of stems from research, but we've gone into a lot of different topics and stuff about that.

In cases where the faculty advisor's research was not related to race or connected with the doctoral student, the students still found opportunities for engagement. There were students in the study who shared how their faculty advisor would ask questions on the respective topic. One student, Lionel, provided an example: "He's asked me about it, and I've explained it to him, and he's talked to other professors about it, and he thinks it's very interesting." Lionel described how his professor was willing to learn more and to assist Lionel in completing his research. Students studying race felt that their faculty advisor had an understanding of the research, was willing to learn more about the topic, or was able to direct them to others who had greater expertise.

For doctoral students who study race, there may exist a greater opportunity for connections between their doctoral experience and their race. Research also provides the doctoral student with a more formal process of connecting aspects of their identity within the context of their profession. This type of cultural connection during the doctoral process expands on the inclusion of social and cultural development in doctoral socialization (Gardner, 2009; Hall & Burns, 2009).

Conclusion

The increasing number of Blacks attaining PhDs has increased scholarly interest in the student experience. The doctoral students in this study described how they managed their doctoral process and how racial experiences impacted their doctoral identity, socialization, and overall experience. Identity for African Americans involves the psychological experience of double consciousness (Bell, 1990; Valentine, 1971). Reflecting on these deep roots, double consciousness influences and shapes the learning experiences of Black doctoral students in complex ways. Using Du Bois's concept of double consciousness, there were three themes identified to help examine the complexity of racial identity of Black doctoral students: a) identifying individuals who share the experience, b) otherness and sense of belonging, and c) at the intersection of doctoral and racial identify. These themes revealed the importance of socializing students into academic and professional roles.

According to Barker (2011), forming positive racial connections is vital for the success of doctoral students in predominantly White institutions (PWIs). When Black students feel marginalized and isolated, this negatively impacts their doctoral experiences and consequently their developmental identity. The literature is clear that there are many challenges for Black doctoral students at PWIs to overcome in order to complete a doctoral program.

Given the nuances of race in doctoral socialization, we recommend that academic programs consider developing doctoral mentoring programs for African American students or consider how existing mentoring programs are culturally responsive, reflective, and affirming (e.g., African American Doctoral Scholars Initiative at the University of Utah connects African American doctoral students with other students and mentors). According to the Council of Graduate Schools' PhD Project (2010), mentoring is one of the most effective and promising practices for successful student outcomes. This type of program will support the development of Black doctoral students at PWIs by providing doctoral students with the opportunity to share their racial experiences while also having more experienced scholars assist doctoral students in better putting their racial experiences in the context of the academic program and discipline. Furthermore, we recommend that programs recognize the critical importance that Black graduate student organizations play in the lives of Black doctoral students. Specific to programs with little diversity, whether among the student body or faculty ranks, student organizations provide a more formal way for students to find community when there is not a critical number within the program. Because students may have a heightened sense of double consciousness, having a support mechanism like a group can have a positive impact on the doctoral student's experience. For larger schools or academic colleges, cohort programs or scholar collectives provide a place where Black doctoral students or doctoral students of color more broadly may come together to discuss their racial experiences and their academic experiences. Previous research validates that Black doctoral students in PWI environments seek relationships with other Blacks to develop a trusted social network (Lewis, Ginsberg, Davis, & Smith, 2004). This type of engagement reinforces a commitment to students to be able see the intersection of racial and doctoral identities.

As an extension of mentoring, career counseling—particularly culturally responsive counseling—might also serve as a process for assisting Black doctoral students in developing their doctoral identity in culturally affirming ways. *The Pathways Through Graduate Schools and Into Careers* report (2012) included a recommendation calling for career counseling for graduate students at the doctoral level given that few doctoral students report receiving "professional skills development, resources, and guidance" for their career path (p. 31). Connecting career counseling to mentoring has the dual capacity to provide psychosocial support and career guidance. According to Felder, Stevenson, and Gasman (2014), students report having the most success with faculty mentoring when the relationships support their racial identity, research interests, and degree completion. In addition to career counseling, mental health and psychological counseling services may also benefit doctoral students. With Black doctoral students facing challenges of isolation and unique racial experiences, counseling can provide students with effective coping strategies. In this context, the students are able to connect with individuals they trust to talk openly about their fears and anxieties (Kram, 1988). Having a strong social support system has been considered beneficial to minorities in graduate school. According to McGaskey, Freeman, Guyton, Richmond, and Guyton (2016), Black doctoral students who developed primarily Black social support networks received emotional and instrumental support and helped to contribute to the doctoral student socialization process. According to Gasman, Hirschfield, and Vuttaggio (2008), African American graduate students seem to have lower levels of social and academic integration. There is research suggesting that students who successfully integrate into their programs' professional and social community (i.e., connecting to the academic community) have higher success rates in completing their degree programs (Hoskins & Goldberg, 2005).

As the number of Black doctoral students continues to rise, it is important to recognize the challenges that Black students face and the level of influence that interactions with faculty and peers has on their overall experience (National Center for Science and Engineering Statistics, 2012). Additionally, this growing number of Black doctoral students in higher education occurs during a time when Black bodies fall under attack, Black Lives Matters has become part of our nation's backdrop, and the souls of Black folk are in danger—both physically and spiritually. This study, and more broadly this book, urges doctoral programs to recognize the need for feeding the souls of Black folks in ways that foster a more inclusive environment and more specifically foster more positive experiences for Black doctoral students that is affirming, supportive, and culturally relevant.

Works Cited

Acosta, M., Duggins, S., Moore, T. E., Adams, T., & Johnson, B. (2015). "From whence cometh my help?" exploring Black doctoral student persistence. *Journal of Critical Scholarship on Higher Education and Student Affairs, 2*(1), 33–48.

Anderson, J. D. (1988). *The education of blacks in the South, 1860–1935.* Chapel Hill, NC: University of North Carolina Press.

Anderson-Thompkins, S., Gasman, M., Gerstl-Pepin, C., Hathaway, K. L., & Rasheed, L. (2004). "Casualties of war": Suggestions for helping African American graduate students succeed in the academy. In D. Clevelend (Ed.), *A long way to go: Conversations about race by African American faculty and graduate students* (pp. 228–240). New York: Peter Lang Publishing.

Astin, A. W. (1993). *What matters in college: Four critical years revisited.* San Francisco, CA: Jossey-Bass Publishers.

Baker, V. L., & Lattuca, L. R. (2010). Developmental networks and learning: Toward an interdisciplinary perspective on identity development during doctoral study. *Studies in Higher Education, 35*(7), 807–827.

Banaji, M. R., & Prentice, D. A. (1994). The self in social contexts. *Annual Review of Psychology, 45,* 297.

Barker, M. J. (2012). An exploration of racial identity among Black doctoral students involved in cross-race advising relationships. In J. Sullivan & A. Esmail (Eds.), *African American identity: Racial and cultural dimensions of the Black experience.* Lanham, MD: Lexington Books.

Barker, M. J. (2011). Racial context, currency, and connections: Black doctoral student and white faculty advisor perspectives on cross-race advising. *Innovative Education & Teaching International, 48*(4), 387–400.

Barker, M. J. (2014). Critiquing doctoral education: Moving toward a cross-race doctoral advising model. In P. P. Felder & E. P. St. John (Eds.), *Supporting* graduate students in the 21st century: Implications for policy and practice (Vol. 27, pp. 109–134). New York, NY: AMS Press.

Barker, M. J. (2010). Cross-race advising relationships: The role of race in advising relationships between Black doctoral student protégés and their White faculty advisors. PhD diss., Louisiana State University, Baton Rouge.

Bell, E. L. (1990). The bicultural life experience of career-oriented black women. Journal of Organizational Behavior, 11(6), 459–477.

Brannon, T. N., Markus, H. R., & Taylor, V. J. (2015). "Two souls, two thoughts," two self-schemas: Double consciousness can have positive academic consequences for African Americans. Journal of Personality and Social Psychology, 108(5), 586–609.

Council of Graduate Schools. (2010). Ph.D. completion and attrition: Policies and practices to promote student success. Retrieved from http://www.phd completion.org/information/executive_summary_student_success_book_iv. pdf

Council of Graduate Schools and Educational Testing Service. (2012). Pathways through graduate school and into careers. Report from the Commission on Pathways Through Graduate School and Into Careers. Princeton, NJ: Educational Testing Service. Retrieved from: http://pathwaysreport.org/rsc/ pdf/19089_PathwaysRept_Links.pdf

Davidson, M. N., & Foster-Johnson, L. (2001). Mentoring in the preparation of graduate researchers of color. Review of Educational Research, 71(4), 549–574.

Du Bois, W. E. B. (1903). The souls of black folk. Chicago, IL: A. C. McClurg & Co.

Felder, P. (2010). On doctoral student development: Exploring faculty mentorship and the shaping of African American doctoral student success. The Qualitative Report, 15(2), 455–474.

Felder, P. P., & Barker, M. J. (2013). Extending Bell's concept of interest convergence: A framework for understanding the African American doctoral student experience. International Journal of Doctoral Studies, 8, 1–20.

Felder, P. P., Stevenson, H. C., & Gasman, M. (2014). Understanding race in doctoral student socialization. International Journal of Doctoral Studies, 9, 21–42.

Gardner, S. K. (2009). The development of doctoral students: Phases of challenge and support. ASHE Higher Education Report Series (Vol. 34). San Francisco: Wiley Periodicals.

Gardner, S. K. (2010). Doctoral student development. In S. K. Gardner & P. Mendoza (Eds.), On becoming a scholar: Socialization and development in doctoral education (pp. 203–222). Sterling, VA: Stylus Publishing.

Gardner, S. K. (2008). Fitting the mold of graduate school: A qualitative study of socialization in doctoral education. Innovative Higher Education, 33, 125–138.

Gardner, S. K. (2007). "I heard it through the grapevine": Doctoral student socialization in chemistry and history. Higher Education, 54, 723–740.

Gardner, S. K., & Barnes, B. J. (2007). Graduate student involvement: Socialization for the professional role. *Journal of College Student Development, 48*(4), 369–387.

Gasman, M., Gerstl-Pepin, C., Anderson-Thompkins, S., Rasheed, L., & Hathaway, K. (2004). Negotiating power, developing trust: Transgressing race and status in the academy. *Teachers College Record, 106*(4), 689.

Gasman, M. Hirschfield, A., & Vuttaggio, J. (2008). "Difficult yet rewarding": The experiences of African American graduate students in education at an Ivy League institution. *Journal of Diversity in Higher Education, 2*, 126–138.

Gildersleeve, R. E., Croom, N. N., & Vasquez, P. L. (2011). "Am I going crazy?!": A critical race analysis of doctoral education. *Equity and Excellence in Education, 44*(1), 93–114.

Golde, C. M. (2005). The role of the department and discipline in doctoral student attrition: Lessons from four departments. *The Journal of Higher Education, 76*(6), 669.

Goto, S. G. (1997). Majority and minority perspectives on cross-cultural interactions. In C. S. Granrose & S. Oskamp (Eds.), *Cross-cultural work groups* (pp. 90–112). Thousand Oaks, CA: Sage Publications.

Green, D. O. N., & Kim, E. (2005). Experiences of Korean female doctoral students in academe: Raising voice against gender and racial stereotypes. *Journal of College Student Development, 46*(5), 487–500.

Hall, L. A., & Burns, L. D. (2009). Identity development and mentoring in doctoral education. *Harvard Educational Review, 79*(1), 49–70.

Harper, S. R., Patton, L. D., & Wooden, O. S. (2009) Access and equity for African American students in higher education: A critical race historical analysis of policy effort. *Journal of Higher Education, 80*(4), 389–414.

Hoskins, C. M., & Goldberg, A. D. (2005). Doctoral student persistence in counselor education programs: Student–program match. *Counselor Education and Supervision, 44*, 175–188.

Johnson, B., & Christensen, L. (2004). *Educational research: Quantitative, qualitative, and mixed approaches* (2nd ed.). Boston: Pearson Education, Inc.

Jones, J. M., & Leitner, J. B. (2015). The Sankofa effect: Divergent effects of thinking about the past for Blacks and Whites. In M. Stolarski, N. Fieulaine, & W. van Beek (Eds.), *Time perspective theory; review, research, and application: Essays in honor of Philip G. Zimbardo* (pp. 197–211). New York: Springer Publishing.

Jones, L. (2000). *Brothers of the academy: Up and coming Black scholars earning our way in higher education.* Sterling, VA: Stylus Publishing.

Kram, K. E. (1988). *Mentoring at work: Developing relationships in organizational life.* Lanham, MD: University Press of America.

Ladson-Billings, G., & Tate, W. F. (1995). Toward a critical race theory of education. *Teachers College Record, 97*(1), 47.

Lovitts, B. E. (2001). *Leaving the ivory tower: The causes and consequences of departure from doctoral study.* Lanham, MD: Rowman & Littlefield Publishers.

Mabokela, R. O., & Green, A. L. (2000). *Sisters of the academy: Emerging Black women scholars in higher education.* Sterling, VA: Stylus Publishing.

Markus, H. (1977). Self-schemata and processing information about the self. *Journal of Personality and Social Psychology, 35*(2), 63.

Markus, H. R., & Kitayama, S. (2010). Cultures and selves a cycle of mutual constitution. *Perspectives on Psychological Science, 5*(4), 420–430.

McGaskey, F., Freeman, S., Jr., Guyton, C., & Guyton, C. W. (2016). The social support networks of Black males in higher education administration doctoral programs: An exploratory study. *Western Journal of Black Studies, 40*(2), 141–158.

Milner, H. R. (2004). African American graduate students' experiences of African American students in higher education. In D. Cleveland (Ed.), *A long way to go: Conversations about race by African American faculty and graduate students* (pp. 19–31). New York, NY: Peter Lang Publishing, Inc.

NCES. (2003). *Work first, study second: Adult undergraduates who combine employment and postsecondary enrollment.* Retrieved from https://nces.ed.gov/pubs2003/2003167.pdf

National Science Foundation, National Center for Science and Engineering Statistics (NCSES). (2012). *Doctorate recipients from U.S. Universities: 2011.* Special Report NSF 13-301. Arlington, VA. Retrieved from https://www.nsf.gov/statistics/doctorates/

Pascarella, E. T., & Terenzini, P. T. (2005). *How college affects students* (Vol. 2, 2nd ed.). San Francisco, CA: Jossey-Bass Publishing.

Patterson-Stewart, K. E., Ritchie, M. H., & Sanders, E. T. W. (1997). Interpersonal dynamics of African American persistence in doctoral programs at predominantly White universities. *Journal of College Student Development, 38*(5), 489–498.

Patton, M. Q. (2002). *Qualitative research and evaluation methods.* Thousands Oaks, CA: Sage.

Rath, R. C. (1997). Echo and Narcissus: The Afrocentric pragmatism of W. E. B. Du Bois. *The Journal of American History, 84*(2), 461–495.

Riley, S., Schouten, W., & Cahill, S. (2003). Exploring the dynamics of subjectivity and power between researcher and researched. *Forum: Qualitative Social Research, 4*(2). Retrieved from http://www.qualitative-research.net/index.php/fqs/article/view/713

Robinson, C. (1999). Developing a mentoring program: A graduate student's reflection of change. *Peabody Journal of Education, 74*(2), 119–134.

Rogers, M. R., & Molina, L. E. (2006). Exemplary efforts in psychology to recruit and retain graduate students of color. *American Psychologist, 61*(2), 143.

Suarez-Balcazar, Y., Orellana-Damacela, L., Portillo, N., Rowan, J. M., & Andrews-Guillen, C. (2003). Experiences of differential treatment. *Journal of Higher Education*, 428–444.

Sulé, V. T. (2009). Oppositional stances of Black female graduate students. In M. F. Howard-Hamilton, C. L. Morelon-Quainoo, S. D. Johnson, R. Winkle-Wagner, & L. Santiague (Eds.), *Standing on the outside looking in* (pp. 147–168). Sterling, VA: Stylus.

Taylor, E., & Antony, J. S. (2000). Stereotype threat reduction and wise schooling: Towards the successful socialization of African American doctoral students in education. *The Journal of Negro Education, 69*(3), 184–198.

Tedla, E. (1995). *Sankofa: African thought and education.* New York: Lang Publishing.

Temple, C. N. (2010). The emergence of Sankofa practice in the United States: A monder history. *Journal of Black Studies, 41*(1), 127–150.

Tinto, V. (1975). Dropout from higher education: A theoretical synthesis of recent research. *Review of Educational Research, 45*, 89–125.

U.S. Census Bureau. (2017). *Current population survey: 2017 annual social and economic supplement.* Retrieved from https://www.census.gov/data/tables/2017/demo/education-attainment/cps-detailed-tables.html

U.S. Department of Education, National Center for Education Statistics, Integrated Postsecondary Education Data System. (2014). *Degrees conferred by sex and race, 2012-2013.*

Valentine, C. A. (1971). Deficit differences, and bicultural models of Afro-American behavior. *Harvard Educational Review, 41*(2), 127–157.

Walker, G. E., Golde, C. M., Jones, L., Bueschel, A. C., & Hutchings, P. (2008). *The formation of scholars: Rethinking doctoral education for the twenty-first century.* San Francisco, CA: The Carnegie Foundation for the Advancement of Teaching. Jossey-Bass Publishing.

Washington, B. T., Du Bois, W. E. B., & Johnson, J. W. (1965). *Three Negro classics: Up from slavery: The souls of Black folk.* New York, NY: Avon Books.

Weidman, J. C., Twale, D. J., & Stein, E. L. (2001). *Socialization of graduate and professional students in higher education: A perilous passage?* (Vol. 28). New York, NY: Jossey-Bass.

Willie, C. V., Grady, M. K., & Hope, R. O. (1991). *African-Americans and the doctoral experience: Implications for policy.* New York, NY: Teachers College Press.

Winkle-Wagner, R., Johnson, S. D., Morelon-Quainoo, C., & Santiague, L. (2010). A sense of belonging: Socialization factors that influence the transitions of students of color into advanced-degree programs. In S. K. Gardner & P. Mendoza (Eds.), *On becoming a scholar: Socialization and development in doctoral education* (pp. 179–199). Sterling, VA: Stylus Publishing.

Wolfenstein, E. V. (2007). *A gift of the spirit: Reading the souls of Black folk*: Ithaca, NY: Cornell University Press.

Conclusion

Pamela Felder Small and Marco J. Barker

"The forces that unite us are intrinsic and greater than the superimposed influences that keep us apart."

—Kwame Nkrumah

The words of Nkrumah, former Ghanaian leader, quoted in the epigraph capture the notion that we owe it to ourselves to understand our strengths, and once we do, we must put that knowledge to use in order to strengthen our communities. In this volume, we seek to expand our understanding of the role of race in doctoral education and the importance of the cultural significance of Black doctoral students' identity at the intersection of professional, doctoral, and personal identities. We use the principle of Sankofa—which speaks to the power of Black doctoral students' narratives and how these narratives could improve doctoral education outcomes for all students—and place Afrocentrism at the center of understanding and critiquing doctoral education. Capturing the racialized experiences of doctoral students is consistent with the Sankofa principle of meaning-making. According to Jones and Leitner (2015), "culture and the meanings that attach to it also give order, coherence, and meaning to events" (p. 197). The narratives and perspectives presented in this volume capture how the journey toward and through a doctoral degree has traditionally left out the voice of Black doctoral students, as well as the role of historically Black colleges and universities (HBCUs) in contributing to the increased number and success of Black doctoral graduates.

The exploration of culturally based frameworks and concepts is essential to unpacking, understanding, and addressing race in doctoral education. The authors in this volume have used or incorporated a range of critical (e.g., critical race theory, or CRT), contextual (e.g., diverse learning environments, or DLE, and sociocultural perspectives of learning), and conceptual (e.g., double consciousness) theories that provided multiple lenses and dimensions for how race shapes individual experiences and how individuals experience their environments. Many of these frameworks illuminate the history of racism and the realization of institutional racism and oppression, which are critical for transforming and designing doctoral education experiences that are inclusive and culturally responsive (Barker, 2014).

Themes

A number of themes emerge across this volume: the importance of HBCUs, the role of faculty, and the intersection of race and gender.

IMPORTANCE OF HBCUs

An important contribution comes from the chapters by Boykins, Felder Small, and McCallum, which draw on the importance of HBCUs in providing supportive environments—whether providing undergraduate students with agency in pursuing the doctorate or providing welcoming and culturally responsive environments that support Black doctoral students and affirm their identity. Many of the scholars in this volume reference the importance of Black doctoral students connecting with faculty, staff, and students who look like them and being affirmed throughout their program, regardless of discipline. HBCUs often provide these opportunities for building community and make supporting community as part of this ethos and mission (Joseph, 2013). The idea of community—and that every individual is connected to their village or community—is steeped in Sankofan tradition (Tedla, 1995). HBCUs foster a sense of self and community that creates an environment of support for doctoral students at HBCUs and fosters confidence and academic preparedness for students who might navigate from HBCUs to predominantly White institutions (PWIs) (Joseph, 2013). While PWIs have the opportunity to build communities among students of color in different ways, the authors of this volume call for deliberate and intentional action in doing so. PWIs (including departments as smaller systems) must wrestle with their histories of exclusion, listen to the voices of their students of color, and disaggregate data to unearth trends and practices that hinder access and persistence among communities of color in order to genuinely create supportive and healthy campus and departmental climates.

THE ROLE OF FACULTY

Another theme across chapters focuses on the role of faculty in shaping experiences. Scholars have consistently posited how faculty or research advisors are critical to the doctoral process (Lovitts, 2001). This is of particular importance given that faculty can significantly shape how minoritized students or students of color progress toward their degrees, experience their learning environments, and participate in scholarly activities (e.g., research, publishing, and teaching) (Graham, 2013).

The doctoral students in these studies reported instances of racism, discrimination, and isolation, which are certainly consistent with the growing research on African American or Black doctoral students. Because faculty often oversee the dissertation process, set the tone for lab behavior and practices, manage classroom engagement, and may interact most often with students, faculty have a crucial responsibility in responding to the needs of students, empowering and affirming students despite the larger context, and setting expectations for what Black doctoral students can achieve and how they navigate their program and discipline.

In the PWI setting, Burt, Griffin et al., and Barker and Washington capture some of the ways in which students encountered faculty and how students begin to make either personal or career decisions based on their interactions. Their studies also highlighted how having an absence of faculty of color as examples or role models was felt by students and how forming community among each other was critical to their success and mental health. Moreover, the chapters by Burt and Griffin et al. demonstrate how STEM Black doctoral students face the growing challenge of developing their STEM identities in the face of racialized experiences where they may lack faculty support and operate in a discipline where their focus on giving back to their communities through science is not as valued.

Intersection of Race and Gender

Burt's study focused keenly on Black graduate men in engineering and challenged the myth that all Black men fit one archetype or could be generalized. Additionally, he offers strategies by which Black men may be oriented, recognized as individuals, and supported in their doctoral programs. While Burt's chapter focuses on Black men, Ramos and Yi's study rounds out this volume through capturing the experiences of two Black women who were challenging and resisting the stereotypes and assumptions made of Black doctoral students. While these women shared similar experiences with students across the chapters, their experiences also captured the intersectionality often faced by women of color. bell hooks (2000) captured the unique positionality of Black women in this way:

> Black women with no institutionalized "other" that we may discriminate against, exploit, or oppress often have a lived experience that directly challenges the prevailing classist, sexist, racist social structure and its concomitant ideology. This lived experience may shape our consciousness in such a way that our worldview differs from those who have a degree of privilege (however relative within the existing system). (p. 16)

Overall, these chapters aim to learn from the experiences of Black doctoral students and to provide empirical, conceptual, and practical considerations of creating environments where Black doctoral students thrive, persist, complete, and successfully enter into the next phase of their careers. By reaching into the experiences of students, the authors of this volume point to very specific actions and efforts that provide researchers, institutions, and policy makers with a beginning.

Contributions to Scholarship

In honor of the Sankofa tradition, we ask readers to consider four outcomes of racial and cultural representation. First, we see this work to be in alignment with notions of CRT. The critical race theoretical approach as a framework embodies the notion of Sankofa. The process of going back to rectify issues of exclusion shaped by systemic oppression, racism, and discrimination provides opportunities for collective acknowledgement, healing, and growth.

Second, by way of a critical race approach, this work creates an artifact of racial and cultural representation focused exclusively on an experience that has been excluded and marginalized in doctoral education research. Researchers (Barker, 2011; Burt, Knight, & Roberson, 2017; Felder & Barker, 2013; Gardner, 2010; Okahana, Allum, Felder, & Tull, 2016) have called for further studies on the ways race shapes doctoral education in varying contexts and disciplines. Third, beyond the racial and cultural representation of this work, it contributes to the process of building community wealth toward the development of similar work and supporting the development of scholarship focused on other historically marginalized student experiences.

Perhaps one of the greatest strengths of this work is its focus on this experience and the value it places on its racial and cultural aspects. On many levels, students are not the same. The daily work of running graduate programs that historically have operated to prioritize legacies of exclusion may inherently serve to marginalize important policies and practices that prioritize belief systems and values that are racially and culturally meaningful to students. This work is important for understanding this racial/ethnic experience among other groups as well as to understand the diversity within it.

Recommendations

In this section, we synthesize major findings across chapters while connecting these findings to relevant recommendations from two key reports developed by the Council of Graduate Schools (CGS) and Educational Testing Service (ETS): *The Path Forward* (2010) and *Pathways Through Graduate School and into Careers* (2012). These two reports discuss the essential role of graduate education in producing a highly skilled workforce for the United States and provide implications and recommendations for universities, employers, and policy makers. Informed by the concept of Sankofa and interweaving the contributions of this volume and the aforementioned reports, we provide additional insights about how these recommendations might be enhanced to strengthen institutional diversity initiatives through the implementation of strategies designed to build and sustain cultural wealth (Yosso, 2005).

Addressing Academic Pathways

University leaders, faculty, and administrators must make early connections with students by meeting them where they are earlier in the academic pipeline—preceding transition into graduate study. The CGS and ETS (2010) found that greater attention was needed to address the pathway to graduate school and to "identify talented undergraduate students, especially those from underrepresented groups and prepare them for entry into graduate education" (p. 29). This approach might involve the development and/or implementation of strategies connecting graduate schools to community colleges and HBCUs to introduce the concept of graduate study as it relates to students' academic and career interests. These pathways should aim to achieve three primary goals:

1. Introduce and make real the possibility of earning a doctorate.

2. Affirm one's cultural, racial, and academic identity—seeing oneself as contributing to a field of knowledge.

3. Identify and minimize barriers of cultural exclusion and maximize opportunities for cultural relevance.

This culturally centered approach may entail the use of a critical race framework while also ensuring that students have access to graduate school environments, meet and engage doctoral students and degree completers who share their cultural or social identities, and participate in research activities—including interactions with diverse faculty and being part of a community where they can share their lived experiences in the academy. We note the importance of "diverse" faculty, as there exists a lack of faculty of color among research graduate faculty ranks and a growing occurrence of cross-race doctoral advising pairs, which Barker and Washington discuss in their chapter. Programs have been established to address this need to connect culture and graduate preparation, such as TRIO Ronald E. McNair Post-baccalaureate Achievement Program and Meyerhoff Scholars Program at the University of Maryland, Baltimore County. These programs have proven successful (CGS & ETS, 2010) but certainly require continued support and funding to sustain their success and to be expanded and replicated. To support the Black/African American experience, strategies should be developed out of sociocultural, contextual, and/or critical race-based frameworks that consider institutional climate and promote inclusivity.

Providing Professional Development on Faculty Advising

There is no doubt that faculty in general and faculty advisors in particular play a crucial role in the successful matriculation, socialization, completion, and overall program satisfaction of the doctoral student (Gardner & Mendoza, 2010; Graham, 2013). Scholars (Gardner & Barker, 2014) have addressed how the faculty advisor and mentor provides a roadmap for navigating the profession, facilitates research and publishing opportunities, assists in reaching program milestones, and identifies future career options. When we consider these functions and the experiences of Black doctoral students, faculty are well positioned to either perpetuate or negate the racist experiences of Black doctoral students and to foster more inclusive environments and practices. Specifically, at PWIs involving cross-race relationships where White faculty advise or mentor Black doctoral students, faculty are not equipped with the lived experiences of navigating these spaces as a person of color and may not recognize the racial and cultural nuances experienced by their students (Barker, 2016). We recommend ongoing professional development for faculty that focuses on understanding institutional racism and the experiences of minoritized doctoral students, working across cultural differences; recognizing and addressing bias; and teaching, advising, and serving through an intersectionality lens. Yi and Ramos's and Burt's findings illustrate how Black doctoral students see their identity as complex and intersecting at their racial, gender, and other identities (e.g., immigrant, advocate).

There is growing attention to the professional development of faculty advisors and the role social identity plays in doctoral advising. Few colleges' and universities' centers for teaching (or variations of teaching and learning), and graduate schools are including these topics as part of their offerings. The University of Michigan's Rackham Graduate School (2018) has a *How to Mentor Graduate Students: A Guide for Faculty*, which references the changing demographics of graduate student composition and the importance of role models. Vanderbilt University's Center for Teaching offers department-specialized workshops on mentoring doctoral students. Furthermore, handbooks and guides have been created that include the importance of considering how race shapes the doctoral experience. In their guide, *How to Get a PhD: A Handbook for Students and Their Supervisors*, Philips and Pugh (2010) address what it means for institutions to create equal opportunities in the context of higher education that is predominantly "white, heterosexual, fit and able-bodied" (p. 148). Gardner and Barnes's (2014) *Advising and Mentoring Doctoral Students: A Handbook* includes an entire section dedicated to understanding students and providing insight into how social identities shape the doctoral experience. There is a real opportunity for departments to provide professional development for graduate students and faculty aimed at creating inclusive environments and practices. Expanding on the CGS and ETS 2010 report's recommendation for federal graduate training programs, there should be an added focus on diversity. Policy makers who award federal or philanthropic monies or grants should consider requiring that institutions not only include aspects of diversity in their projects but also require that grant recipients complete professional development focused on diversity with race as a component.

OFFERING INTENTIONAL CAREER COUNSELING

It's important to consider the extent to which career counseling services support the belief systems of historically marginalized students. One strategy for strengthening support of Black/African American students is to consider ways career services embrace culturally relevant tools and resources to assist students with decision-making processes for their careers. For instance, how might graduate programs prepare Black/African American students for making the transition into faculty careers, and in what ways are career counseling strategies culturally relevant and supportive? CGS and ETS (2010, 2012) found there was little known by doctoral students of their career options. This problem may be a more compounded issue for Black doctoral students who struggle to connect with faculty advisors who may differ racially or who might feel isolated by a racially chilling environment.

The reports also discuss the value in the acquisition of disciplinary knowledge and the importance of graduate students building competencies to support their interests. Findings in this work suggest that Black/African American doctoral students transitioning into career pathways must be cognizant of their racial and cultural presence within their disciplinary communities. Having this understanding is essential to recognizing their professional positionality and their capacity to participate within various systems. For instance, Griffin, Gibbs, and English note in their chapter how graduate programs can facilitate a sense of belonging by creating intentional strategies that foster community membership. Building community can be done by expanding professional development to incorporate ways race and culture are relevant to the cultivation of professional skills and competencies. Additionally, race may shape career mapping, as Black doctoral students must also consider future workplaces and spaces that are supportive and committed to their success; have a record of fostering inclusive and equitable work environments; and, in the case of some faculty roles, appreciate and value scholarship related to race, gender, and intersectionality. Similar to our recommendations on professional development, we agree with the CGS and ETS recommendation that departments develop intentional career counseling as part of faculty advising or a separate function, but we recommend that this counseling factor in the needs and expectations of student of color.

Developing and Strengthening Policies and Practices That Encourage Diversity and Promote Mental Health and Wellness

As indicated by the research across this volume, Black doctoral students have unique experiences and accordingly have unique needs. Particularly in predominantly White contexts, they are faced with managing their social, racial, and professional identities in ways that White students do not. Winkle-Wagner, Johnson, Morelon-Quainoo, and Santiague (2010) found that having a sense of belonging was important to students of color. Consistent with other recommendations (Barker, 2016; Felder & Barker, 2013; Felder, Stevenson, & Gasman, 2014; Gildersleeve; Croom & Vasquez 2011), we recommend that there be greater institutional accountability for departments to create inclusive spaces and reward systems and accountability for faculty who are responsive to the needs of students of color. For example, departments should conduct faculty searches that include an assessment of candidates' demonstrated ability to support diverse students. In terms of faculty development, faculty awards and budget allocations take into consideration the faculty member's participation in professional development activities focused on diversity; or a commitment to diversity becomes part of the review process. Specific to mental health and wellness services, there should be partnerships between departments, graduate schools, and counseling services to ensure that (1) students are presented with resources; (2) students become familiar with counseling staff; and (3) seeking mental health services becomes normalized. Some attention must also be given to graduate student use of mental health services and the accessibility of such services.

Addressing climate and culture is as important as individual actions. Departments might develop a series of sessions or workshops that bring students together while connecting them with the department. Winkle-Wagner et al. also recognize that offering more departmental activities will provide a greater opportunity to explicitly and consistently communicate program expectations, which might often be unspoken or unclear. Because racial climate remains an issue for institutions and departments, the institution and graduate school should make sure that students are aware of how to best manage and report bias in the context of doctoral programs; in doctoral programs, faculty hold a position of power, which calls for a careful process or procedure for students to share concerns or report without retaliation.

EXPANDING RESEARCH

The research in this volume spanned the intersections of race and gender, STEM doctoral students, the role of faculty interactions at HBCUs, the experiences of students in cross-race doctoral advising relationships, and the examinations of programs. While these areas of research represent a broad range of topics, there remain other areas of scholarship that might advance our knowledge of the Black doctoral experience. First, there is more to learn about the dynamic of gender identity and sexual orienta- tion in STEM. How might Black lesbian, gay, bisexual, trans, queer, and questioning (LGBTQ) doctoral students or Black women doctoral students in STEM fields experience these White, male-dominated fields? Second, the role of faculty in doctoral education has been echoed in the literature, but less is known about what interactions lead to more positive outcomes when factoring in the race of the faculty advisor, discipline, and institu- tional context. Furthermore, how might institutional context, environment, and mission influence Black doctoral student success? Last, we have only scratched the surface of how Afrocentric theories or principles manifest in doctoral education. In other words, how does Afrocentricity or Black culture and history guide Black doctoral students' decision making and behaviors through doctoral matriculation? While Yi and Ramos's chapter highlights how a greater purpose of advocacy and social justice fueled the persistence and engagement of their participants, it is still unclear whether other Black doctoral students are driven by the same notions or if there are other aspects of Black culture that influence Black doctoral students' decisions to enroll, persist, and complete.

Conclusion

The development of doctoral education in the 20th century represents national prominence focused on the cultivation of disciplinary ideas, knowledge dissemination, and increased representation of populations historically excluded from doctoral degree attainment. This Sankofa volume is, in large part, retrospective in its premise to build on the emergence of research centralizing racial and cultural experiences as a critical contribution to doctoral education in the United States and throughout the world. Through critical analysis of narratives and empirical evidence, Sankofa also provides a bridge toward future scholarly endeavors that emphasize historically marginalized communities and their contributions to our national and global systems of graduate education.

We developed this volume in August 2017, during and following the period of White nationalist protests on the University of Virginia campus and a resurgence of racist incidences and signage occurring on campuses across the country (Bauer-Wolf, 2017). These events exemplify racist and vitriolic sentiments that continue to exist on our nation's college and university campuses. These events constitute evidence that research, practice, and policies focused on supporting historically marginalized communities must be prioritized to combat systemic oppression. Furthermore, Sankofan principles empower us all to look back so that we can move forward in ways that interrogate institutional legacies of exclusion, spark social justice and equity efforts, and ensure that Black and other marginalized voices are heard.

References

Barker, M. J. (2011). Racial context, currency, and connections: Black doctoral student and white faculty advisor perspectives on cross-race advising. *Innovative Education & Teaching International, 48*(4), 387–400.

Barker, M. J. (2014). Critiquing doctoral education: Moving toward a cross-race doctoral advising model. In P. P. Felder & E. P. St. John (Eds.), *Supporting graduate students in the 21st century: Implications for policy and practice* (Vol. 27, pp. 109–134). New York: AMS Press.

Barker, M. J. (2016). The doctorate in Black & White: The experiences of Black doctoral students in cross-race advising relationships. *Western Journal of Black Studies, 40*(2), 126–140.

Bauer-Wolf, J. (2017). A September of racist incidents. *Inside Higher Ed.* Retrieved from https://www.insidehighered.com/news/2017/09/22/racist-incidents-colleges-abound-academic-year-begins

Burt, B. A., Knight, A., & Roberson, J. (2017). Racializing experiences of foreign-born and ethnically diverse Black male engineering graduate students: Implications for student affairs practice, policy, and research. *Journal of International Students, 7*(4), 925–943.

Chatora, A. (2015, September). 10 quotes from Kwame Nkrumah. Retrieved from https://thisisafrica.me/10-quotes-from-kwame-nkrumah/

Council of Graduate Schools and Educational Testing Service. (2010). *The path forward: The future of graduate education in the United States.* Report from the Commission on the Future of Graduate Education in the United States. Princeton, NJ: Educational Testing Service.

Council of Graduate Schools and Educational Testing Service. (2012). *Pathways through graduate school and into careers.* Report from the Commission on Pathways Through Graduate School and Into Careers. Princeton, NJ: Educational Testing Service.

Felder, P. P., & Barker, M. J. (2013). Extending Bell's concept of interest convergence: A framework for understanding the African American doctoral student experience. *International Journal of Doctoral Studies, 8*, 1–20.

Felder, P. P., Stevenson, H. C., & Gasman, M. (2014). Understanding race in doctoral student socialization. *International Journal of Doctoral Studies, 9*, 21–42.

Gardner, S. K. (2010). Doctoral student development. In S. K. Gardner & P. Mendoza (Eds.), *On becoming a scholar: Socialization and development in doctoral education* (pp. 203–222). Sterling, VA: Stylus Publishing.

Gardner, S. K., & Barker, M. J. (2014). Engaging graduate and professional students. In S. R. Harper & S. J. Quaye (Eds.), *Student engagement in higher education: Theoretical perspectives and practical approaches for diverse populations* (2nd ed., pp. 339–350). New York: Taylor & Francis.

Gardner, S. K., & Barnes, B. J. (2014). *Advising and mentoring doctoral students: A handbook.* CreateSpace Independent Publishing Platform.

Gildersleeve, R. E., Croom, N. N., & Vasquez, P. (2011). "Am I going crazy?!": A critical race analysis of doctoral education. *Equity & Excellence in Education, 44*, 93–114.

Graham, E. (2013). The experiences of minority doctoral students at elite research institutions. In K. A. Holley & J. Joseph (Eds.), *Increasing diversity in doctoral education: Implications for theory and practice* (No. 163, pp. 77–87). *New Directions for Higher Education*. San Francisco: Jossey-Bass.

hooks, b. (2000). *Feminist theory: From margin to center* (2nd ed.). Cambridge, MA: South End Press.

Jones, J. M., & Leitner, J. B. (2015). The Sankofa effect: Divergent effects of thinking about the past for Blacks and Whites. In M. Stolarski, N. Fieulaine, & W. van Beek (Eds.), *Time perspective theory; review, research, and application: Essays in honor of Philip G. Zimbardo* (pp. 197–211). New York: Springer Publishing.

Joseph, J. (2013). The impact of historically Black colleges and universities on doctoral students. In K. A. Holley & J. Joseph (Eds.), *Increasing diversity in doctoral education: Implications for theory and practice* (No. 163, pp. 67–76). *New Directions for Higher Education*. San Francisco: Jossey-Bass.

Lovitts, B. E. (2001). *Leaving the ivory tower: The causes and consequences of departure from doctoral study*. Lanham, MD: Rowman & Littlefield Publishers.

Okahana, H., Allum, J., Felder, P. P., & Tull, R. G. (2016). *Implications for practice and research from Doctoral Initiative on Minority Attrition and Completion* (CGS Data Sources PLUS #16-01). Washington, DC: Council of Graduate Schools.

Phillips, E. M., & Pugh, D. S. (2010). *How to get a PhD: A handbook for students and their supervisors*. Berkshire, England: Open University Press.

Tedla, E. (1995). *Sankofa: African thought and education*. New York: Lang Publishing.

University of Michigan. (2018). *How to mentor graduate students: A guide for faculty*. University of Michigan Rackham Graduate School, MI. Retrieved from http://www.rackham.umich.edu/downloads/publications/Fmentoring.pdf

Vanderbilt University. (n.d.). *Mentoring graduate students*. Center for Teaching. Retrieved from https://cft.vanderbilt.edu/guides-sub-pages/mentoring-graduate-students/

Winkle-Wagner, R., Johnson, S. D., Morelon-Quainoo, C., & Santiague, L. (2010). A sense of belonging: Socialization factors that influence the transitions of students of color into advanced-degree programs. In S. K. Gardner & P. Mendoza (Eds.), *On becoming a scholar: Socialization and development in doctoral education* (pp. 179–199). Sterling, VA: Stylus Publishing.

Yosso, T. J. (2005). Whose culture has capital? *Race, Ethnicity and Education, 8*(1), 69–91.

Contributors

Marco J. Barker is vice chancellor for diversity and inclusion and associate professor of practice for education administration at the University of Nebraska–Lincoln. In his administrative role, he serves as the chief diversity officer and is responsible for providing leadership for campus diversity initiatives, with a focus on strengthening programs, community relations, and strategic planning. His research, publications, and consultations address cross-race mentoring and advising relationships, doctoral education, diversity, and leadership in higher education. Barker earned his undergraduate degree in industrial engineering from the University of Arkansas, an MBA from Webster University, and his PhD in educational leadership and research, with an emphasis in higher education from Louisiana State University.

Brian A. Burt is assistant professor of higher education in the School of Education at Iowa State University, and is a National Academy of Education/Spencer Postdoctoral Fellow. Burt has received funding from the National Science Foundation for *CAREER: Leveraging Learning and Engineering Identity to Broaden Participation of Black Men in Colleges of Engineering*. He received his PhD in higher education from the University of Michigan. His research draws upon learning theories and critical theories to study institutional practices related to the educational and workforce pathways of graduate students of color, particularly Black men in engineering.

Tiffany Fountaine Boykin is dean of Student Engagement at Anne Arundel Community College. Boykin provides leadership and strategic direction for programs that support student belonging, development, leadership, and wellness. In addition, Boykin interprets, articulates, and implements institutional compliance with appropriate federal and state laws, regulations, and policies. She is also an adjunct professor in the Community College Leadership Doctoral Program at Morgan State University, where she primarily instructs courses in research methods and legal aspects of higher education. Boykin's research examines success and participation for Black students in postsecondary settings, the role of historically Black colleges and universities, and legal aspects of higher education. Boykin earned a BA in communication from the University of Maryland, College Park; an MS in communications management from Towson University; a PhD in higher education from Morgan State University; and a JD from the University of Baltimore School of Law.

Fanuel Chirombo is a PhD student in the Organizational Leadership program at the University of Maryland Eastern Shore. His research interests include transformational leadership, organizational culture, and organizational communication climate and employee engagement. He earned a master of science degree in management from the University of Maryland University College and a master of library science degree from the University of Maryland, College Park. Currently, he serves as the Acquisitions and Serials Librarian at Morgan State University.

Shelvia English is the coordinator for Student Services for the University of Maryland Incentive (UMD) Awards and a doctoral candidate in the University's Higher Education, Student Affairs, and International Education Policy program. She received her master of education degree from the University of Massachusetts Amherst. Her research interests center on issues of identity and equity, particularly for Black immigrants; undergraduate and graduate students of color; and first-generation and low-income students. Prior to arriving at UMD, Shelvia was an assistant director of Student Life at Loyola University Maryland.

Pamela Felder Small is an Independent Scholar and Founder of #Black DoctoratesMatter, a research-based social media initiative dedicated to providing knowledge of marginalized students pursuing doctoral studies. Her professional experience includes being a faculty member at the University of Maryland Eastern Shore; the Graduate School of Education at the University of Pennsylvania; Morgan State University; Teachers College, Columbia University; and Camden County College. Felder Small's research explores the relationship between the belief systems and behaviors of doctoral students and their impact on academic socialization, success, and degree completion. She received her undergraduate degree from the University of Maryland Eastern Shore, a master's degree in educational policy and leadership from Temple University, and a PhD in education from the University of Pennsylvania. Her work has been published in *Teachers College Record*, *The Western Journal of Black Studies*, the *International Journal of Doctoral Studies*, and the *Journal of African American Studies*. She is Consulting Editor for the *Journal of Diversity in Higher Education*.

Sydney Freeman Jr. is an associate professor of adult, organizational learning and leadership at the University of Idaho. His research investigates the challenges facing higher education administration programs, specifically higher education as a field of study and the university presidency. Freeman has published numerous journal articles and is the lead editor (with Linda Serra Hagedorn, Lester F. Goodchild, and Dianne A. Wright) of *Advancing Higher Education as a Field of Study: In Quest of Doctoral Degree Guidelines* (Stylus Publishing, 2014), which received the 2015 Auburn University Graduate School "Book of the Year" Award. He also serves on the Board of Directors of the American Association of University Administrators and was honored with the "2015 Emergent Leader of the Year" award by the same professional society. He serves on multiple academic journal editorial and review boards, including serving as managing editor of the *Journal of HBCU Research + Culture*. He also is the founder and editor-in-chief of *The Journal for the Study of Postsecondary and Tertiary Education*.

Marybeth Gasman is professor of higher education in the Graduate School of Education at the University of Pennsylvania. Her areas of expertise include the history of American higher education, minority-serving institutions (MSIs) (with an emphasis on historically Black colleges and universities), racism and diversity, fundraising and philanthropy, and higher education leadership. Marybeth is the founding director of the Penn Center for Minority Serving Institutions, which works to amplify the contributions of MSIs and to strengthen and support MSIs and those scholars interested in them. Having authored or edited more than 22 books, Gasman most recently published *Educating a Diverse Nation* with Clif Conrad (Harvard University Press, 2015) and *Academics Going Public* (Routledge Press, 2016). She earned her bachelor of arts degree in political science and communications from St. Norbert College and a master of science degree in higher education, and a PhD in higher education and law from Indiana University.

Kenneth Gibbs is director of the Postdoctoral Research Associate Training (PRAT) program and program director in the Division of Training, Workforce Development, and Diversity at the National Institute of General Medical Sciences (part of NIH). Prior to joining NIH, Gibbs completed a PhD in immunology at Stanford University and the American Association for the Advancement of Science's Science and Technology Policy fellowship at the National Science Foundation, where he studied the career decision-making process of recent STEM PhD graduates.

Kimberly A. Griffin is an associate professor in the Higher Education, Student Affairs, and International Education Policy program at the University of Maryland. Her research interests are focused on diversity in graduate education and the professoriate, mentoring and career development, campus climate issues, and diversity within the Black higher education community. Griffin earned her doctoral degree in higher education and organizational change from UCLA. Prior to completing her doctoral work, she worked in higher education administration, primarily focused on diversity recruitment, admissions, and retention in undergraduate and graduate education.

Girvin Liggans received his PhD from the University of Maryland Eastern Shore (UMES). His research interests include public policy analysis, food safety and security, and decision making within teams. He obtained his bachelor's degree in environmental science from UMES and his master's degree in environmental health sciences from the University of Michigan. Dr. Liggans has more than 15 years of environmental health and retail food regulatory experience. He has conducted environmental health research with various organizations, including the Environmental Protection Agency; the Food and Drug Administration; the U.S. Army Corps of Engineers; the University of Maryland at Baltimore; and the University of Natal in Durban, South Africa.

Carmen McCallum is an assistant professor at Eastern Michigan University. Her research interests include access and retention within graduate education; graduate students mentoring experiences; and African American students and faculty. She is particularly interested in understanding how race, ethnicity, gender, and socioeconomic status influence students' graduate school experiences. Her work has been published in the *Journal of Diversity in Higher Education, Readings on Equal Education,* and *About Campus.* She has received funding from the National Science Foundation to support her study of graduate education.

Delma Ramos earned her PhD in higher education with an emphasis on research methods and statistics at the University of Denver. She is currently an assistant professor of higher education at the University of North Carolina at Greensboro. Her research focuses on college success, specifically examining the role of family, community, and culture in empowering students to navigate college. Her work engages historically marginalized populations and employs critical methodologies and theories to uncover systems of oppression that perpetuate inequity in education. Ramos earned a bachelor's degree in social work and a master's degree in student affairs and higher education from Colorado State University.

C. Ellen Washington is an associate professor of psychology at The Chicago School of Professional Psychology in the BA Online Program. Her previous position was the director of STEM Continuing Education at Fielding Graduate University in Santa Barbara, CA. Her current research interests are leadership development for minorities in STEM and organizational change. She is also an avid proponent for diversity in the workplace, and leadership and social competencies. Dr. Washington has published articles in the *Oxford University Public Policy Journal* and the *International Journal of Business and Social Science.* She earned her PhD in industrial organizational psychology from the University of Minnesota, a master's degree in counseling psychology from the Georgia School of Professional Psychology, and a bachelor's degree in psychology from the University of Arkansas.

Varaxy Yi earned her PhD in higher education from the University of Denver. She conducts research on educational access and equity for historically underserved communities, including first-generation, refugee and immigrant populations, and students of color, with a special focus on Southeast Asian college students. She is currently an assistant professor in educational leadership at California State University Fresno. Yi earned bachelor's degrees in English and business administration from University of the Pacific and a master's degree in library and information science from San Jose State University.

Index

www.ingramcontent.com/pod-product-compliance
Lightning Source LLC
Chambersburg PA
CBHW020348270326
41926CB00007B/344